Making People Illegal

This book explores the relationship between illegal migration and globalization. Under globalizing forces, migration law has been transformed into the last bastion of sovereignty. This explains the worldwide crackdown on extra-legal migration, and informs the shape this crackdown is taking. Even as states ratchet up provisions to end illegal migration, the phenomenon becomes increasingly significant legally, politically, ethically, and numerically. This book makes the innovative argument that the current state of migration law is vital to understanding globalization. It shows the intertwining of refugee law, security, trafficking and smuggling, and new citizenship laws, with particular attention to how the United States and the European Union define and defy what counts as global. *Making People Illegal* evaluates why migration law in the twenty-first century is markedly different from even the recent past, and argues that this is a harbinger of paradigm shift in the rule of law.

Catherine Dauvergne is Professor and Canada Research Chair in Migration Law at the University of British Columbia Faculty of Law. She is author of the book *Humanitarianism Identity and Nation: Migration Laws of Australia and Canada*, and is editor of *Jurisprudence for an Interconnected Globe*. She has published articles in the *Modern Law Review, Theoretical Inquiries in Law, Social and Legal Studies, International Journal of Refugee Law, Sydney Law Review, Melbourne Law Review, Res Publica*, and the *Osgoode Hall Law Journal*, among others.

The Law in Context Series

Editors: William Twining (University College London)
and Christopher McCrudden (Lincoln College, Oxford)

Since 1970 the Law in Context series has been in the forefront of the movement to broaden the study of law. It has been a vehicle for the publication of innovative scholarly books that treat law and legal phenomena critically in their social, political, and economic contexts from a variety of perspectives to bear on new and existing areas of law taught in universities. A contextual approach involves treating legal subjects broadly, using material from other social sciences, and from any other discipline that helps to explain the operation in practice of the subject under discussion. It is hoped that this orientation is at once more stimulating and more realistic than the bare exposition of legal rules. The series includes original books that have a different emphasis from traditional legal textbooks, while maintaining the same high standards of scholarship. They are written primarily for undergraduate and graduate students of law and of the disciplines, but most also appeal to wider readership. In the past, most books in the series have focused on English law, but recent publications include books on European law, globalization, transnational legal processes, and comparative law.

Books in the Series
Anderson, Schum, & Twining: *Analysis of Evidence*
Ashworth: *Sentencing and Criminal Justice*
Barton & Douglas: *Law and Parenthood*
Beecher-Monas: *Evaluating Scientific Evidence: An Interdisciplinary Framework for Intellectual Due Process*
Bell: *French Legal Cultures*
Bercusson: *European Labour Law*
Birkinshaw: *European Public Law*
Birkinshaw: *Freedom of Information: The Law, the Practice and the Ideal*
Cane: *Atiyah's Accidents, Compensation and the Law*
Clarke & Kohler: *Property Law*
Collins: *The Law of Contract*
Cranton, Scott & Black: *Consumers and the Law*
Davies: *Perspectives on Labour Law*
De Sousa Santos: *Toward a New Legal Common Sense*
Diduck: *Law's Families*
Elworthy & Holder: *Environmental Protection: Text and Materials*
Fortin: *Children's Rights and the Developing Law*
Glover & Thomas: *Reconstructing Mental Health Law and Policy*
Gobert & Punch: *Rethinking Corporate Crime*
Goodrich: *Languages of Law*
Harlow & Rawlings: *Law and Administration: Text and Materials*
Harris: *An Introduction to Law*
Harris: *Remedies, Contract and Tort*
Harvey: *Seeking Asylum in the UK: Problems and Prospects*
Hervey & McHale: *Health Law and the European Union*
Lacey & Wells: *Reconstructing Criminal Law*
Lewis: *Choice and the Legal Order: Rising above Politics*
Likosky: *Law, Infrastructure and Human Rights*
Likosky: *Transnational Legal Processes*
Maughan & Webb: *Lawyering Skills and the Legal Process*

Continued after the index

Making People Illegal

What Globalization Means for Migration and Law

Catherine Dauvergne
University of British Columbia

CAMBRIDGE
UNIVERSITY PRESS

182553062

CAMBRIDGE UNIVERSITY PRESS
Cambridge, New York, Melbourne, Madrid, Cape Town, Singapore, São Paulo, Delhi

Cambridge University Press
32 Avenue of the Americas, New York, NY 10013-2473, USA

www.cambridge.org
Information on this title: www.cambridge.org/9780521895088

First published 2008

Printed in the United States of America

A catalog record for this publication is available from the British Library.

Library of Congress Cataloging in Publication Data

Dauvergne, Catherine.
Making people illegal : what globalization means for migration and law / Catherine Dauvergne.
    p.   cm.
Includes bibliographical references and index.
ISBN 978-0-521-89508-8 (hardback)
1. Aliens.   2. Emigration and immigration law.   3. Refugees – Legal status, laws, etc.   I. Title.
K3274.D38   2008
342.08′2–dc22   2007048447

ISBN   978-0-521-89508-8 hardback

Contents

Acknowledgments

I could not possibly have completed this book without help. Acknowledgments such as these are as inadequate as they are customary. They are truly the most satisfying part of the book to write because of the warm memories their composition conjures.

For inspiration, draft reading, long conversations, and general encouragement with this endeavor, I am grateful to Ruth Buchanan, Peter Fitzpatrick, Jim Hathaway, Audrey Macklin, Jenni Millbank, Peter Showler, and Jeremy Webber. I have so enjoyed your company.

Portions of the book were refined in the conversations that grow out of having an audience. For these opportunities I am grateful to the Department of Law at Carleton University; the CERIUM project at the University of Montreal; the Faculty of Law at the University of New South Wales; the Citizenship, Borders, Gender Conference at Yale University; the Faculty of Law at the University of Toronto; the "Why Citizenship?" Workshop convened by Guy Mundlak and Audrey Macklin; the 2006 Demcon meeting; the College of Law at the University of Saskatchewan; and the 2007 Law and Society Association meeting in Berlin.

I have been very lucky to have had a group of terrific research assistants during the evolution of the book, most of whom have now graduated or will soon do so from the University of British Columbia Faculty of Law, all of whom have tremendous adventures before them. For their solicitous attention to detail and their patience, in chronological order, I am grateful to Robert Russo, Catherine Wong, Megan Kammerer, Ashleigh Keall, and Jacqueline Fehr. There must be a special mention of Megan, who spent two years with me, and Jacqueline, who lived through the final hours. Of course, none of this assistance would have been possible without the support of the Canada Research Chairs Program and the Social Science and Humanities Research Council of Canada.

Duncan, Nina, and Hugh I must thank for constancy and love. And Peter for everything, and also titles.

Catherine Dauvergne
Vancouver,
December 2007

Publication acknowledgments

Chapter 4 is based upon my article "Refugee Law and the Measure of Globalization" (2005), 22:2 *Law in Context* 62–82, and is revised and published here by permission of The Federation Press, the journal's publishers.

Part of Chapter 6 was published by Sage Publications as "Security and Migration Law in the Less Brave New World" (2007), 16:4 *Social and Legal Studies* 533–549.

Part of Chapter 7 was published as "Citizenship with a Vengeance" (2007), 8:2 *Theoretical Inquiries in Law* 489–508, and is republished with permission of the Cegla Center for Interdisciplinary Research of the Law.

CHAPTER ONE

Introduction

In any given week in 2007, newspapers around the world carried reports of "illegal" migration. This did not start in 2007. It is not poised to end any time soon. While many of the accounts are about the United States or the European Union, unauthorized migration is newsworthy in all corners of the globe. Russia has a large and growing extralegal population.[1] China stopped more than 2,000 illegal border crossers in 2006.[2] Thailand and Malaysia have launched a cooperative approach to their shared illegal populations.[3] The Gulf of Aden is a key human smuggling route.[4] South Africa is attempting to grapple with its unauthorized occupants.[5] Morocco and Ethiopia face similar issues.[6] Brazil both sends and receives extralegal migrants, as does Mexico.[7] Illegal migrants come in droves to India, and in lesser

1 Biznes-Vestnik Vostoka, "Uzbekistan, Russia to Sign Agreements on Counteracting Illegal Migra-tion," *Nationwide International News* (June 28, 2007); "Over 230 Illegal Migration Cases Opened in Russia – Official," *RIA Novosti [Russian News and Information Agency]* (November 17, 2005); "Improvement of Russian-Chinese Ties Gives Rise to Illegal Migration – Official," *ITAR-TASS [Russian News Agency]* (December 7, 2005); Kirill Vasilenko, "Illegal Immigration on the Rise," *Vremya Novostey [Russian Press Digest]* (January 27, 2006) 5.
2 "China Cracks Down on Illegal Migration, Cross-border Drug Trafficking," *BBC Worldwide Monitoring* (January 24, 2007).
3 "Malaysia and Thailand to Cooperate in Managing Illegal Workers," *Deutsche Presse-Agentur [German Press Agency]* (July 29, 2005).
4 "At Least 100 Reported Dead, Missing in Latest Smuggling Tragedy in Yemen," UNHCR Press Release (March 26, 2007).
5 Ann Bernstein and Sandy Johnston, "Immigration: Myths and Reality," *Business Day [of South Africa]* (May 11, 2006) 13; "Zimbabwe Migration Office Discourages "Border Jumping," *Voice of America News* (May 16, 2007).
6 "Ethiopia; Human Trafficking Rises at an Alarming Rate – Police," *The Daily Monitor [of Addis Ababa, Ethiopia]* (August 15, 2005); "Feature: Illegals Brave Increasing Dangers to Enter Spain," *Deutsche Presse-Agentur [German Press Agency]* (September 18, 2005); "Spain May Use Six Satellites Against African Illegal Immigration," *Deutsche Presse-Agentur [German Press Agency]* (May 29, 2006).
7 "Brazil, Paraguay to Work on Border Disputes," *Xinhua General News Service [of Shanghai]* (March 31, 2005); "Illegal Immigration: Removed from Reality," *The [London] Guardian* (May 18, 2006) 36; Alan Clendenning, "Seeking Better Life Back Home, Brazilians Heading Abroad in Droves," *The Associated Press* (July 30, 2005); Francis Harris, "Bush Under Pressure on Influx from Mexico," *The Daily Telegraph [of London]* (August 17, 2005) 13; Alan Clendenning. "Brazilian Police Launch Crackdown on Illegal Immigration to U.S.," *The Associated Press* (September 14, 2005); Ginger Thompson, "On a Border in Crisis, There's No Bolting a Busy Gate," *Josefa Ortiz de Dominguez Journal* (September 15, 2005).

numbers to Pakistan.[8] Whatever term we choose, extralegal migration is a global phenomenon.

The rise of the moral panic that accompanies this phenomenon is a marker of the twenty-first century. At the outset of the twentieth century, migration was in the process of becoming "legalized." It was not until early in that century that a robust system of passports and visas was fully established to regulate border crossing.[9] The great waves of migration of earlier eras took place largely without the framework of migration laws, fostered instead by the legal structures of colonial empires and the image of great unpopulated spheres of the globe.[10] In contrast with the legalization of migration that took place at the outset of the previous century, we are currently witnessing the "illegalization" of migration. This is made up in part of the increasing regulatory focus on extralegal migration, in part by the rhetoric and hyperbole of constructing the accompanying moral panic, and in part by the migration flows themselves. It is a potent mixture. The border control imperative has become a headline maker around the globe, and is a vital domestic political issue in all prosperous Western states, and elsewhere as well.

This book examines the relationship between globalization and illegal migration, arguing that the worldwide crackdown on extralegal migration is a reaction to state perceptions of a loss of control over policy initiatives in other areas. One response to this loss of control is a reinterpretation of the highly malleable concept of sovereignty. In contemporary globalizing times, migration laws and their enforcement are increasingly understood as the last bastion of sovereignty. This shifts their character, their content, and their politics. Because of this shift in importance of migration laws, these legal texts become an ideal site to observe key aspects of the debates within globalization theory. Migration laws function almost as a laboratory setting for testing globalization's hypotheses. That is, migration law presents a response to questions like: Is the demise of the nation-state inevitable? Is globalization primarily or exclusively an economic force? Is globalization merely Americanization? Can globalization be resisted? The dilemmas of illegal migration offer a detailed engagement with each of these debates.

---

8 "India Proposes High-level Meeting on "Illegal" Bangladesh Migration," *Agence France Presse* (August 6, 2005); "Steps Being Taken to Check Illegal Immigration – Kasuri," *Pakistan Press International Information Services* (December 28, 2005); Sanjoy Hazarika, "North by North East Ticket to Ride but No Law," *The Statesman [of India]* April 17, 2006); "India to Increase Outposts along Bangladesh Border," *The Asian Age [of India]* (April 26, 2006).

9 Ann Dummett and Andrew Nicol, *Subjects, Citizens, Aliens, and Others: Nationality and Immigration Law* (London: Weidenfeld and Nicolson, 1990). John Torpey, *The Invention of the Passport: Surveillance, Citizenship, and the State* (Cambridge: Cambridge University Press, 2000) makes the important point that the use of passports began as early as 1669 and evolved gradually as a mechanism of state surveillance. The twentieth-century marker is tied to the global use of this technique and the concomitant closing of borders in response.

10 The doctrine of *terra nullius*, dating from the 1600s, was instrumental in European colonization and subsequent migration as it established that indigenous people did not have ownership of the land they inhabited. This facilitated the establishment of settler societies in the United States, Canada, and Australia, all key destinations in contemporary migration and migration mythology.

To make the most compelling version of the argument that migration law informs debates about globalization, the book has an ambitious breadth. Taking unauthorized migration as its starting point, the argument proceeds by considering the categories and mechanisms used to identify and construct extralegal migration. The book examines labor migration, trends in refugee law, trafficking and smuggling of human beings, the migration security nexus, and shifts in citizenship law. Every one of these areas is itself the subject of entire scholarly literatures. This argument, however, focuses on the way these topics are intertwined. Using the dilemmas of globalization theory, I aim to develop the story that emerges from combining these areas of study rather than analytically separating them. In that sense, the book works to make the points so often confined to introductory or concluding remarks as being "beyond the scope of this study" or "analytically distinct." The central argument *is* the parallel arguments in each of these areas, and the insights that come from a focus on similarities of this sort.

With this breadth of potentially distinct topics, the narrative challenge then becomes how to avoid superficiality, the potential pitfall of presenting an analysis that merely skates across the surface of neighboring ponds but that fails to hold together because the ice cracks under the slightest pressure arising from a more detailed engagement with what lies below. The countermeasure applied in this analysis is to adapt the ice scientist's methodology of core sampling. To understand the layers, the scientist extracts a narrow sample that contains a trace of each element under examination. This is the antidote to breadth. Core sampling in the context of my argument means drilling into each topic under consideration to extract a sample that in key ways reveals something about the whole. Some sampling choices are easier than others, but they are all choices. The book does not, therefore, aspire to be a comprehensive source of information about any of the diverse topics it addresses. It does aspire to select sample instances for analysis that offer original insights regarding each of these areas. The persuasive effects of these choices will be one of the crucial ways to assess the book.

The final element in understanding the book's logic is to recall that it is about law and that its author is a legal scholar. This makes sense of its broad ambitions and of the way the core is sampled. The overarching story of the book is that of how globalizing forces align with particular shifts in migration law. Within this story is a jurisprude's desire to situate law within theoretical accounts of globalization. For this reason, each case study addresses one part of the story of law in globalizing times. In the final chapter I gather these strands together into a commentary on the place of law within analyses of globalization. This considers the consequences for law of transforming control over migration into the last bastion of sovereignty. It also aims to disturb the view that law is a mere tool that can be applied in a straightforward way to dilemmas of the global; that it can be deployed to either facilitate global forces or shore up states against them. Instead, the evidence from migration law shifts shows that law has consequences independent of state aims. In particular, the ideological commitment of rule of law gives legal changes independent and sometimes unpredictable force. Migration law, with its international and domestic elements, constructs an important platform from which to observe the internationalization of nation-bound legal principles and to consider the increasingly law-like character of international law. In this sense, the central argument of the book takes up the challenge issued by Boaventura de Sousa Santos to investigate at an empirical level the question of law's potential for progressive social transformation.[11] To unfairly paraphrase Peter Fitzpatrick, the vantage point constructed here offers a glimpse of the new gods he conjured for international law.[12] Any such sighting brings a test of faith. Part of my jurisprudential aspiration is to consider how migration law's authority is surviving this test.

Given all of this, the easiest way to convey the book's method is to introduce the stories recounted within each of its chapters – the core samples that are woven together in the overall story of globalization and illegal migration. The book begins by considering illegal migration broadly. "Illegal" is one of the most derogatory terms applied to the type of border crossing I am concerned with here. My choice to use it in spite of this is deliberate. A number of other terms are used synonymously in popular and scholarly literature: unauthorized, undocumented, clandestine, irregular, and more. My first reason for using "illegal" in contrast to all of these is that it directly implicates the law. The role of the law in constructing illegality is essential to this study and I keep a close focus on it throughout. A related second reason for this selection is that the term "illegal" with its reference to the law has an allure of crisp precision. In the early twenty-first century, xenophobic paranoia thrives. Many foreigners are undesirable and law-abiding folk in many Western states yearn for simpler, exclusionary times. The laws of migration run through the middle of those who are targeted by this exclusionary impulse. Their status within the texts of migration law is vital to how xenophobia and racialization are enacted upon them, and vital to the analysis I want to make. Finally, I choose the term "illegal" because of its broad popular and political currency. I want to consider this popularity, and to use the language that has the most traction in naming it. The opening chapter, "On Being Illegal," takes up this challenge. It introduces the range of phenomena under the illegal migration umbrella and looks at how and why the label "illegal" works. The chapter then turns to the relationship of illegal migration and the law through analyzing the fledgling International Convention on the Protection of the Rights of All Migrant Workers and Members of Their Families.[13] This analysis reveals the reciprocal relationship of illegality and sovereignty.

---

11 *Toward a New Legal Common Sense: Law, Globalization, and Emancipation,* 2nd ed. (London: Butterworths LexisNexis, 2002).
12 Peter Fitzpatrick "'Gods Would Be Needed . . . ': American Empire and the Rule of (International) Law" (2003), 16 *Leiden Journal of International Law* 429.
13 *International Convention on the Protection of the Rights of All Migrant Workers and Members of Their Families,* GA Res. 45/158, UN GAOR, 45th Sess., Supp. No. 49A, UN Doc. A/45/49 (1990) 261 (entered into force July 1, 2003).

The following chapter, "Migration in the Globalization Script," extends the analytic platform of the central argument in two directions. First, this chapter situates migration and law within the "stock story" of globalization. It sets out how accounts of globalization typically talk about migration. It also looks for traces of the law in renditions of globalization. Talk of legal globalization clusters in two areas. First, there is a focus on the rapid expansion of human rights. Second, there is intense interest in the spread, over multiple sites of norm creation, of economic law. Migration law is a challenge on both these fronts. It has proven extraordinarily difficult to meaningfully extend human rights norms to those with an "illegal" status. Similarly, economic discourse has made very little space for extralegal migrants, despite the compelling evidence that they provide vital support to prosperous economies. The chapter also considers elements of the debates that form the core of what can be called "globalization theory." In doing this it builds the argument that a close reading of contemporary migration law reveals something about these debates. Together, these two chapters ground the core sampling that follows.

The first core sampling case study comes from the domain of refugee law in the chapter "Making Asylum Illegal." The central concern of this chapter is the damage done to refugees, and to refugee law, by the global crackdown on illegal migration. The tightening of migration restrictions makes refugee law a more important constraint on sovereignty than ever before. It is also the case that over the last decade or so, refugee law is becoming more law-like in character, in part because of the global spread of human rights norms. Ironically, the increasing importance of human rights to refugee law is vital to states' desire to narrow the constraint on sovereignty to the smallest point possible. This chapter canvasses recent state moves to restrict refugee protection while expanding refugee rhetoric. What these shifts reveal about refugee law's relationship with both human rights law and migration law is the key contribution of this chapter. They also show a key transformation of sovereignty under global pressures.

"Trafficking in Hegemony" situates human trafficking and the rapid rise of law regarding it within the overall argument. My focus here is on the annual United States' *Trafficking in Persons Report*.[14] Important aspects of the story of international law in global times can be gleaned from considering the United States' role in developing international legal instruments in this area and then turning away from those instruments to instead take up a foreign policy initiative

---

14 U.S. State Department, *Trafficking in Persons Report 2000* (U.S. State Department, 2000); U.S. State Department, *Trafficking in Persons Report 2001* (U.S. State Department, 2001); U.S. State Department, *Trafficking in Persons Report 2002* (U.S. State Department, 2002); U.S. State Department, *Trafficking in Persons Report 2003* (U.S. State Department, 2003); U.S. State Department, *Trafficking in Persons Report 2004* (U.S. State Department, 2004); U.S. State Department, *Trafficking in Persons Report 2005* (U.S. State Department, 2005); U.S. State Department, *Trafficking in Persons Report 2006* (U.S. State Department, 2006); U.S. State Department, *Trafficking in Persons Report 2007* (U.S. State Department, 2007). Subsequent references will provide the title and date of the report. All other publication data remain the same.

in the form of the annual report with its ranking and sanctioning of nations. I am particularly interested in the way this story is illuminated by looking at how the *Trafficking in Persons Report* is illustrated. The photographs of real and pretend trafficking victims, taken consensually and nonconsensually, reflect and refract the contours of the debate and also tell us something about its intractability. To round out the argument, the chapter concludes by considering the intertwining of trafficking and smuggling and how and why the law seeks to police this boundary. This chapter contributes an understanding of the feminization of trafficking law and the consequences of this for law and sovereignty.

"The Less Brave New World" considers the security turn in migration discourse and its consequences for migration law. These consequences are closely linked to the breadth of discretion that has traditionally been associated with migration decisions and the consequently large scope for unchecked executive action in the area of migration. Securitization is increasingly global and its discourse is shifting the us-them line that was once such a close fit for the national boundary. In this chapter I examine the use of migration laws to achieve the indefinite detention of terror suspects. These unlaw-like spaces within migration law texts are presently being examined by courts in many liberal democracies and found lacking. This is in no small part due to the fact that the legal fiction of using migration laws to achieve criminal law ends is fracturing. This is important to contemporary reconceptualization of migration laws and to the exception and exclusion that have been their mainstay since their inception.

The final migration law subject area that I take up is citizenship. In talking of illegal migration, it is impossible to avoid slipping over into the plane of citizenship discourse. This is true both in terms of formal legal citizenship and in terms of the broader understanding of citizenship as social inclusion, robust participation, and rights entitlement. These themes are addressed in "Citizenship Unhinged" by considering the role that amnesties play in state responses to illegal migration. Amnesties construct a bridge across the citizenship law–migration law dichotomy. Reflecting contemporary pressures, the pillars of such bridges are changing. As citizenship laws are transformed to open additional avenues of inclusion, the increasing illegalization of migration ensures that exclusion is also multiplied. Citizenship law stands as the final circle of inclusion when read as a migration law text (a one-dimensional reading to be sure). Changes in these laws conform to the broader argument of the book that migration law is emerging as the center of sovereignty. New citizenship laws, forged as part of the global crackdown on illegal migration, show this transition clearly.

Following these core samples from a series of migration law topics, the book turns to situating these within globalization theory and to examining what they reveal about law in a global era. The "Myths and Giants: The Influence of the European Union and the United States" chapter does this by looking directly at the European Union and the United States. In accounts of the global, both of these geographies loom large. Europe does so because it stands as a beacon of cooperation and human rights, and unending peaceful expansion. Particularly for legal scholars, the legal innovation that is Europe holds endless fascination. Situating this fascination within the globalization script is crucial. I do this through a consideration of Europe's journey toward harmonization of migration laws, and why this is stalled at the crossroads of asylum and illegality. The United States is an equally important avatar of globalization. American economic hegemony is an enormous part of the substance of globalization. Indeed there is contestation about whether the phenomenon should be known simply as Americanization. The American economy is a huge draw for migrants of all sorts, including those outside the law. The notion that illegal migration strikes at the heart of sovereignty needs to be confronted squarely on this terrain. Why does the most powerful nation of the global era tolerate such an enormous illegal population? The response to this begins in economic terms, but cannot end there. It also involves understanding the laws and myths of migration and what they mean to the state and the nation. The contrast between how these strands of analysis are situated in the European Union as compared to the United States contributes another piece to our understanding of globalization.

This contrasting view of the giants of the global narrative takes the book to its culminating chapter, "Sovereignty and the Rule of Law in Global Times." In these global times, the United States and the European Union have emerged as twinned loci of power. Their responses to illegal migration both reveal something of how contemporary power makes and uses sovereignty, and of how important migration laws are to this function. The final chapter begins at this point and gathers the insights of the core samples to create a full picture of the intertwining of migration law and sovereignty at the outset of the twenty-first century. Drawing on this picture, I then turn to the law.

The shifting parameters of our economic and social boundaries have deep consequences for the law, which throughout the modern era has been inextricably linked to national spheres. Considerable work has been done to demonstrate how this linkage is degraded by contemporary eruptions of law in both local and supranational spheres. The work in this book is distinct from both these trends. Instead, it looks at that law which is quintessentially national – as migration law is at its core a border construction site – and considers how this nationally bound law is affected by global trends. Migration laws have become a site of contestation, in which nations inscribe their resistance to human rights norms and global convergence trends. This inscription, however, encounters the partial and constrained autonomy of law, revealing both that law has some immunity from pure political control, and thus is a sometimes valuable resistance strategy, and also that law continues to reflect national aspirations even as these are losing their meaning across many other spheres.

Migration laws are solidifying. Even very recently, migration laws of prosperous Western states functioned primarily as sieves through which the shifting whims of national policy could be poured and made law in short order. Migration laws have typically been marked by high degrees of discretion, conflicting objectives, and direct political control over key elements such as quotas. The inherent flexibility of migration laws has made them an ideal border for the nation because of their capacity to maintain a fixed and law-like appearance while also being infinitely malleable. They provided both the appearance of a boundary and the convenient absence of fixity, like melting and refreezing ice sheets. This is changing. Migration laws are now imbued with more rule of law character. The speed of this change, happening almost exclusively since the early 1990s, is instructive regarding contemporary globalization. This shift reveals how global forces limit the border construction role of migration laws. This in turn highlights why the migration law battleground is so crucial to understanding whether and how globalizing forces are a threat to nation-states, and how states are responding to these threats.

Illegal migration and the laws that construct and confront it are vital political currency at present. This phenomenon has much to tell us about the forces that define our present, and about directions for the future. The movement of states to make people themselves illegal shifts understandings of criminality and raises the stakes for all rights arguments. This book aims to make sense of the forces behind this illegality and to consider options for strategizing against it. Echoing the concerns of globalization theorists, the book considers, from several vantage points, the question of whether illegal migration is simply inevitable given the vast disparities of wealth around the globe. Illegal migration is largely invisible. This invisibility serves the interests of states, of the migrants themselves, and of complacent populations. It also facilitates dehumanizing the people whose lives are shaped by the contours of migration law. More than any other phenomenon, illegal migration points up the immense and arbitrary privilege of birth in a prosperous state. The currently popular strategy of building bigger fences quite literally uses might to construct rights. This book is devoted to exploring other alternatives, and to arguing in support of a progressive direction to emerge in the global paradigm shift that is already in train.

CHAPTER TWO

On being illegal

In September 2003, five Britons released their "No One Is Illegal!" manifesto.[1] With the opening salvo, "For a world without borders! No Immigration controls!" they called for the elimination of all border controls, for opposition to all deportations and for a massive trade union campaign to organize undocumented workers. Their opposition to border controls is grounded in a conviction that immigration laws cannot be "reformed" in a way that will meaningfully sever them from what they label racist and fascist origins. The "No One Is Illegal" manifesto asserts the impossibility of grounding thoroughgoing reform in compassionate exceptions to the immigration laws, and the inability of liberalism to do more than reinforce a demarcation between inclusion and exclusion. Beginning in 2002, "No One Is Illegal" groups began to make their voices heard in a number of Canadian cities.[2] The Canadian groups identify themselves as a "campaign" and, in a perhaps typically Canadian political posture, take a less ideologically articulated position than the British group. The Canadian groups do not, for example, highlight an opposition to all forms of immigration control. They instead focus on a broad integration of social justice issues:

> The No One Is Illegal campaign is in full confrontation with Canadian colonial border policies, denouncing and taking action to combat racial profiling of immigrants and refugees, detention and deportation policies, and wage-slave conditions of migrant workers and non-status people.

> We struggle for the right of our communities to maintain their livelihoods and resist war, occupation, and displacement, while building alliances and supporting indigenous sisters and brothers also fighting theft of land and displacement.

Similarly named groups have appeared in other European nations over the past few years, including Kein Mensch Ist Illegal in Germany, Ninguna Persona Es Ilegal in Spain, Ingen Manniska Ar Illegal in Sweden, Geen Mens Is Illegal in Holland, and

---

1 Steve Cohen, Harriet Grimsditch, Teresa Hayter et al., "Our Manifesto: No One Is Illegal!" on-line: No One Is Illegal, UK, www.noii.org/no-one-is-illegal-manifesto.
2 In Canada, "No One Is Illegal" is organized city by city in Montreal, Ottawa, Toronto, and Vancouver, and is poised to expand.

Zaden Czlowiek Nie Jest Nielegalny in Poland.[3] "No One Is Illegal" campaigns have also had a voice in Australia and the United States. Although the British group traces its origins to campaigns in the 1970s and 1980s, the manifesto and the widespread proliferation of this organizing imperative belong to the twenty-first century.

The emergence of these groups at the opening of this century highlights the fact that public and political discourse has reached a point where "No One Is Illegal" makes sense as a rallying cry. This is a distressing evolution of the English language. In the mid-twentieth century the noun "illegal" was used in reference to Jewish migrants in various places. By the late 1960s, it was used in quotation marks, or as a repeat reference, once illegal immigrants had already been discussed. Now it is used without drawing any special attention at all.[4] In English, "illegal" has become a noun. This is a key anchor for the book; to examine the law and politics behind the increasingly relevant notion of "illegal" people. It used to be impossible to call people themselves "illegal." But the fight against this elision has been lost. The emergence of "No One Is Illegal" as a resistance campaign is at once a capitulation and a call to examine the construction of such illegality.

Such examination is the work of this chapter. The first section considers the global phenomenon of illegal migration and its relationship to the increasingly important efforts by Western nations to confront this population flow. The next section interrogates the label "illegal," considering what it accomplishes analytically and rhetorically. The final section examines the potential of law to confront this "illegality" through considering the attempt made by the International Convention on the Protection of the Rights of All Migrant Workers and Members of Their Families[5] to treat both regular and irregular migrant workers as rights-bearing persons.

The globalization of illegal migration

Located just underneath the worldwide panic about illegal migration is an assumption that everyone everywhere is talking about the same thing. News stories rarely bother with precise definitions, but even statistical documentation by state agencies often does not define illegality. In Michael Jandl's words, "[a]s most estimates do not specify their definition of 'illegal migrant,' we have to assume a common-sense approach."[6] Jandl believes a commonsense approach is possible but rare. I am not

---

3 Web sites for the groups are as follows: Kein Mensch Ist Illegal (Germany) http://www.kmii-tuebingen.de; Ingen Manniska Ar Illegal (Sweden) http://www.ingenillegal.org; Geen Mens Is Illegal (Holland) http://www.defabel.nl; Zaden Czlowiek Nie Jest Nielegalny (Poland) http://www.zcnjn.most.org.pl. The official web site for Ninguna Persona Es Ilegal (Spain) could not be accessed in July 2007 but the group and its goals are discussed at: http://www.noborder.org/camps/01/esp/display.php?id=8.

4 *The Oxford English Dictionary,* on-line ed., *s.v.* "illegal."

5 *International Convention on the Protection of the Rights of All Migrant Workers and Members of Their Families,* GA Res. 45/158, UN GAOR, 45th Sess., Supp. No. 49A, UN Doc. A/45/49 (1990) 261.

6 Michael Jandl, "The Estimation of Illegal Migration in Europe" (2004), 41 *Studi Emigrazione/Migration Studies* 141 at 142.

certain I share Jandl's optimism. The veneer of precision and neutrality embedded in the term "illegal" is an apt guise for assumption and stereotype. What is common in public discourses about illegal migration may not be sensible at all.

Moving toward precision, however, is not easy. By definition, those who are on the move without legal sanction attempt to avoid state surveillance. In general, migration statisticians are interested in "stocks" and "flows," the former referring to ongoing population and the latter to border crossings per year.[7] Methodologies for estimating the stock of illegal migrants involve extrapolating from census data, making assumptions based on known quantities such as legal migrant populations, surveying those – like employers – who might come in regular contact with illegal migrants, and calculating based on regularization statistics.[8] Flows of illegal migrants are estimated based on border apprehension statistics as compared to related figures such as asylum claims. While these techniques tend to yield more precise figures, in Jandl's view they are generally less reliable. All of the methods, however, rest on making assumptions that embed an understanding of people and their behaviors in areas where this is notoriously difficult to do and where social scientists are, in any case, just beginning to work at figuring out these factors. Given the myriad difficulties, it is hardly surprising that the British Director of Enforcement and Removals in the Home Office Immigration and Nationality Directorate would state in May 2006 that he had not the "faintest idea" how many people were in Britain illegally.[9]

The most straightforward way to define illegal migration is by reference to the migration law of the state doing the counting. Under this method, anyone who is currently in contravention of the law has an "illegal" status. This will include people who enter the country in breach of the law and those who overstay their permission to remain. More ambiguously, it may include those who intend to make an asylum claim but have not yet made one. Because refugees are not to be punished for extralegal entry, such a claim usually removes one from the illegal entry statistics, but if the claim is rejected the statistical assessment may shift again.

---

7 Charles B. Keely, "Demography and International Migration" in *Migration Theory: Talking Across Disciplines* (New York and London: Routledge, 2000) 43 at 48:

   Migration, therefore, typically refers to change of usual residence that includes crossing a political boundary. Data can count the size of the movement in a given period, the flow, or the cumulative number of migrants, the stock. The stock can be increased or decreased in any period by in and out migration or deaths of previous migrants.

8 Jandl, *supra* note 6, discusses each of these methods along with some variations. See also Jeffrey S. Passel, "The Size and Characteristics of the Unauthorized Migrant Population in the U.S.: Estimates Based on the March 2005 Current Population Survey" (Research Report prepared for the Pew Hispanic Center, March 7, 2006); Franck Düvell, "Irregular Migration: a Global, Historical and Economic Perspective" in Franck Düvell, ed., *Illegal Migration in Europe: Beyond Control?* (New York: Palgrave MacMillan, 2006) 14; John Salt, *Current Trends in International Migration in Europe* (Strasbourg: Council of Europe, 2001); Peter Futo, Michael Jandl, and Liia Karsakova, "A Survey of Illegal Migration and Human Smuggling in Central and Eastern Europe" (2005), 21 *Migration and Ethnic Studies* 35.

9 Alison Little, "Now We Give Up Chasing Illegals; Immigration Chief's Shameful Confession," *The [U.K.] Express* (May 17, 2006) 1; "Illegal Immigration: Removed from Reality," *The [London] Guardian* (May 18, 2006) 36.

In most migration regimes it is possible to have legal permission to remain but restrictions on work rights. This is common with tourist and student visas and with some types of temporary residence permits. Those working in breach of their right to do so may or may not be captured by statistics based on estimates of migration law breaches, even though their contravention is clear. However it is defined, illegality is a creation of the law. Broad shifts in legal regimes make this point more clearly. While Dave Roberts was pilloried in the press for his "faintest idea" comment, there was a rational account available for those who followed this story beyond the sound bite. The most recent Home Office study of numbers had been conducted in 2001. Given the expansion of the European Union in 2004, nationals of ten additional states had some mobility rights in the United Kingdom. The effect of this shift had not been subject to government analysis by May 2006,[10] providing some basis, but not political appeal, for the comment. A similar but more broadly reaching legal shift has occurred with the border changes in the former Soviet Union. The reestablishment of Russian national borders has left Russian citizens stranded and rightless throughout the region. Newly emerging nationalities and rights have created pockets of illegality in many of the new states.

Despite all of this, estimates of illegal population numbers are still compelling. The respected Pew Hispanic Center estimated the "unauthorized" population of the United States at 11.5 to 12 million in March 2006.[11] Of this number 7.4 million are Latin American, of which 5.9 million are Mexican. Journalists, some allegedly drawing on Pew Center data, report the illegal population of the United States as ranging from eleven to twelve million.[12] The U.S. government estimates the figure to be seven to twelve million.[13] The Russian press digest reported in January 2006 that there are up to fourteen million "illegal migrant workers" presently in

10 At the 2004 expansion, the United Kingdom imposed a Worker's Registration Scheme for nationals of eight of the ten new member states (exempting Cyprus and Malta), further complicating counting in May 2006 when this had just recently been renewed. The Home Office made estimates of the illegal migrant stock available in 2005, but these were derived from applying the "indirect residual method" to 2001 census data.
11 Passel, *supra* note 8 at 3. This estimate draws on the 2005 Current Population Survey, monthly Current Population Surveys up to January 2006, and the 2000 census.
12 The Associated Press estimated the number at twelve million in May 2006 (Brock Vergakis, "Fox: Mexico Wants to be Part of Solution to U.S. Immigration Problem," *The Associated Press* (May 24, 2006)); The Guardian Weekly's Suzanne Goldenberg used the figure eleven million ("Bush Orders National Guard to Secure Mexican Border," *The [London] Guardian* (May 19, 2006)); The Financial Express reported twelve million ("How Many Aliens," *The Financial Express [of Mumbai]* (May 7, 2006)); *The (London) Financial Times* used the figure 11.5 to 12 million (Edward Alden, "Illegal Immigration in U.S. Grows by 500,000 Annually," *The [London] Financial Times* (March 8, 2006)). This figure is also used by the *New Zealand Herald* ("Twelve Million Aliens in the U.S.," (March 9, 2006)).
13 The most recent INS estimate was released in 2003 and estimates the illegal population to be seven million in 2000 (U.S., Immigration and Naturalization Service, *Estimates of the Unauthorized Immigration Population Residing in the United States: 1990–2000* (Office of Policy and Planning, 2003). In 2003 Homeland Security Secretary Tom Ridge estimated the illegal population to be eight to twelve million (Dan Eggen, "Ridge Revives Debate on Immigrant Status," *The Washington Post* (December 11, 2003) A08.

Russia.[14] International Organization for Migration (IOM) data published in 2005 indicates "up to ten million irregular migrants" in the Eastern Europe and Central Asia region.[15] In 2006, the IOM estimated five to ten million irregular migrants in Russia alone.[16] Novosti reports the Russian Interior Ministry giving figures of between 400,000 and 700,000 for illegal Chinese migrants in Russia's Far East.[17] The French illegal migrant population has been estimated at between 200,000 and 400,000.[18] The Home Office study based on 2001 numbers, led to an average estimate of 430,000 in the United Kingdom, but other estimates put the number as high as one million.[19] One estimate for Italy puts the illegal population at 150,000.[20] In May 2006, reports from Spain estimated that "more than 9,000 Africans" had already reached the Canary Islands in the calendar year, all as illegal migrants.[21] The IOM gave a total figure of three million illegal residents across Europe for 1998.[22] Canada's extralegal population is estimated at 200,000,[23] and Australia's is precisely rendered as 47,798.[24]

Concerns and estimates are not limited to prosperous Western countries. The extralegal population of India has been estimated at fifteen to sixteen million.[25] Malaysia reports up to one million illegal "workers" and neighboring Thailand has an illegal population of two million, with another report suggesting one million new illegal entries to Thailand each year.[26] Estimates of the illegal population in

---

14 Kirill Vasilenko "Illegal Immigration on the Rise," *Vremya Novostey [Russian Press Digest]* (January 27, 2006) 5.
15 International Organization for Migration (IOM), *World Migration 2005: Costs and Benefits of International Migration* (Geneva: International Organization for Migration, 2005) at 154. This region includes Armenia, Azerbaijan, Belarus, Georgia, Kyrgyzstan, Moldova, the Russian Federation, Tajikistan, Turkmenistan, Ukraine, and Uzbekistan. New data not released by December 2007.
16 Natalia Voronina "Outlook on Migration Policy Reform in Russia: Contemporary Challenges and Political Paradoxes," in Roger Rodríguez Rios, ed., *Migration Perspectives Eastern Europe and Central Asia* (Vienna: International Organization for Migration, 2006) at 71.
17 "Russian Official Alarmed by Illegal Migration from China," *Novosti [Russian News and Information Agency]* (March 15, 2006).
18 Jon Henley, "France Rejects Migrant Amnesty," *The [London] Guardian* (May 12, 2005).
19 Little, *supra* note 9; Graeme Wilson, "Million Illegal Immigrants 'Have Set Up Home in UK,'" *The [London] Daily Mail* (January 12, 2005) 32.
20 "Italian Minister Warns of Sharp Rise in Illegal Migration," *BBC Worldwide Monitoring* (January 1, 2006).
21 "Zapatero Pledges Controls after 800 Africans Enter Spain," *Deutsche Presse-Agentur [German Press Agency]* (May 30, 2006).
22 IOM, *supra* note 15 at 78. Although the estimate references 1998, the data were published in 2005, signifying the more cautious approach of this international organization.
23 Nicholas Keung, "Illegals Afraid to See a Doctor," *The Toronto Star* (May 23, 2006) A04; Thulasi Srikanthan, "Afraid Every Morning I Wake Up," *The Toronto Star* (May 28, 2006) A04.
24 Australia, Department of Immigration and Multicultural Affairs, *Population Flows: Immigration Aspects, 2004–2005 Edition* (Commonwealth of Australia, 2006) at 142.
25 Sanjoy Hazarika, "North by North East Ticket to Ride but No Law," *The Statesman [of India]* (April 17, 2006).
26 "Malaysia's Crackdown on Illegals Is No Solution," *South China Morning Post* (February 28, 2006) 16; "Malaysia and Thailand to Cooperate in Managing Illegal Workers," *Deutsche Presse-Agentur [German Press Agency]* (July 29, 2005); "Thailand: Massive Check Up to Take Place to Solve Illegal Immigration Problems," *Thai Press Reports* (June 21, 2005).

South Africa have ranged from 500,000 to 8 million over the past decade.[27] Fiji reported the arrival of "up to 7,000" illegal migrants from China in the two years leading up to October 2005.[28] Paraguay has concerns about illegal migrants in its Brazilian population.[29] Brazil, the Philippines, and Pakistan have each expressed concern about their nations' illegal residents elsewhere.[30]

Although there is clearly a great deal of ambiguity and uncertainty underpinning these numbers, they portray an overall picture of a vast amount of population movement outside legal frameworks. The various estimates may total as many as fifty million people illegally resident somewhere at present. This compares with the aggregated UN estimate of just over 190,634,000 migrants in 2005.[31] That is, currently about 2.9 percent of the world's population is living outside its country of birth for a period of at least a year.[32] Given this number, illegal migration is an important part of the contemporary story of globalization. In the prosperous Western states that have been tracking these figures for a decade or more, it is perceptibly on the increase.

One factor that accounts for the growth of illegal migration is the law. Since the early 1990s, prosperous Western states have been engaged in a worldwide crack-down on illegal migration. This has included constitutional changes in Germany;[33] a range of restrictions introduced in France by the notorious Pasqua laws;[34] extensive reduction of asylum seeker rights in Britain;[35] shifts in Italian law;[36] moves toward European Union harmonization in matters of illegal migration and asylum

27 Ann Bernstein and Sandy Johnston, "Immigration: Myths and Reality," *Business Day [of South Africa]* (May 11, 2006) 13.
28 "Fiji Military Briefs Australia on Illegal Migration from China," *Radio Australia* (October 3, 2005).
29 "Brazil, Paraguay to Work on Border Disputes," *Xinhua General News Service [of Shanghai]* (March 31, 2005).
30 Alan Clendenning, "Brazilian Police Launch Crackdown on Illegal Immigration to U.S." *The Associated Press* (September 14, 2005); Nikko Dizon, "Come Home Now 'Na,' DFA Tells Filipino Illegals in U.S.," *Philippine Daily Inquirer* (April 1, 2006) 1; "Steps Being Taken to Check Illegal Immigration Kasuri," *Pakistan Press International Information Services Limited* (December 27, 2005).
31 United Nations, *International Migration 2006* (United Nations Publication, 2006), on-line: Department of Economic and Social Affairs: Population Division, http://www.un.org/esa/population/publications/2006Migration_Chart/Migration2006.pdf.
32 IOM, *supra* note 15 at 13. See also Demetrios G. Papademetriou, "The Global Struggle with Illegal Migration: No End in Sight," (September 1, 2005), on-line: Migration Policy Institute, http://www.migrationinformation.org/feature/display.cfm?ID=336.
33 In 1993, Germany changed the form of its constitutional right to seek asylum. See Terrence Petty, "Germany Closes Borders to Asylum-Seekers, 'European Fortress' Feared," *The Associated Press* (June 30, 1993); Ariane Genillard, "German Court's Ruling Allays Asylum Law Fears," *Financial Times [of London]* (July 20, 1993) p. 2.
34 So named after Interior Minister Charles Pasqua, who introduced these laws; see Susan Soltesz, "Implications of the Conseil Constitutionnel's Immigration and Asylum Decision of August 1993," (1995), 18:1 *Boston College International and Comparative Law Review* 265.
35 This has been accomplished through a series of amendments beginning in 1999. The most recent restrictions in state support are reflected in section 55 of the *Nationality, Immigration and Asylum Act 2002* (UK), 2002, c. 41.
36 A new Immigration Act was introduced in 2002 ("*Bossi-Fini*" Law, no. 189 of July 30, 2002, amendment to legislation on immigration and asylum).

admission.[37] Canada has introduced stricter penalties for migration infringements and has lowered thresholds for deporting permanent residents.[38] The United States has increased border and inland scrutiny.[39] Most innovatively, Australia has moved to excise whole tracts of territory from its "migration zone," rendering parts of the state "nonterritory" for the purposes of claiming asylum.[40] These are not the only changes of the past fifteen years, but they give a sense of the geographic breadth and range of legal options deployed. Each extension of the law regulating migration increases illegal migration through defining increasingly larger categories as being outside the law. In addition, states have stepped up migration enforcement. This too increases the number of illegal migrants through technologies of surveillance. Just as the physicist calibrates her instrument differently to find a wave or a particle, state migration agencies will find illegal migration when they set out to look for it. The recent increase of border patrol officer numbers by the United States along its border with Mexico will certainly raise the number of people detected while attempting clandestine crossings.[41]

Both these effects mean that the current "crackdown" on extralegal migration cannot help but increase it. It is impossible to "observe" illegal migration in any other way. In the absence of law, there can be no illegal migration. In the absence of state enforcement attempts, illegal migration is no more than the proverbial tree falling silently in the forest. The obvious implication of this is that illegal migration would be significantly reduced by halting all moves to enforce existing laws. It would be completely eliminated by repealing all laws regulating it. Neither of these options is politically possible at present, a topic I address directly in Chapter 3. Both, however, reflect part of the rhetorical stance of the "No One Is Illegal Movement." Migration law is being used to make people "illegal" and this rhetoric is resonating as never before.

Meanings of illegality

The "illegality" of people is a new discursive turn in contemporary migration talk. People who transgressed migration law were recently referred to as "illegal aliens" or "illegal migrants." These labels are still current, but so is the simple descriptor "illegal." People themselves are now "illegal"; states are concerned about "illegals."

---

37 These are discussed in detail in Chapter 8.
38 Introduced by the *Immigration and Refugee Protection Act*, S.C. 2001, c. 27.
39 These changes result principally from changes in discretionary practice rather than legislative change, reflecting the capacity of immigration laws generally to shift rapidly in response to political change.
40 *Migration Amendment Regulations 2005* (No. 6) (Cth.). The Coral Sea Island Territory, Queensland islands north of latitude 21 degrees south, Western Australian islands north of latitude 23 degrees south, and Northern Territory islands north of latitude 16 degrees south are all excised.
41 Peter Baker, "Bush Set to Send Guard to Border; Assignment Would be Temporary; Critics Cite Strain on Troops," *The Washington Post* (May 15, 2006) A01; David Jackson, "Bush Plan Calls for Thousands of Guard Troops Along Border; Conservatives Maintain Doubts," *USA Today* (May 16, 2006) 1A.

The lived quality of language means that correctness follows common usage. One of globalization's markers is an ever-faster pace of change on all social, cultural, and economic fronts. This is another example.

This shift in discourses permits several important observations.[42] Although the term "illegal" is precise in its relationship with the law, it is empty of content. It says even less than other identity markers in the migration hierarchy: resident, visitor, guest worker, or refugee. It circumscribes identity solely in terms of a relationship with law: those who are illegal have broken (our) law. Discourse about illegals gathers together a shred of common meaning, some pejorative connotation, and a fixed idea of The Law. The minimal content of the term "illegal" obscures the identities of those to whom it is affixed. While any number of people may infringe migration laws and regulations, the label adheres better to some than to others. We imagine illegals as poor and brown and destitute. The backpacking tourist who overstays her visa and the businessperson who fails to renew papers on time are not who comes to mind. In Australia in 2005–06 the largest group of "illegals" was visitors who had outstayed their legal welcome, and among these the largest nationality group was American,[43] hardly those who occupy our imaginary sweatshops and brothels. These data are not systematically available for other states, but there is no strong reason to expect wide variation.[44] When we think of the boatloads in southern France, in the Timor Sea, or the Atlantic, of those running the Channel Tunnel or the Sonoma Desert, we imagine lean brown faces, poverty, desperation. Despite persistent evidence that, for example, many fleeing Afghans were educated professionals or that remittances to Fujian province have moved families into China's burgeoning middle class, the image of illegals persists.

The predominance of the term "illegal" also underscores a shift in perception regarding the moral worthiness of these migrants. While previously immigration infringements were not widely regarded as criminal, those who enter and remain without authorization are increasingly perceived as "criminal" in a *mala in se* sense. This identification as transgressor first and migrant second facilitates political and public acceptance of the broad range of crackdown measures currently being

---

42 This section of the chapter draws on my earlier paper, "Making People Illegal" in Peter Fitzpatrick and Patricia Tuitt, eds., *Critical Beings: Law, Nation, and the Global Subject* (Aldershot: Ashgate Press, 2004).

43 The United States is ranked first on the list of countries with the most overstayers as of June 30, 2006, with approximately 4,800 overstayers, approximately 10 percent of the total. The United Kingdom is second with approximately 3,800 overstayers. Third on the list is the PRC with approximately 3,700 overstayers. Australia, Department of Immigration and Multicultural Affairs, *Population Flows: Immigration Aspects 2005–2006 Edition* (Commonwealth of Australia, 2007) at 79, on-line: Australian Government, Department of Immigration and Citizenship: Publications, Research and Statistics, http://www.immi.gov.au/media/publications/statistics/popflows2005–6/index.htm. This information published in January 2007.

44 The universal visa requirement in Australia makes data collection feasible. In countries where visas are not required, they cannot be "overstayed." It would be near impossible to gather data on the number of individuals who outstay permission to remain that is merely stamped in their passport on arrival.

implemented, including stripping these individuals of procedural and substantive rights. The morality of immigration discourses is important to contemporary politics, as well as to efforts to shift those politics. Many citizens of prosperous states experience their right to enter and remain there as a morally imbued entitlement, rather than an accident of birth. Those who seek to enter can therefore be cast as "rorters" seeking to unjustly exploit the system or circumvent the (just) rules that confine them to poorer states with fewer life chances.

The term "illegal" also operates to move migration law's "us-them" line in response to globalizing forces. Migration laws make national borders meaningful for people, determining who can enter and who must be turned away. Through this process such laws constitute the community of insiders, and also spell out degrees of belonging and entitlement through the hierarchical systems they establish. Globalization brings a range of pressures to national borders, and they are increasingly permeable to flows of money and ideas. Migration laws have long been a key site of national assertions – of power, of identity, of "nationness." The central argument I am pursuing here is that this site is even more important now that "nationness" is threatened across a range of policy areas. One way to understand the present importance of the term "illegal" is to consider how it reinforces migration law's exclusionary capability when faced with these threats.

Although it is evident that prosperous states would like to assert complete control over those who cross their borders, it is equally evident that this is not possible. Or, at least, that states (especially democratic capitalist ones) are not willing to undertake the trade-offs (mostly economic) that would be necessary to come anywhere close to achieving this goal. The labeling of part of the population as "illegal" accomplishes this exclusion when the border itself does not. Capturing the moral panic about extralegal migrants and enshrining it in law allows governments control that their borders lack. When a part of the population is labeled "illegal" it is excluded from within. Despite their (sometimes long-term) presence and their contribution to the economy, debate about appropriate participation in the political and social community is all but silenced by the label "illegal." This is markedly different from the tenor of debate that surrounds the entitlements of long-term guest workers, for example.[45] The difference is underlined by the arguments that Legomsky musters to urge that restricting the sizable illegal population of the United States is counterproductive: as illegals, they provide labor that Americans will not, receive no state benefits, and abide by the law to avoid deportation.[46] When the nation is unable to assert its traditional sovereignty by closing its borders, it retains its power to separate "us" from "them" through this labeling, although the exclusion is now diffuse and no longer lines up neatly with the clear bright lines of

45 William R. Brubaker, "Introduction" in William R. Brubaker, ed., *Immigration and the Politics of Citizenship in Europe and North America* (Lanham: University Press of America, 1989) 1.
46 Stephen Legomsky, "Employer Sanctions: Past and Future" in Peter Duignan and Lewis H. Gann, eds., *The Debate in the United States Over Immigration* (Stanford, Calif.: Hoover Institution Press, 1998).

a map. Those excluded are outside The Law, regardless of which nation they enter or attempt to enter.

The desperation of the illegal other appears in contrast to our prosperity as a nation. We "have" and they "have not"; entitlement to membership is ours to bestow. One of the shifts occurring at present is that as "illegal" emerges as a globally meaningful identity label, the characteristics of all of those nations against which this other is imagined also tend to merge. The line between having and not having can no longer be easily conceived as fitting around the border of *a* nation and must instead fit around the border of *all* prosperous nations, creating a global understanding of "insiders" and "outsiders." This conception also resonates with the pedigree of the emotive term nation: prosperous Western nation-states are closer to the ideal of nation than others are. Their desirability as destination for extralegal migrants functions as a measure of their status and standing as nations. While globalization may bring some characteristics of the nation under threat, it also allows the exclusion that is essential to the existence of nations to expand. National actions designed to assert traditional sovereignty also contribute to a globalizing of sovereignty in this new way. Typically, the content of migration law – especially the most important parts for determining who will be admitted and who will not – is easily and frequently altered. As the label "illegal" has no content aside from being against the law, it accommodates similarly frequent changes. The law and the nation name the other in this way as not-us and not-legal.

Making people illegal reflects an increasingly globally coherent view that there are proper and improper reasons to migrate. The force of sanctions against extralegal migration is often aimed at "mere economic migrants." Being destitute, or even being poor or "average" and wanting a better life in return for abandoning all that is familiar and starting one's life over again, are insufficient reasons to migrate today. Those who are "merely" seeking a better life are the prime targets of the constricting global migration net. This is a key marker of migration regimes in the twenty-first century. The massive population movements of the nineteenth and twentieth centuries were made up in significant part of people seeking to better their life circumstances. Being poor and willing to start one's life again was formerly a primary reason to migrate, not to be excluded from doing so. People with an abundance of education, training, labor, and entrepreneurial experience are welcome and encouraged to migrate. Globalization has in this sense reframed traditional "class" lines. Although the basic contours of privilege remain, shifts are visible along the edges. Workers in the emerging IT industry servicing globalization's technology increasingly enjoy worldwide mobility despite comparatively low levels of education and no connections to traditional wealth. Knowledge workers such as academics are included in the global elite despite often being paid little enough that they may never own their own homes. It is common in both groups to develop career patterns that span the globe.

In addition to asserting sovereignty, this newest round of regulation against illegal migrants is also part of a new facet of the migration law – nation relationship. The moral panic over illegal migration and the legal responses to it are not limited to one nation. Globalization gives both factors the appearance of happening all over the world, all at once. This is not true, of course, but that matters little to the mythologizing of globalization. It is equally not true that McDonald's restaurants exist the world over or that everyone can access the Internet – globalization is marked by uneven penetration.[47] The impression that the problem of illegal migration is a global one, and the fact that those who seek to migrate outside the law have access to a geographically broader range of options than in earlier eras, contribute to the construction of an identity category of people named by the new noun "illegal." We create in this way the impression that the people who seek entry to Australia via Indonesia by boat are *the same as* those who attempt to walk the length of the Channel Tunnel or swim the Rio Grande. This allows talk of "illegals" in international and intranational discourses as though the term had some fixed meaning besides being an adjectival description of legal transgression.

The emergence of "the illegal" as a subject and object of migration law thus reflects features of the crackdown currently being pursued by prosperous Western states. The term, however, has moved well beyond its legal moorings. "Illegal" is now established as an identity of its own, homogenizing and obscuring the functioning of the law and replicating layers of disadvantage and exclusion. Even as it is difficult to accurately track numbers of extralegal migrants, the discursive phenomenon magnifies this difficulty and makes accurate social and political understandings of this migration near to impossible. For extralegal migrants seeking legal protection or redress for harms, the status of "illegal" has been almost insurmountable. This will eventually prove to be one of the most important tests of the global spread of human rights.

Countering illegality with the law

Living without legal migration status is precarious. Illegal migrant workers do not command minimum wage, have no social welfare protections, generally do not have health care or disability insurance, and lack job security. Of the potentially fifty million illegal migrants today, a considerable portion move to work. The work they do is often in the "three D" categories: dirty, dangerous, or degrading. It is now accepted that illegal migrant labor is an important support to prosperous economies because these workers are available on no notice and will simply "disappear" when the need for them passes. It is commonplace to argue that one of the great strengths of the massive American economy depends to a large extent on the perpetual availability of cheap, dispensable, illegal labor. Similarly, urban myth now has it that if all the illegal workers were rounded up and deported, London would

---

47 William Twining writes compellingly of this unevenness in "The Province of Jurisprudence Re-Examined" in Catherine Dauvergne, ed., *Jurisprudence for an Interconnected Globe* (Aldershot: Ashgate Press, 2002) 13 at 24–25.

stop functioning overnight. While some illegal migrants are literally enslaved, the majority simply inhabit the margins of prosperous societies, invisible because of their illegality to the surveillance mechanisms of contemporary states.

In economic terms illegal migrants are not people but labor, an input for which demand waxes and wanes. Shifts in the globalizing economy have changed the parameters of work, facilitating demand for extralegal workers.[48] An increasing number of jobs are part-time or seasonal; work is increasingly "outsourced."[49] Each of these changes makes workers with no ties to the economy and no formal rights a more useful commodity. A good example of this trend is the importance of "just in time" delivery for supermarkets. Consumers in prosperous Western states have become accustomed to the perpetual availability of fresh fruits and vegetables. In the United Kingdom, the 2004 tragedy of the Morcambe Bay cockle pickers brought public attention to the role of illegal migrants in keeping supermarkets in business.[50] The British supermarket sector is now able to respond to fluctuations in demand that occur, for example, when the weather warms and more people decide they would like to eat lettuce as a result. On short notice, supermarkets order more lettuces. Gangmasters – the name a descriptor of their work – facilitate the instant delivery of more produce by coordinating workers willing to pick and work in pack houses for long hours on short notice and to find themselves without work the next day.[51]

Saskia Sassen has written that the most important distinction in the contemporary era is the one between those with legal migration status and those without it.[52] This is the result of a spread of human rights norms, in tandem with legal recognition in domestic courts, which combine to reduce the importance of citizenship as a determinant of life chances. David Jacobson makes a similar argument, asserting that human rights norms have overtaken citizenship status as the basic common denominator of human entitlement.[53] In Chapter 7, I set out the argument for

---

48 Saskia Sassen describes these transformations and others in *Globalization and its Discontents* (New York: New York Press, 1998).

49 Outsourcing has both domestic and international dimensions. In some cases, outsourced work moves from the factory to the home, such as piecework in the garment industry. In other cases, outsourced work crosses national borders, as is typical of the growing importance of India to northern IT interests.

50 On February 5, 2004, twenty-one illegal migrant workers drowned while picking cockles, a delicacy that must be consumed fresh, in Morcambe Bay, Lancashire. Although the Bay was notoriously dangerous, it appeared that no effort was made to warn those who were working there under supervision of a gangmaster. The public outcry following this mass drowning contributed to the passage of the *Gangmaster Licensing Act 2004* (UK), 2004, c. 11.

51 Rachael Levene, *Irregular Migrant Workers in the UK: A Story of Marginalization* (LL.M. Thesis, University of British Columbia Law School, 2005) [unpublished]; U.K., H.C., Environment, Food and Rural Affairs Committee, *Gangmasters, Fourteenth Report of Session 2002–2003* (London: The Stationary Office Limited, 2003); U.K., Select Committee on Environment, Food and Rural Affairs, *Memorandum Submitted by the Transport and General Workers Union* (2004).

52 Saskia Sassen, *Losing Control? Sovereignty in an Age of Globalization* (New York: Columbia University Press, 1996).

53 David Jacobson, *Rights Across Borders: Immigration and the Decline of Citizenship* (Baltimore: John Hopkins University Press, 1996); David Jacobson, "Courts Across Borders: The Implications of Judicial Agency for Human Rights and Democracy," (2003), 25 *Human Rights Quarterly* 74.

tempering this view of citizenship. Nevertheless, I am in full agreement with Sassen that the gulf between those with some kind of migration status and those without it is vitally important. This is because the capacity of the law to span this gulf is sharply limited. Considering the limits of the law in this regard is crucial to unearthing the place of law in accounts of globalization, and to understanding both how and why globalizing forces are making people illegal.

The proliferation of human rights norms is an important marker of the contemporary era of globalization. From the rapid development of rights statements following the Second World War, to the more recent widespread attention to genocide and torture, human rights norms have become common currency. Mechanisms for human rights enforcement have also proliferated. The European Court of Human Rights has gained importance within its jurisdiction and influence beyond. Constitutional reform in South Africa, Canada, and emerging post-Soviet states has given prominence to human rights commitments at a national level. Key to Sassen and Jacobson's arguments is the persuasive evidence that domestic courts extend human rights protections to immigrants and nationals equally. Indeed, this trend is the key to Joppke's thesis that liberal states have lost control over immigration policy, because of liberal courts' interference with such on a human rights basis.[54]

Despite all of this, human rights norms have done little to assist illegal migrants. This is true for two reasons: ironically, because of law's power and its impuissance. The power of the law is implicated in the failure of human rights norms to reach those who are most marginalized because of the tyranny of jurisdiction. Despite the "human" in human rights, being merely human is not enough to ensure legal standing in many instances. Only a handful of individuals have ever used the complaints procedures available in broad international human rights documents such as the International Covenant on Civil and Political Rights[55] and the Convention on the Elimination of All Forms of Discrimination Against Women,[56] even for those few states that have accepted the optional obligation for individual complaints. A number of legal doctrines have developed that limit access of illegal people to the courts, such as the common law rule that an employment contract will not be binding contractually when the worker is "illegal" to begin with,[57] or the conspicuous

---

54 Christian Joppke, "Why Liberal States Accept Unwanted Immigration" (1998), 50 *World Politics* 266 at 267; Christian Joppke, "Immigration Challenges the Nation State" in Christian Joppke, ed., *Challenge to the Nation State: Immigration in Western Europe and the United States* (New York: Oxford University Press, 1998) 5. Interestingly, Joppke seems to separate courts from "states" in this regard.

55 *International Covenant on Civil and Political Rights*, December 19, 1966, 999 U.N.T.S. 171; 6 I.L.M. 368 (entered into force March 23, 1976).

56 *Convention on the Elimination of All Forms of Discrimination Against Women*, December 18, 1979, 1249 U.N.T.S. 13 (entered into force September 3, 1981).

57 The doctrine of illegality will usually render a contract, such as an employment contract, unenforceable. This is an important feature of the USSC decision in *Hoffman Plastic Compounds v. National Labor Relations Board* 535 U.S. 137 (2002). This doctrine has been deployed routinely to the detriment of migrant workers in the United Kingdom. See, for example, *Sharma v. Hindu Temple and Others* (1990) EAT/253/90.

absence in the Refugee Convention of any explicit right to enter another country.[58] These doctrines mean that even when people without status find the resources to engage with rights seeking legal processes and overcome the fear of reprisal that publicly approaching the courts entails, they will often be unsuccessful. Law's incapacity, on the other hand, means that securing a rights entitlement before the courts will not necessarily translate into a meaningful change of circumstances. This is a commonplace of rights discourse. Rights talk in the absence of other forms of privilege is often just that: talk.

For these reasons, despite the fact that "human" rights – of which a dizzying array have now been propagated – seem by definition to apply to "humans," advocates for migrants at the margins have worked to establish special rights that apply only to them. The Refugee Convention is the first example of this phenomenon, and I consider its evolving relationship with human rights law as the principal subject of Chapter 4. The Refugee Convention does provide a type of remedy for illegality for those who seek and later obtain refugee status, but the number of people who benefit from this provision is a tiny fraction of those considered illegal migrants.[59] At this point, I want to consider briefly the short history of the International Convention on the Protection of the Rights of All Migrant Workers and Members of Their Families [Migrant Workers' Convention].[60] The existence of this Convention attests to the inability of "human" rights to adequately extend to all "humans." Even more revealing, however, is the steadfast attempt in this treaty to protect the rights of even those migrant workers who have no legal migration status. The result of this attempt is a text that demonstrates precisely how few rights these workers have, and how narrowly their entitlement to "human" rights has been read. The document in the end accords a greater place to sovereignty than to the rights of illegal migrants, and as such, is a paragon of the inabilities of law to address the new illegality of people. To examine this inability, I will first spell out my contentions about this Convention.

The Migrant Workers' Convention came into force on July 1, 2003, twelve and a half years after it was opened for signature, accession, and ratification. At that time, twenty-two countries had ratified it.[61] As of December 2007, the number of states party had climbed to thirty-seven, with an additional fifteen signatories. In

58 *Convention Relating to the Status of Refugees*, July 28, 1951, 189 U.N.T.S. 150, (entered into force April 22, 1954) [*Refugee Convention*].
59 In 2006, there were 303,430 asylum claims lodged in the 50 countries that the UNHCR considers to be "industrialized." This number has steadily declined from 628,660 in 2002. UNHCR, Field Information and Coordination Support Section, Division of Operational Services, *Asylum Levels and Trends in Industrialized Countries, 2006: Overview of Asylum Applications Lodged in European and Non-European Industrialized Countries in 2006* (Geneva: UNHCR, 2007) at 10, on-line: UNHCR – The UN Refugee Agency: Statistics, http://www.unhcr.org/statistics/STATISTICS/460150272.pdf. Even the 2002 figure is only 1.2 percent of an estimated 50 million illegal migrants, and not all those who lodge asylum claims eventually benefit from the protections of the Refugee Convention.
60 *International Convention on the Protection of the Rights of All Migrant Workers and Members of Their Families*, *supra* note 5.
61 Twenty ratifications were required to bring the Convention into force (Article 87(1)).

addition to the length of time required to meet the comparatively low requisite number of ratifications, it is notable that the states party to this Convention are comprised entirely of countries who primarily send rather than receive migrants, with Chile, Mexico, Guatemala, and Turkey among the wealthiest states party.[62] All the states party are in the lowest two-thirds of countries according to 2006 statistics for GDP per capita.[63] The Convention does direct some provisions to obligations of sending states, such as an obligation to readmit nationals (Article 8), a right to vote and to be elected at home for those who are working elsewhere (Article 41, only for workers in a "regular" situation), and an obligation to provide appropriate information to potential migrants (Article 65). Furthermore, sending states are covered by the Convention because it explicitly addresses the entire migration trajectory from preparation to return (Article 1).[64] Obviously, however, the majority of the provisions are aimed at receiving states, referred to as employment states in the Convention. The absence of major receiving states as signatories underlies the present weakness of the Convention. This is further emphasized by considering the Convention's contents.

The articles defining the Convention's scope are cast in apparently broad language, opening with references to "all migrant workers . . . without distinction" and the "entire migration process" (Article 1). A migrant worker " . . . refers to a person who is to be engaged, is engaged, or has been engaged in a remunerated activity in a State of which he or she is not a national" (Article 2 (1)). In addition to the long migration trajectory, Article 1 also specifies that the Convention applies to " . . . all migrant workers and members of their families without distinction of any kind such as sex, race, color, language, religion or conviction, political or other opinion, national, ethnic or social origin, nationality, age, economic position, property, marital status, birth or other status" (Article 1(1)). What is omitted here is crucial. Among the enumerated grounds of the nondiscrimination provision, migration status, or even more specifically, irregular or nondocumented migration status is a conspicuous absence. This may yet be read into the "other status" category, but given the specific attention elsewhere in the Convention to lack of status it may also plausibly be argued that this omission was deliberate and ought to be read as an exclusion. Similarly, the definition of migrant worker does not include those seeking work. Possibly work seekers might be covered by the reference to "a person who is to be engaged . . . in a remunerated activity"; however, this interpretive

---

62 Parties to the Convention include: Albania, Algeria, Argentina, Azerbaijan, Belize, Bolivia, Bosnia and Herzegovina, Burkina Faso, Cape Verde, Chile, Colombia, Ecuador, Egypt, El Salvador, Ghana, Guatemala, Guinea, Honduras, Kyrgyzstan, Lesotho, Libyan Arab Jamahiriya, Mali, Mauritania, Mexico, Morocco, Nicaragua, Peru, Philippines, Senegal, Seychelles, Sri Lanka, Syrian Arab Republic, Tajikistan, Timor-Leste, Turkey, Uganda, and Uruguay.

63 As reported in August 2007 by Millennium Development Goals Indicators: The Official United Nations site for the MDG Indicators, http://unstats.un.org/unsd/mdg/default.

64 See Theresa Lawson, "Sending Countries and the Rights of Women Migrant Workers: The Case of Guatemala" (2005), 18 *Harvard Human Rights Journal* 225 for an interesting analysis of the potential reach of obligations of sending states.

extension could only be made after that fact. That is, someone actively seeking work could not be protected by the Convention, although they might possibly, after finding work, be able to complain of their treatment along the way to attaining their position (if their state of employment had signed up to the individual complaints procedure[65]). The Convention does not contain a right to cross borders to work.[66] Each of these limitations constrains the Convention in its potential application to the most vulnerable migrants.

Most important, however, the scope of the Convention is defined by work itself. A specific rights document aimed at migrant workers and their families excludes those who might migrate for other reasons, in addition to those who would migrate in the hope of finding work but who may not do so. Refugees and stateless persons are explicitly excluded from the protections of this Convention (Article 3). This has several effects, all tied to the hegemony of economic discourses and rationales. In the first place, defining rights in this way subtly fosters a view that there are no other reasons to move. Legitimate human choices and motivations are reduced to this singular one. This is particularly important when we consider those for whom this Convention might possibly, at some distant future time, make a difference. For prosperous, sought-after, globetrotting migrants, the rights set out in this Convention go without saying. One would be hard pressed to find anywhere in the world an investment banker, software engineer, or law professor who would migrate without a prospect of freedom of speech and association or rights to consular services – the types of things set out here. Similarly, migration of the privileged may have some financial angle, but is rarely solely about the money. Those who are literally citizens of the world take into account conditions of life and work, family ties, where their children will be educated, retirement, cultural affinities, tax advantages, and countless other small and large factors. The assumption that decisions are not so complex for those without privilege is misleading.

Reducing migration to economic factors alone functions to reduce our capacity to think fully about the life experiences of those who are differently situated from us. This is one of the "othering" mechanisms that serve to facilitate migration law's distinction between "us" and "them." The economic focus of this discourse also marks the Convention as belonging to the contemporary era of globalization. Whatever other factors we use to define and interpret globalizing forces, economic

---

65 Article 77 provides that States Party may declare that individuals under their jurisdiction may submit complaints to the oversight Committee of the Convention. The procedure will not enter into force until ten states have made declarations of acceptance. To date, no countries have joined in this procedure (*The International Convention of Migrant Workers and its Committee: Fact Sheet Number 24 (Rev. 1)*, Office of the United Nations High Commissioner for Human Rights (2005) at 12).

66 International law contains no border crossing rights, save that which can be read from the obligation of states to admit their own nationals. This is also important to the *Convention Relating to the Status of Refugees*, July 28, 1951, 189 U.N.T.S. 150 (entered into force April 22, 1954), discussed in Chapter 4.

functions are at the core of any understanding of the rapid changes of the past two decades. The trend toward making people illegal is linked to understanding people increasingly as labor, as ingredients in an economic process. The underlying rationale of human rights commitments goes against this trend, but any assessment of the Migrant Workers' Convention demonstrates the significant hurdles involved in attempting to counter economic hegemony.

The Convention explicitly includes both legal migrant workers and those it defines as "nondocumented" or "in an irregular situation" because they are not "... authorized to enter, to stay and to engage in a remunerated activity in the State of employment..." (Article 5). Part III of the Convention sets out rights for all migrant workers and Part IV addresses rights for those who are in a "regular situation." The key difference between these sets of provisions is that the Part III rights are almost exclusively reiterations of commitments set out in other, generally applicable, human rights documents. These include a right to enter and remain in one's state of origin (Article 8), right to life (Article 9), freedom from torture (Article 10), freedom from slavery (Article 11), freedom of thought and religion (Article 12). Some of the rights are expressed more explicitly than they are in other more generally applicable documents. For example, the Article 17 rights to security and liberty include specific remarks about immigration detention and costs of detention, and the trial rights discussed in Article 19 make specific reference to nonretroactivity of criminal law and taking migration status into account in sentencing. The only provisions here that are related specifically to migration status include a prohibition on unauthorized destruction of identity and travel documents and a protection against collective expulsion (Articles 21 and 22). While these provisions are specifically related to migration status, they could possibly be read into early rights documents as a matter of interpretation. The Migrant Workers' Convention does not offer illegal migrant workers much that is not already supposedly available to them. From this we can draw two conclusions. Either the Convention was never intended to extend new rights to those without legal status, or the rights protections generally available to all "humans" are inadequately available to extralegal workers without this additional reinforcement, as are the myriad of rights available to all "workers" set out in the plethora of international labor conventions. (Sadly, the drafters found it necessary to include in this Convention the right to "recognition everywhere as a person before the law" (Article 24).) Both these conclusions may be true. The drafters averted to the particular concerns of illegal migrant workers as evidenced by the Preamble, but these concerns were not reflected in the substantive text of the Convention.[67] I do agree with Saskia Sassen that this is "one of the most important documents seeking

---

67 The Preamble contains the following statements:

Bearing in mind that the human problems involved in migration are even more serious in the case of irregular migration and convinced therefore that appropriate action should be encouraged in

to protect the rights of migrants."[68] But even if the Convention were universally ratified, her conclusion must be read with deep irony.

The Convention does offer an array of distinct rights for authorized migrant workers. Their rights of liberty of movement and freedom of association can only be restricted by concerns related to national security and public order (Articles 39 and 40). Migrant workers are guaranteed treatment equal to nationals in health and social services provided by the state (Article 43). States are to consider on humanitarian grounds granting equal status to the family members as to workers themselves (Article 44), and similarly to consider granting families the right to remain even after the death of a worker or a marriage breakdown (Article 50). Migrant workers have a right to transfer savings (Article 47) and protection from inequitable taxation and other deductions from income (Article 48). Restrictions on free choice of employment must be specified in legislation (Article 52). A number of other important rights are also spelled out. This is, therefore, a significant rights document for legal migrant workers, aiming to address specific vulnerabilities related to work outside one's home state. This important achievement also means that the Convention serves to broaden the gap between legal and illegal migrant workers. This raises the perpetual question of the potential that rights documents carry for social transformation, otherwise known as the question of whether law does any good whatsoever. In this case, however, the question is moot for at least the time being as those states most affected by the obligations of the Migrant Workers' Convention are not bound by it.

The Migrant Workers' Convention also importantly affirms state sovereignty and validates migration controls. Article 68 reads in full:

1. States Parties, including States of transit, shall collaborate with a view to preventing and eliminating illegal or clandestine movements and employment of migrant workers in an irregular situation. The measures to be taken to this end within the jurisdiction of each State concerned shall include:
   (a) Appropriate measures against the dissemination of misleading information relating to emigration and immigration;

order to prevent and eliminate clandestine movements and trafficking in migrant workers, while at the same time assuring the protection of their fundamental human rights,

Considering that workers who are nondocumented or in an irregular situation are frequently employed under less favorable conditions of work than other workers and that certain employers find this an inducement to seek such labor in order to reap the benefits of unfair competition,

Considering also that recourse to the employment of migrant workers who are in an irregular situation will be discouraged if the fundamental human rights of all migrant workers are more widely recognized and, moreover, that granting certain additional rights to migrant workers and members of their families in a regular situation will encourage all migrants and employers to respect and comply with the laws and procedures established by the States concerned....

68 *Supra* note 52 at 94.

(b) Measures to detect and eradicate illegal or clandestine movements of migrant workers and members of their families and to impose effective sanctions on persons, groups or entities which organize, operate or assist in organizing or operating such movements;

(c) Measures to impose effective sanctions on persons, groups or entities which use violence, threats or intimidation against migrant workers or members of their families in an irregular situation.

2. States of employment shall take all adequate and effective measures to eliminate employment in their territory of migrant workers in an irregular situation, including, whenever appropriate, sanctions on employers of such workers. The rights of migrant workers vis-à-vis their employer arising from employment shall not be impaired by these measures.

These provisions indicate that states that commit to the Convention are also undertaking to implement a variety of crackdown measures, and to collaborate in doing so. Article 69 commits states to taking actions to ensure that irregular situations do not persist. Reference is also made to regularizing status, but this is clearly not the only option. Similarly, the threshold question of whether or not an individual's migration status is irregular is to be determined by domestic law. That is, sovereignty is reinforced by leaving states in firm control of who can be a migrant worker and under which conditions, and by requiring states to reinforce their borders.

Within the text of the Convention, illegality and sovereignty have a reciprocal relationship. Domestic legal attempts to crack down on illegal migration signal an assertion of sovereign power, which is extended within state territory by the label "illegal" itself. Within the text of the Convention, a similar relationship between illegal migration and sovereignty is present. The objective of addressing extralegal migration brings into being a strong positioning of the state. The definition of extralegal migrants depends on domestic law, and the aim of eliminating such migration conjures powerful state actions: "preventing," "eliminating," and "eradicating." In this way, the relationship between sovereignty and illegal migration parallels what happens in domestic law when migrants and potential migrants bring rights arguments to bolster their claims. Once an argument is shifted to the terrain of rights, the right of the nation to shut its borders tends to overshadow rights claims of individuals.[69] In this instance, any attempt to make a discursive space for illegal migrants is hemmed in by its reference to the sovereign power to make migration illegal.

This points in two directions. The first is toward the difficulties of using law to alleviate illegality. The law is a necessary site for constructing illegality, but is much less apt for remedying it. The contents and current status of the Migrant

---

69 I have explored this argument and its relationship to constitutional rights protections in *Humanitarianism, Identity and Nation: Migration Laws of Australia and Canada* (Toronto and Vancouver: UBC Press, 2005), see especially Chapter 7.

Workers' Convention provide a key illustration of this. In the first instance, it is difficult or impossible for states to agree to any document creating new rights for illegal migrants because even naming such rights requires creating a space for those individuals whom states are exercising considerable resources to erase. Thus even while the Preamble may name the problems, the legal text itself cannot. The true remedy for illegality is an erasure of the law that creates it, not any rights within it that will always in a reciprocal fashion conjure the right of the state to create illegality in the first place. Rather than erasing laws, illegal status is sometimes pardoned through amnesty. This device, as we shall see in Chapter 7, is always framed outside of the law as an exception rather than a challenge. The exclusionary device of making people illegal is so complete that those so labeled scarcely even have human rights. Drawing on Agamben, we can say here that the contemporary trend toward making people illegal counters the modern move toward giving bare life a place in the political sphere. Illegality is exclusion from that sphere, to a status diminished even beyond bare life.[70]

The second direction indicated by the reciprocity of sovereignty and illegality is to search for the source of this intertwining. This, I believe, can be puzzled out by considering how migration law is positioned within the vortex of globalization. It is to this that I turn in Chapter 3. The contemporary crackdown on extralegal migration has changed the central preoccupations of migration law. There is a much greater emphasis in the law on security concerns and exclusions, even though these elements were present throughout migration law's first century. Heightened attention to illegality predates the terrorist assaults of September 11, 2001, and, at any rate, these events are part of the story of globalizing forces, not an isolated pressure on migration laws. The rallying cry "No One Is Illegal" only makes sense in a world where people increasingly *are* made "illegal." The remainder of this book analyzes the modes and mechanisms of this illegality and offers globalization as the explanation for its prevalence.

---

70 Giorgio Agamben, *Homo Sacer: Sovereign Power and Bare Life,* trans. by Daniel Heller-Roazen (Stanford: Stanford University Press, 1995).

CHAPTER THREE

Migration in the globalization script

The intertwining of sovereignty and illegal migration presented in Chapter 2 is intelligible against a backdrop of the changes that have accompanied the recent era of globalization. This chapter is devoted to demonstrating why migration law is an ideal setting for understanding and testing the nature of globalization. In order to do this, I examine two relationships. The first is that of globalization and the law and the second is that of nation and migration. The increasing focus on migration regulation, resulting in heightened attention to illegal migration, is situated at the intersection of these two relationships.

The argument proceeds by first considering globalization. To make sense of the burgeoning literature of globalization, I isolate four central concerns that permeate discussions of globalization. The next step is to consider where migration law fits into the story of how law writ large is situated within globalization. This involves solving the riddle of how migration can be viewed as a paradigmatic global event yet migration law can have little role in legal conceptualization of globalization. Having canvassed the terrain in these two areas, the chapter then turns to explaining why migration law is an ideal laboratory for observing globalization because of how it relates to the central debates of the theoretical cacophony about globalization. This requires a reexamination of the traditional role migration law has played over the past century and the specific challenges that the contemporary pace and nature of change bring to this role. This chapter lays the foundation for the "core sampling" chapters that follow, each of which takes up a particular instance of illegal migration and considers where it fits in globalizing trends.

Mapping globalization

In an ironic mirroring of the phenomenon it describes, the term globalization has grown out of control. There is no longer much to be gained in pinning down a definition for this shape shifter. Rather, it makes sense to use it with full consciousness of its fluidity, and its inevitable incorporation by reference of layers of meaning from the popular to the erudite. When precision is required, we must look elsewhere; globalization is hopelessly imprecise. Among the meanings that have accreted to globalization, a common theme is economic. Thus globalization is often understood as being about the interconnectedness of world markets, the hegemony of the American dollar, the worldwide predominance of transnational corporations, and the McDonald's on Tiananmen Square.[1] All of these economic phenomena and more are symptoms or signifiers of globalization. Another key aspect of globalization, which facilitates the economic, is technological: from email and real-time chat rooms, to live, around-the-world television broadcasts and the possibly-still-new wireless era. These too are symbols and symptoms of globalization, literally shrinking the globe by making all corners of it simultaneously imaginable and accessible.

Most accounts of globalization go further than the economic or the technological, but these two elements are the ever-present backdrop to whatever follows. While some theorists assert that globalization is predominantly economic and that its noneconomic effects therefore are interpreted as a secondary offshoot,[2] those who hold this view are being outnumbered by others who find the most compelling aspects of globalization to be related to how people experience the world, their place in it, and their relationships with others. In Giddens' analysis, although everyone lives a local life, phenomenal worlds for the most part are truly global.[3] To take one of his examples, "When the image of Nelson Mandela may be more familiar to us than the face of our next-door neighbor, something has changed in the nature of our everyday experience."[4] Gill links the economic and the psychological elements, asserting that globalization, " . . . in its present mythic and ideological representations, . . . serves to reify a global economic system dominated by large institutional investors and transnational firms."[5] For Held and McGrew, the key to globalization is in " . . . the multiplicity of linkages and interconnections between the states and societies which make up the modern world system."[6] What each of these perspectives has in common is an emphasis on a reordering of the social. Whether this is cast in terms of phenomenal worlds, or mythic and ideological representations of the global, or in societal interconnections, the focus is on something beyond a mechanically conceived economic and technological shift.

A decade ago, it was possible to imagine that scholarly and popular interest in globalization might be a passing fad. By the early 1990s, discussions of globalization had appeared in economics, political science, sociology, international relations, and

---

1 So much so that George Ritzer's account of globalization is the "McDonaldization" thesis; *The McDonaldization of Society* (Thousand Oaks, Calif.: Pine Forge Press, 2004) and Benjamin Barber's influential treatise uses the same title device *Jihad vs. McWorld* (New York: Times Books, 1995).

2 See, for example, Kenichi Ohmae, *The End of the Nation State: The Rise of Regional Economies* (London: Harper Collins, 1995); Robert B. Reich, *The Work of Nations: Preparing Ourselves for 21st Century Capitalism* (London: Simon & Schuster, 1983).

3 Anthony Giddens, *The Consequences of Modernity* (Stanford: Stanford University Press, 1990).

4 Anthony Giddens, *Runaway World: How Globalization is Reshaping Our Lives* (New York: Routledge, 2000) at 29–30.

5 Stephen Gill, "Globalization, Market Civilization, and Disciplinary Neo-liberalism," (1995), 24 *Millennium* 3.

6 David Held and Anthony McGrew, "Globalization and the Liberal-Democratic State," in Yoshikazu Sakamoto, ed., *Global Transformation: Challenges to the State System* (Tokyo and New York: United Nations University Press, 1994).

even law. Looking at this literature in 2007, however, suggests that far from fading away, globalization is close to becoming a field of study in and of itself.[7] The speed with which new works concerning globalization appear parallels the increase in velocity of all phenomena, which is itself a marker of globalization. In this literature and elsewhere there is a conversation about whether globalization is actually a new thing, but the extent to which it has captured our contemporary intellectual interest most certainly is novel.[8] My contention is that migration and the laws that regulate it are uniquely positioned to provoke insights about what is taking place under the banner of globalization. To ground this claim I look briefly at some of the central preoccupations of the burgeoning globalization scholarship.[9] The core sampling chapters then show how recent migration law shifts, most importantly the myriad ways that people are being made illegal, reflect these preoccupations.

The predominant question in the globalization debate is whether globalization threatens the nation-state. The centrality of this question is partially due to the vigor with which opposing sides stake their claims. Those asserting that globalization has rendered the nation-state redundant have put their case in the strongest possible terms. Ohmae states that " . . . in terms of real flows of economic activity, nation-states have already lost their role as meaningful units of participation in the global economy of today's borderless world."[10] Reich similarly argues that nation-states are now no more than local authorities of the global economic system.[11] The counterarguments are equally assertive. Linda Weiss claims that in the future, " . . . nation-states will matter more rather than less. . . . "[12] In her assessment, globalists have both overstated and overgeneralized state powerlessness, particularly because they have not taken account of state variety and adaptability. Weiss argues that the enhanced importance of nation-states will in fact advance the development of the world economy. In between these polarized positions, others assert a range of options. Hirst and Thompson argue that the state remains a crucial institution, even though some aspects of its governance capacity have been weakened.[13] This argument highlights a range of aspects of "nation," including their view of the still

---

7 Some sense of the enormity of scholarship on globalization, and of the diverse scholars and opinion leaders involved, is gained by perusing compendious volumes such as David Held et al., eds., *Global Transformations: Politics, Economics, and Culture* (Cambridge: Polity Press, 1999) or more recently Frank Lechener and John Boli, eds., *The Globalization Reader* (Malden: Blackwell Publishing, 2004), David Held, Anthony Barnett, and Caspar Henderson, eds., *Debating Globalization* (Cambridge: Polity Press, 2005).

8 See David B. Goldman, "Historical Aspects of Globalization and Law" in Catherine Dauvergne, ed., *Jurisprudence for an Interconnected Globe* (Aldershot: Ashgate Press, 2003) 43 for an overview of the new-old debate.

9 In their comprehensive volume tracking approaches to and effects of globalization, Held, McGrew, Goldblatt, and Perraton take a different approach to classifying the literature by identifying three schools of thought about globalization: skeptics, transformationalists, and hyperglobalizers. See Held et al., *supra* note 7 at 2–8.

10 See Kenichi Ohmae, *supra* note 2 at 11.   11 See Robert B. Reich, *supra* note 2.

12 Linda Weiss, *The Myth of the Powerless State: Governing the Economy in a Global Era* (Cambridge: Polity Press, 1998) at 195.

13 Paul Hirst and Grahame Thompson, *Globalization in Question: The International Economy and the Possibilities of Governance*, 2nd ed. (Malden, Mass.: Polity Press, 1999).

central role of national economies.[14] Ruggie asserts that states are "anything but irrelevant,"[15] in opening his argument that notions of territoriality are shifting, and with them the settled position of the nation-state. Held and McGrew claim that the state has some continued importance, but that current theory does not adequately situate it within the global system.[16]

The debate over the relative health of the nation-state is sometimes cast in terms of sovereignty. Jayasuriya argues that sovereignty is being transformed by globalizing forces.[17] MacCormick sees it ebbing away to the benefit of all concerned.[18] In this version of the narrative, sovereignty is thus viewed as the distinguishing characteristic of the nation-state and its erosion is seen as a measure of impaired state capacity. The question of state capacity has a great deal in common with the question of sovereignty, but sovereignty is not merely state capacity for exclusive action in a particular policy area, or even territory. The concept of sovereignty has a pedigree far longer than that of globalization, and it is claimed as a centerpiece, in different ways, for international relations scholars and legal theorists. For these reasons, and even in spite of them, I have set sovereignty at the center of my analysis of the transformation of migration laws. Accordingly, I return to it later and at greater length, in Chapter 9. At this point I merely want to join the analysis of sovereignty to the ongoing concern about the health of nation-states.

A second vital question in globalization theory is whether globalization is essential to economic growth. There is a posited relationship between globalization and free trade, and between free trade and market efficiency. Following on from this is increasing tension between support among the governments of prosperous nations for a variety of initiatives that foster free trade (from strengthening regional trading alliances to supporting the World Trade Organization) and resistance from non-governmental actors arguing that free trade will damage conditions of local lives. The contemporary "anti-globalization" protests, which plausibly began in Seattle and are now an anticipated accompaniment to high-level heads of government meetings, reflect this tension.[19] A somewhat different take on this issue is to regard

---

14 For a more recent iteration of this perspective, see Grahame Thompson's 2005 essay "The Limits of Globalization: Questions for Held and Wolf" in David Held et al., eds., *Debating Globalization: Politics, Economics, and Culture* (Cambridge: Polity Press, 2005) at 52.

15 John Gerrard Ruggie, "Territoriality and Beyond: Problematizing Modernity in International Relations," (1993), 47 *International Organization* 139 at 142.

16 David Held and Anthony McGrew, *supra* note 6 at 57.

17 Kanishka Jayasuriya, "Globalization, Law, and the Transformation of Sovereignty: The Emergence of Global Regulatory Governance" (1999), 6 *Indiana Journal of Global Legal Studies* 425.

18 Neil MacCormick, "Beyond the Sovereign State," (1993), 56 *Modern Law Review* 1.

19 Like many phenomena in the globalization cluster, this genre of protest can be traced back hundreds of years. Some would include under the heading "anti-globalization" protests indigenous activism directed against European colonists. Others date this genre of protest to the 1968 protests in Paris or the reaction in the United States against the Vietnam War. The 1999 Seattle protests then provide a good marker of the argument that "globalization" in the contemporary era is both connected to this long history, and differing in its contemporary format. The Seattle protests were surprising, unruly, newly worrisome. The "taming" of this protest movement, its capture by international superstars (Geldof, Bono) and the way in which the protests are now an accepted accompaniment

it as a debate over whether economic growth is a value to be pursued. To the extent that the debate takes that form, it shifts ground somewhat and operates on the assumption that globalization *does* promote economic growth, but that economic growth is not to be presumed as a common good. As globalization theory advances, the debate becomes more nuanced. Hurrell and Woods make an important contribution in this area by arguing that globalization exacerbates existing inequalities between states and therefore contributes differentially to both economic growth and state capacity.[20] The pursuit of a "deglobalization" and "decommodification" agenda also challenges the value of economic growth as a way of alleviating human suffering.[21]

A third issue that circulates through the literature on globalization theory is whether globalization is a liberal phenomenon or a "transmission belt" for liberal values, or, in a variation on this theme, whether globalization ought to be understood simply as "Americanization." For Young, globalization and liberalism are inextricably intertwined. He asserts that " ... from the beginning, it [liberalism] has always been about globalization"[22] and argues that since the end of the Cold War the universalizing aspects of the liberal project have become more prominent. The question of liberal values has economic resonance, but reaches beyond that. The global spread of ideas such as Western human rights norms, with their strong liberal pedigree, is also an aspect of this question, as is the counter-cry of cultural imperialism. Often the two are tied, as in discussions of tied aid or linking trade status with human rights "performance." The question of Americanization has become particularly important since the onset of the "war on terror," and more ominous. Whereas human rights and democratic governance often pass as unqualified positives for human development, cast as Americanization this is rarely the case. De Sousa Santos stakes a middle ground in this conversation by arguing that because the globalization of a neo-liberal political and legal form is already in train, the question of the social role of law is now important around the globe. This question, he asserts, is not itself Western but is firmly grounded in the Western (liberal) tradition.[23]

A final preoccupation of globalization theory is the question of global governance, whether this is possible or desirable and the extent to which it is already

to key head of state meetings, are all part of what is "new" about the present era of globalization. For further analysis see Donatella della Porta, "The Social Bases of the Global Justice Movement: Some Theoretical Reflections and Empirical Evidence from the First European Social Forum," United Nations Research Institute for Social Development, Civil Society and Social Movements Programme Paper, Number 21, December 2005. Porta names Seattle as the "turning point" at 6.

20 Andrew Hurrell and Ngaire Woods, "Globalization and Inequality," (1995), 24 *Millennium* 447.
21 Patrick Bond, "Top Down or Bottom Up? A Reply," in David Held et al., eds., *Debating Globalization* (Cambridge: Polity Press, 2005) at 82.
22 Tom Young, "'A Project to be Realized': Global Liberalism and Contemporary Africa," (1995), 24 *Millennium* 527 at 527.
23 Boaventura de Sousa Santos, *Toward a New Legal Common Sense: Law, Globalization, and Emancipation*, 2nd ed. (London: Butterworths LexisNexis, 2002) at 445.

happening. David Held, for example, sets the objective of global governance at the center of his work *Global Covenant*, arguing for a new multilateral treaty setting the terms of world rule according to social democratic principles.[24] Anne Marie Slaughter asserts that interrelationships among bureaucrats, technocrats, judges, and legislators affect global governance perspectives both formally and informally.[25] The question of legitimacy arises in this exchange both in debates about the democratic deficit of international institutions formed solely by states, and in the question of how global civil society movements fit into the global terrain.

The four questions of the prevalence of the nation-state, the value of economic growth, the homogenization of cultural values, and the dilemma of global governance provide a simplified map of the preoccupations of scholarly engagement with globalization. These questions overlap and intertwine. Most theorists who assert that the capacity of the nation-state is affected by globalization, for example, rely in their argument on assertions about economic growth and the place of liberalism. In addition, few would dispute that globalization is an uneven and paradoxical process. These features are not subject to debate in the same way, perhaps coming closer to the core of globalization's emerging orthodoxy. Examining contemporary shifts in migration law provides a way of assessing each of these debates. This provides, in turn, a set of answers to the questions about the nation-state, economic growth, value export, and the potential for global governance. The answers generated at the migration law site are not always broadly generalizable; their strength is, rather, in their grounding. In addition, considering law in this setting has the benefit of allowing an engagement with legal accounts of the global, a particular subset of globalization's cacophony.

Conceptualizing law within globalization

There is an enormous amount written about globalization and law. Lawyers seeking to illustrate the influence of global forces on their discipline tend to point to two areas: the immense growth of economic law – the new *lex mercatoria* – and the proliferation of human rights law.[26] Both of these areas lend themselves to the third

---

24 David Held, *Global Covenant: The Social Democratic Alternative to the Washington Consensus* (Cambridge and Malden, Mass.: Polity Press, 2004).
25 Anne-Marie Slaughter, *A New World Order* (Princeton: Princeton University Press, 2004).
26 This is reflected in the contents of the *Indiana Journal of Global Legal Studies* or by reviewing symposia volumes such as Volume 41, No. 3 (2003) of the *Alberta Law Review* entitled *Globalization and the Law*. See also Volkmar Gessner and Ali Cem Budak, eds., *Emerging Legal Certainty: Empirical Studies on the Globalization of Law* (Aldershot and Brookfield, USA: Ashgate Publishing, 1998); Jarrod Wiener, *Globalization and the Harmonization of Law* (London and New York: Pinter, 1999); N. Douglas Lewis, *Law and Governance: The Old Meets the New* (London: Cavendish, 2001); Errol Mendes and Ozay Mehmet, *Global Governance, Economy, and Law: Waiting for Justice* (London and New York: Routledge, 2003); Ronald Charles Wolf, *Trade, Aid, and Arbitrate: The Globalization of Western Law* (Aldershot and Burlington: Ashgate Publishing, 2004); Franz von Brenda-Beckmann, Keebet von Brenda-Beckman, and Anne Griffiths, eds., *Mobile People,*

prevalent theme in this discussion: that international law is becoming increasingly important and authoritative. Migration law is instructive in thinking about how law is responding to globalizing forces because it can be made to speak to each of these three topics. In the case of economic law, this is possible because of the extent to which migration policy is increasingly conceptualized in economic terms. Human rights norms are immensely important to migrants, and the difficulties of meaningfully extending these standards to those without migration status reveals a vital problem with being "merely human." Finally, the story of the rise and rise of international law is challenged by an almost complete absence of international regulation of migration – a quintessentially international phenomenon that states are clearly desperate to control. Why international law is not the first recourse to achieve this objective is an important part of the puzzle.

All of this contributes to seeing the importance of migration law as a key legal site for understanding globalization. On the one hand, it is possible to set the question of migration aside and say that it is one small area that simply fails to fit the trends. This is perhaps a reasonable perspective from within the discipline of law where migration law has been primarily regarded as a specialized subset of administrative law scholarship. This is changing, but not rapidly. Migration law is not a required or even recommended course at most law schools. It is not considered a leading practice area. Refugee law, the international legal cousin of the story, has fared somewhat better in this regard, but is nonetheless considered a confined niche. It rarely merits a chapter in international law textbooks, for example. Its practitioners are often mired in the diverse intricacies of the national decision-making regimes, rather than arguing principles of international treaty interpretation. This is deeply ironic given that the *Refugee Convention* is the most frequently applied international treaty in the world: since 2000, it has governed approximately 500,000 asylum decisions each year in industrialized countries.[27] While other conventions apply every day, none is subject to adjudication to this extent. The lack of attention to migration and refugee law helps explain why their lack of fit with the stock story of legal globalization has not been particularly troubling. It does not suggest that this should continue to be so.

Mobile Law: Expanding Legal Relations in a Contracting World (Aldershot and Burlington: Ashgate Publishing, 2005); Alison Brysk and Gershon Shafir, eds., *People Out of Place: Globalization, Human Rights, and the Citizenship Gap* (New York: Routledge, 2004).

27 *Convention Relating to the Status of Refugees,* July 28, 1951, 189 U.N.T.S. 150 (entered into force April 22, 1954). Statistics drawn from UNHCR, Field Information and Coordination Support Section, Division of Operational Services, *Asylum Levels and Trends in Industrialized Countries, 2006: Overview of Asylum Applications Lodged in European and Non-Euorpean Industrialized Countries in 2006* (Geneva: UNHCR, 2007) at 10, on-line: UNHCR – The UN Refugee Agency: Statistics, http://www.unhcr.org/statistics/STATISTICS/460150272.pdf. These numbers reflect claims for refugee status made in fifty industrialized states party that are thus obligated by the Refugee Convention to make a determination. The Convention is also used by the United Nations High Commissioner for Refugees in determining refugee status outside of host countries.

The question of how globalizing forces challenge the nature of law is the central focus of jurisprudential concern about globalization.[28] Boaventura de Sousa Santos has argued that law is facing a paradigm shift, poised to move from modern to postmodern underpinnings and assumptions.[29] In his analysis, the hegemonic form of legal globalization is for the time being liberal legalism, but the conditions of globalization also unleash myriad possibilities for the development of what Santos calls subaltern cosmopolitan globalization. That is, law with a renewed emancipatory and transformative potential to alter conditions of those who are not simply exploited but also excluded from the globalizing social sphere.

Santos' work is apposite to an analysis of contemporary migration law because of three features of his diagnosis. The first is his call for an "unthinking" of the law. Key to this unthinking is the initial step of detaching law from the nation. This is partially a project of legal pluralism, to which Santos' own work has made seminal contributions.[30] However, his call for unthinking law in the face of the global is more far-reaching than simply looking for alternative sources of authority. In his words, "Unthinking is epistemologically complex because it involves both thorough but not nihilistic destruction and discontinuous but not arbitrary reconstruction." The constructive movement in unthinking must be outside the disciplinary boundaries of modern law: ". . . unthinking amounts to a new cultural synthesis."[31] Migration law is vital to the unthinking project. Santos identifies the migration context, particularly where illegal migrants confront the laws of the nation-state, as one of what he terms the "contact zones" where emancipatory subaltern cosmopolitan law may emerge.[32] The overarching challenge, however, is beyond what Santos names in his sketch of an emerging research agenda. Indeed, unthinking migration law

---

28 The project of jurisprudence in globalization is discussed by William Twining in "The Province of Jurisprudence Re-examined" in Catherine Dauvergne, ed., *Jurisprudence for an Interconnected Globe* (Aldershot: Ashgate Press, 2003) at 13. See also Catherine Dauvergne, "New Directions for Jurisprudence" in Catherine Dauvergne, ed., *Jurisprudence for an Interconnected Globe* (Aldershot: Ashgate Press, 2003) at 1. Twining addresses this question at greater length in *Globalisation and Legal Theory* (London: Butterworths, 2000).

29 *Supra* note 23.

30 Santos' work on Pasargada law in particular has been crucial to the project of legal pluralism. He summarizes this project in Chapter 4 of the second edition of *Toward a New Legal Common Sense, supra* note 23, and gives a fuller account in the first edition of *Toward a New Legal Common Sense* (London: Routledge, 1995). Santos' early accounts of this work were published in the 1970s. See *Law Against Law: Legal Reasoning in Pasargada Law* (Cuernavaca: Centro Intercultural de Documentacion, 1974) and "The Law of the Oppressed: The Construction and Reproduction of Legality in Pasargada" (1977), 12 *Law and Society Review* 5.

31 *Supra* note 23 at 83.

32 Santos says, "Contact zones are social fields in which different normative life worlds meet and clash. . . . The contact zones that concern me here are those in which different legal cultures clash in highly asymmetrical ways, that is, in clashes that mobilize very unequal power exchanges" (*supra* note 23 at 472). Santos considers that exclusion has replaced exploitation as the central mechanism of disentitlement. He expresses this in terms of a narrowing of the social contract, both excluding more from joining the contract in the first place and excluding those who belong to the social contract from full participation (at 451–2). These exclusions drive profound social dislocations in the privileged nations of the globe. There is clearly much in this analysis that maps onto the question of illegal migration as discussed in Chapter 2.

requires us to consider whether this law, which is at the core of state power and national community definition, can be unhinged from the state and yet remain law-like. This is a challenge that the core sampling of my analysis takes up directly.

Closely related to this point is Santos' analysis of law as poised at a moment of paradigm shift. His evocative description of problems that can be solved within a modern paradigm and those that cannot, can be cast as a framing of the dilemmas of illegal migration.[33] The bounded, sovereign nation-state and its law is at the center of the modern world. This state exerts absolute control over its borders, in the name of identity, or community, or simple power. The present worldwide crackdown on illegal migration is an attempt to address the dilemmas of illegal migration within the paradigm of modernity. The failure of these attempts to achieve their objectives (assuming these to be a reduction in numbers of illegal migrants) suggests these approaches are not working. The question arises whether any proposal aiming to use law to shore up the borders of modernity in this way can succeed. Even more vital is the question of whether law can shore up modern borders and at the same time protect people who are outside the borders assigned to them by modernity. This is the question of law's emancipatory potential.

This raises the third and most challenging aspect of Santos' critique that I draw on in this work. Santos recognizes that the hegemonic neo-liberal globalization brings with it an embrace of rule of law and judicial adjudication.[34] To this extent it is fair to say that he diagnoses globalization as a legalizing process. The growth of *lex mercatoria* and human rights law clearly fits into this picture. Santos' project is animated, however, not by a description of this process, but by the question of the social consequences of this massive increase in law measured by volume. He concludes his analysis in *A New Legal Common Sense* by asking the question, "Can law be emancipatory?" This question returns us to Chapter 2 and the mobilization of the "No One Is illegal" activists. In the illegal migration context, the question of law's emancipatory potential is positioned squarely here: Can law do anything to alleviate the harms of illegality or does its deployment merely endlessly reproduce categories of illegal at its boundaries? Is there an alternative between withdrawing altogether from law, on the one hand, and endlessly reifying nation and its sovereignty on the other? This inquiry is the core of this book. It amounts to addressing the question of whether law can draw its authority from any source other than the nation.

My approach to this question is a return to the central pillar of jurisprudence, the rule of law. The rule of law has thick and thin versions as its terminal poles. The thick version is imbued with process rights so strong they form a platform of human dignity at the core of the law itself, the thin one so narrow it is a bare ledge of formalism. When Santos offers up the rule of law and an obsession with adjudication as marks of neo-liberal globalization, it is not a rule of law as a social good in and of itself that he implies. Over a range of migration law sites,

---

33 *Supra* note 23 at 13–14.   34 Ibid. at 445.

I test the emerging forms of the rule of law and attempt to assess their potential to improve conditions for individuals. This inquiry mirrors the jurisprudential obsessions of the mid-twentieth century when the legal legacy of the Nazi regime made it imperative that jurisprudes give an account of the morality of law. That debate queried whether pronouncements that meet the formal requirements of law are still law if their substantive content is heinous.[35] The contemporary setting of illegal migration raises a parallel inquiry in regard to the rule of law. That is, is the rule of law an empty concept that will bear the weight of whatever political agenda it is conjured to support (as Santos suggests[36]), or does the rule of law embed its own emancipatory potential that can, under some conditions, pull away from the substantive thrust of the legal text itself?

In examining the rule of law in this way, I turn to the work of Peter Fitzpatrick and draw on his analysis of the rule of law and the place of sovereignty under conditions of globalization.[37] The central starting point for much of Fitzpatrick's analysis of law and the global is his description of the relationship between law and nation. While both law and nation tend to the universal in their aspirations, they are each essentially bounded and limited to some particularity, relying for their operating logic on an excluding and othering movement. The universal cannot be achieved because there would then be nothing outside it against which meaning can be derived. The symbiotic relationship between the two exists because each provides the boundary condition for the other. Law sets the limits of the nation, and nation sets the limits of the law, and each ensures fluidity for the other.[38] This relationship is crucial to understanding how migration law and nation are

35 See Lon L. Fuller, *The Morality of Law*, rev. ed. (New Haven and London: Yale University Press, 1969); Christian Joerges and Navraj Singh, eds., *Darker Legacies of Law in Europe: The Shadow of National Socialism and Fascism over Europe and Its Legal Traditions* (Oxford: Hart Publishing, 2003).

36 *Supra* note 23 at 85, Santos states:

> ... law has both a regulatory potential or even repressive potential and an emancipatory potential, the latter being much greater than the model of normal change has ever postulated. The way law's potential evolves, whether towards regulation or emancipation, has nothing to do with the autonomy or self-reflexivity of the law, but rather with the political mobilization of competing social forces.

37 The principal text in which Peter Fitzpatrick makes this argument is *Modernism and the Grounds of Law* (Cambridge and New York: Cambridge University Press, 2001). This argument is also developed in a different setting in Peter Fitzpatrick, "'We Know What It Is When You Do Not Ask Us': The Unchallengeable Nation," (2004), 8 *Law/Text/Culture* 263. It is echoed in subsequent texts as well.

38 This is a base oversimplification of one of the central threads of Fitzpatrick's analysis. A flavor of his expression of the intertwining of law and nation can be seen here:

> ... neither the negative nor the transcendent constitution of law can be entirely sufficient because law's determinant dimension must have some existent ground. A modern response to this imperative has been the constituent attachment of law to territorial space. Although the resort to territory may import a satisfying solidity grounding law's determinant dimension, it also cannot be entirely sufficient since law is unable to endure solely in that dimension. Determination itself depends integrally on law's responsiveness and this responsive dimension is always beyond the determinant. [...] Law's operative ground, then, must be animated by a responsive dimension. There is a type of territory which would combine determinant and responsive dimensions matching those of law, and that territory is the nation, or at least the nation of modern nationalism.

intertwined, a point I elaborate next. For the time being, however, I want to follow this central Fitzpatrick insight into a consideration of what then happens to law under globalizing pressures, the central thrust of which is a challenge to nation itself, particularly as a site of sovereignty.

Fitzpatrick resists a conclusion that nation is displaced by globalizing forces. In his consideration of the evolution of the European Union, he asserts that the logic of nation itself is extended to this new entity, rather than transformed in some way.[39] On the other hand, in his diagnosis of the shifting ground of international law, he outlines effects of globalizing forces that are unique. These dual insights parallel effects I observe in migration law settings throughout the book, and thus it is important to examine their jurisprudential underpinnings, which in each case lead back (or around) to the question of sovereignty. Fitzpatrick's inquiry into the contemporary health of international law wades into the debate about the legitimacy of international law by asking how it could be that international law is nothing more than an assertion of bare power of nation-states when the United States itself is condemned as transgressor in the face of its war on terror: "If, then, international law is merely or ultimately the receptacle and instrument of power, this section on international law and American empire could now end with an abrupt and obvious conclusion."[40] Yet it does not. In searching for an explanation of the traction that international law has in confronting the United States (seen through the effects of " . . . disregard, active opposition and violation"), Fitzpatrick grounds international law's authority in an existent ethics of a community of law.[41] This grounding admits, therefore, of a distinction between the substance of any given law in the instance of any judicial pronouncement on the one hand – where the powerful nation may in fact prevail – and the ethical commitment of law on the other – where power cannot furnish authority. In his words:

> Here the effect of disregard, active opposition, and violation merge. They cumulatively conform to that definitive difference between *imperium* and a community of law. It is not as if law's determinate content, responding as it does to the demands of a predominant power, would be likely to pose a ruptural challenge to American empire. That challenge would come from an ethics of the existent within law, from an insistence this ethics would carry into law made determinate, an insistence on equality, freedom, and impartiality within law, and an insistence on a regardful community of law.[42]

> . . . It is not the case, however, that in matching law's constituent dimensions nation provides an integrally positive grounding of law. Rather, the irresolution of law's dimensions typifies that of the nation as well. And as with law, the resulting alternation between dimensions should not be seen as a corrosive defect in the formation of identity but, rather, as the dynamic of that formation. Deficiency does have connective consequences, however. Through their sharing the same irresolution, nation and law mutually compensate for their ineluctable instabilities. (Ibid., *Modernism*, at 107.)

39 See Peter Fitzpatrick, Ibid., *Modernism*, at Chapters 5 and 6.
40 Peter Fitzpatrick, "'Gods Would Be Needed . . . ' American Empire and the Rule of (International) Law," (2003), 16 *Leiden Journal of International Law* 429 at 457.
41 Ibid.   42 Ibid. at 466.

My guess is that the profound optimism of this conclusion may account for why Fitzpatrick borrows Rousseau's incantation that "Gods would be needed . . . " [to give men laws] as the title for this piece. Such a hope for international law is an act of faith and jurisprudes are skeptical by nature. Finding authority in an act of faith fits with Fitzpatrick's assessment of sovereignty as a secularized theological concept.[43] That is, in modernity sovereignty no longer references the transcendental; it is transcendent. To achieve this, sovereignty needs law. Indeed, sovereignty cannot be sovereign without the law.[44] "If sovereign claims are to be any more than evanescent, if they are to assume an operative continuance, they then become integrally tied to law."[45] Fitzpatrick sees "constituent complicities" between law and sovereignty, which parallel those he elaborates between law and nation.[46]

Fitzpatrick's account of the intertwining of law, sovereignty, and nation provides an account of the persistence of nation and its law in globalizing times. This account fits with much of what the story of globalization and illegal migration reveals. The settings I examine in this book ground Fitzpatrick's account and suggest elaborations, which I turn to in Chapter 9. I am particularly interested in Fitzpatrick's act of faith and in his useful suggestion that international law may be law-like in its authority even without prevailing in each instance. In finding an ethics insisting on equality, freedom, and impartiality, Fitzpatrick is describing a thick version of the rule of law. I think this description is consistent with his earlier evocation of the protean potential of the rule of law.[47] Here the question is raised of the potential of a thick version of the rule of law overlapping the boundaries of national legal systems. In recent transformations of migration laws, this emerges in my view as the sole location for the emancipatory potential. As I illustrate over the next several chapters, an assessment of any progressive potential of migration law is discouraging from the perspectives of international law (especially international human rights law) and domestic law. But almost in the spaces between these texts, there is the hint of something else. This is what is so intriguing about exploring the globalization of law in this context. If what can be glimpsed here is a thick and unhinged (in the Santos sense of a first step toward "unthinking") rule of law, we are indeed on the cusp of a paradigmatic shift in thinking about the law. If what is making this possible is a "regardful community of law," a new faith may emerge.

---

43 Ibid. at 434–36. This formulation draws on Jacques Derrida and Carl Schmitt, whose work Fitzpatrick discusses over these pages.
44 Ibid. at 436.
45 Peter Fitzpatrick, "Bare Sovereignty: *Homo Sacer*, and the Insistence of Law," in Andrew Norris, ed., *Politics, Metaphysics, and Death: Essays on Giorgio Agamben's Homo Sacer* (Durham: Duke University Press, 2005) 49 at 63. This goes to the nub of Fitzpatrick's disagreement with Agamben, who sees bare life and creating and sustaining sovereignty without any place for law in the equation. Fitzpatrick finds we cannot live an unmediated life, and law provides an irreducible mediation (at 69).
46 *Supra* note 40 at 431.
47 Peter Fitzpatrick, "Introduction" in Peter Fitzpatrick, ed., *Nationalism, Racism, and the Rule of Law* (Aldershot: Dartmouth Press, 1995).

To all of this there are two crucial qualifiers. The first is in tempering optimism. My assessment of developments across a range of migration settings is that most of the legal shifting visible at present belongs to a conservative tradition of shoring up modern nation-states, using law as an instrument to advance this agenda, and thus elevating rule of law as a formal rather than a robust principle. Since the opening salvo of the war on terror, there has been much talk by the American administration, and by those opposed to American actions, of the rule of law.[48] This flurry of interest in the rule of law is a form of politics and reflects an anxiety on all sides about a perception of increased lawlessness. The call may just as well be for "law" full stop, but rule of law makes better politics. This increase in rule of law "talk" is not what appears to hold some new promise. Indeed, the present politics of the rule of law holds many signals of dark times ahead. To the extent that I am optimistic at all (and I imagine this would be true also of Santos and Fitzpatrick), it is not because of some clear direction that presents itself, but rather because of some possibilities vaguely discernable in spite of the fog of rule of law hysteria.

The second and quite different qualifier to all of this must take the form of an apology to both Boaventura de Sousa Santos and Peter Fitzpatrick for invoking their work in pursuit of a project that follows only part of the paths each has marked. Alternatively, I could offer a straightforward apology for what may possibly be viewed as dilettantism but which I hope is instead an applied engagement with this theoretical debate that is grounded in the area of migration laws and thus does not aspire to cover the field of globalizing jurisprudence more broadly. Reading Fitzpatrick and Santos together, especially as informed by William Twining, almost calls upon one to pronounce on postmodernism. This is beyond the province of migration lawyers. The concern with migration law and the nation belongs resolutely to modernity. It is increasingly clear that the intertwining of sovereignty and nation is the barrier to any large steps in resolving the dilemmas of illegal migration, and that this is more and more true given contemporary developments. I do not follow Santos onto the plain of subaltern oppositional cosmopolitan legality as the shape of future potential. Rather, I draw on his work because of its acuity in diagnosis, and because I am motivated by the creativity and optimism it shows. In this sense, my approach is closer to that of William Twining, who positions his own work in relation to postmodernism in general and Santos in particular as " . . . broadly in sympathy with some of the[ir] central concerns and ideas at less abstract levels."[49] Fitzpatrick's work is an essential grounding because his insights

---

48 An excellent example of this is the document "The National Security Strategy of the United States of America," (September 2002), on-line: The White House http://www.whitehouse.gov/nsc/nssall.html.

49 *Globalisation and Legal Theory, supra* note 28 at 195. In full, Twining writes:

I side with Haack in rejecting several of the more extravagant philosophical claims made by post-modernists, while being broadly in sympathy with some of their central concerns and ideas at less abstract levels. I shall argue that this does not quite amount to accepting Santos's conclusions while rejecting his premises, but there is a puzzle that needs teasing out.

limn the migration law-nation relationship in such a way that I remain astonished that this was not his starting point.

Migration law as a testing ground

The final movement in this chapter is drawing on the central debates that mark globalization theory, and with regard to key jurisprudential concerns about globalization, to explain why migration law sits at the intersection of these crosscutting currents. In part, this is because migration itself occupies a curious place in the grand narrative of globalization. One of the hardest globalization myths to assess is whether it is true that more people are on the move now than at any other time in history. Held and his coauthors tackled this question in comprehensive detail, assessing human migration patterns over history on the basis of extensity, intensity, velocity, and impact on host and home states and societies.[50] Their conclusion was tentative, stating that if present trends continue the contemporary pattern of migration " . . . may supersede its predecessors in terms of intensity as well as extensity."[51] This conclusion was published in 1999, an eternity ago by globalization's ever more rapid clock, but in subsequent work Held and his coauthors have not reframed this conclusion.[52] If any aspect of the "more people on the move" idea holds true, it is probably that international travel has increased greatly. Nonetheless, the proportion of the world's population that travels across borders may not have changed significantly if we consider the recent exponential growth of the world's population and that most people in the most densely populated parts of the earth do not participate in either the backpacking or sun-seeking rituals.

Saskia Sassen is one of the few leading figures of globalization analysis who has grappled with migration at length. She writes, "Immigration is . . . one of the constitutive processes of globalization today, even though not recognized or represented as such in mainstream accounts of the global economy."[53] Sassen argues that while territory has been "denationalized" to facilitate global economic development,

---

50 David Held and Anthony McGrew, "People on the Move: Globalization and Migration" in David Held et al., eds., *Global Transformations: Politics, Economics, and Culture* (Cambridge: Polity Press, 1999) at Chapter 6.

51 Ibid. at 312. In full, they state:

In the end, it is a close call. The transatlantic surge of 1880–1920 was certainly more intense than the early colonial emigrations, the slave trade, or the Asian migrations of the nineteenth century. It was probably more intense than the global flows of the postwar era – but only just. The comparison between nineteenth-century Asian migrations and contemporary ones is more clear-cut. The former were greater. However, intra-Asian migratory flows are only just beginning to mount as differential rates of economic development generate the preconditions for large movements of labor. If these migrations continue to expand, and American migrations continue – and there is no sign of them abating – then the contemporary pattern of migration may supersede its predecessors in terms of intensity as well as extensity.

52 David Held and Anthony McGrew, *Globalizaton/Anti-Globalization* (Cambridge and Oxford: Polity Press, 2002) at 39 and 121. In more recent work such as *Global Covenant, supra* note 24, and *Debating Globalization, supra* note 7, David Held does not pursue an analysis of migration trends.

53 Saskia Sassen, *Globalization and Its Discontents* (New York: The New Press, 1998) at xxi.

politics have been "renationalized," in part explaining the rise of anti-immigrant feelings.[54] Sassen also asserts that while new forms of legality have been created to facilitate capital flow, there has been a lack of legal innovation surrounding people's movements.[55] As I demonstrated in Chapter 2, I disagree in part with Sassen's assessment of the constraints states face in enacting immigration control and with the significance of human rights instruments in the border-crossing context. It is vital, however, for legal scholars to take up her provocative suggestion about the way legal innovation, or lack thereof, is implicated in the construction and advance of globalizing forces. This book makes a detailed assessment of the innovative potential of migration laws and, in particular, explores the linkages between migration laws and state power that are implicit in Sassen's work.

The mobility of people, or in economists' terms "labor," is never assumed to be as great as that of capital within the globalized economy. Although money and ideas circumvent the globe, people remain in place. The removal of most passport controls within the European Union is so far an isolated example, which covers a relatively small geographic area. Increased options to move within Europe are not yet challenging national or cultural identity groupings. The most pressing migration issue in European public discourse at the outset of the twenty-first century is the question of illegal migration, the one area where increased potential mobility within Europe makes little difference. There is little evidence that the removal of passport controls has triggered widespread permanent migration between European nations.[56] The North American Free Trade Agreement (NAFTA) loosens some migration controls, but primarily for businesspeople and service providers.[57] Sassen points out that the NAFTA and the General Agreement on Tariffs and Trade (GATT) both have the effect of transforming what would have formerly been temporary labor migration into a nonmigratory flow of services.[58] Neither the Asia Pacific Economic Cooperation group nor the narrower Association of South East Asian Nations sets out any migration provisions in their constituting agreements, although the former has

54 Ibid., see Chapter 2, "The De Facto Transnationalizing of Immigration Policy" and Chapter 3, "America's Immigration Problem." An overview of this argument is also presented in Saskia Sassen, *Losing Control?: Sovereignty in an Age of Globalization* (New York: Columbia University Press, 1996).
55 *Globalization and its Discontents, supra* note 53.
56 See annual net migration rates reported at "Migration and Asylum in Numbers," on-line: EU Statistical Migration Data, http://ec.europa.eu/justice_home/doc_centre/asylum/statistics/printer/doc_asylum_statistics_en.htm. This conclusion holds generally in the longer term but must be tempered by considering the migration restrictions that accompanied the 2004 and 2007 expansions of the European Union. These are discussed in Chapter 8.
57 *The North American Free Trade Agreement Between the Government of Canada, the Government of Mexico and the Government of the United States,* December 17, 1992, Can. T.S. 1994 No. 2, 32 I.L.M. 289 (entered into force January 1, 1994) [NAFTA]. See "NAFTA: Key Provisions," on-line: U.S. Department of Commerce International Trade Administration, www.mac.doc.gov/nafta/3001.htm, which notes that the key beneficiaries of the NAFTA's easing of entry for businesspersons are after-sales service providers, sales representatives/agents/buyers/market researchers, and financial service personnel, professionals, and company executives and managerial personnel.
58 *Globalization and Its Discontents, supra* note 53 at 15.

developed a fast-track travel-pass program.[59] In sum, even these regional groupings have not fundamentally altered migration: they have made movement easier for those who would have been able to obtain permission, and an incentive, to move anyway under earlier regimes. Even Hirst and Thompson's pilloried "ideal type" global economy does not operate primarily by actual labor mobility from country to country but "by mobile capital selecting locations with the best deal in terms of labor costs and supply."[60]

There are a number of factors that make migration's legal text – as distinct from its occurrence – a key site for evaluating and exploring globalizing effects. The most straightforward of these is that migration law's features occupy a place in accounts of globalization that are produced by those who hold no interest in either the law or this branch of it. For example, Hirst and Thompson argue that one persistent bastion of strength of the nation-state is its control over the mobility of its population: "People are less mobile than money, goods, or ideas: in a sense they remain 'nationalized,' dependent on passports, visas, and residency and labor qualifications."[61] In Sundhya Pahuja's terms, migration law plays a role in the "globalization script."[62] Assumptions about migration, and the laws that control it, are embedded in the stock stories of globalization at all levels of the discursive spectrum from popular to political to theoretical. The reason for this, in turn, leads to the other features of migration law that suit it to this analysis: its importance for the liberal nation-state, the absence of international law in the area, and its symmetry with sovereignty.

Migration law is constitutive of liberal communities, both as "nations" and as "states."[63] The modern political world is divided into nations. Subject only to exceptions such as the high seas and Antarctica, the geography of the globe is "nationalized." There is no empty, non-national space where people can live beyond the reach of nation. The importance of "state" in disciplines such as international relations, the precise definition it is afforded in law through the *Montevideo*

---

59 This program is aimed at facilitating speed and efficiency in short-term business travel within APEC member countries. As of February 2007, seventeen members (Australia, Chile, Hong Kong, Korea, China, Philippines, Malaysia, New Zealand, Thailand, Peru, Indonesia, Japan, Papua New Guinea, Singapore, Chinese Taipei, Vietnam, and Brunei Darussalam) were participating in the scheme, which has allowed governments and customs personnel to share a large amount of information with each other before arrivals. Once a businessperson is issued with the APEC Business Travel Card she is able to travel visa-free to participating countries, as well as enjoy the benefits of accelerated customs processing on arrival. For a brief overview of the scheme under APEC's Mobility of Business People Working Group, see http://www.businessmobility.org.

60 *Supra* note 13 at 12 (of the first edition).

61 Ibid. at 257.

62 Sundhya Pahuja, "'Normalizing' Pathologies of Difference: The Discursive Functions of International Monetary Fund Conditionality," in Lyndsay M. Campbell et al., eds., *International Intersections: Law's Changing Territories: Papers Presented at Green College, University of British Columbia, April 3–May 2, 1998* (Vancouver: University of British Columbia, Faculty of Law, Graduate Program, 1998) at 181.

63 This is also true of nation-states that are not presently governed by liberal regimes; however, because the nation-state paradigm is a product of liberalism and because the nations that are most active in defining illegal migration and the most attractive to illegal migrants are liberal states, it is appropriate to put primary focus on liberal states in this argument.

Convention on the Rights and Duties of States 1933, and the ambiguity of the nation-state couplet have not succeeded in diminishing the prevalence of nation. Despite this prevalence, however, nation is elusive. Attempts to pin nation down with academic precision have resorted to central terms that themselves suggest instability. Smith's attempt to define nation by reference to ethnicity nonetheless conceded that this could not be the case with new nations such as the United States, Australia, or Canada, and presumably a large number of colonially constructed nations as well.[64] Given the importance of his exceptions he instead asserted that these nations existed by providing a sense of belonging to individuals that in a mythic sense created a parallel with ethnic nations. The importance of mythic fabrication is a good part of what sustains this account in the world beyond Europe. Gellner's conception of nation puts myth in a central role, and Anderson's seminal work isolates collective imagining as vital in forming the "imagined communities" of his title.[65] Hobsbawn asserts the importance of invented traditions and of the " . . . assumptions, hopes, needs, longings, and interests of ordinary people . . . "[66] Brubaker's analysis pushes beyond these accounts of nation, arguing that nation must be read as a contingent event.[67]

These trends in scholarship point up two significant things at this juncture. First is that nation is inseparable from people – its people – ultimately its citizens. Accordingly, in each of these analyses nation and national identity – a perception of myth, symbol, imagination – are linked. Second, in contrasting the difficulty of defining nation and the instability woven into all attempts to do so with the predominance of nation in the political world, we are confronted with a concept that must have, against these odds, a stable appearance. This stability is necessary for any particular nation to be defined, and is at the crux of nation's relationship with law and especially migration law, mirroring Peter Fitzpatrick's analysis of the ways in which law and nation each provide the other with a necessary limit.

The importance of people, therefore, is one aspect of the interweaving of migration law and nation. Of all the subcategories and subdivisions of law, migration law is that which controls the membership of the nation. Legal frameworks for controlling entry – systems of passports, visas, entry permits, refusals, deportations – are inscribed in the texts of migration laws. For the "new" nations of migration like the United States, Australia, Canada, or New Zealand, migration laws are crucially bound up with populating the nation and the exercise of nation building. In only slightly earlier times, they provided a framework for "settlement" and regulated the

---

64 Anthony D. Smith, *National Identity* (London and New York: Penguin, 1991) at 40.
65 Ernest Gellner, *Nations and Nationalism* (Ithaca, New York: Cornell University Press, 1983); Benedict Anderson, *Imagined Communities: Reflections on the Origin and Spread of Nationalism* (London and New York: Verso, 1991). Peter Fitzpatrick offers a compelling critique of these attempts to define nation in *Modernism and the Grounds of Law, supra* note 37 at 114–20.
66 Eric Hobsbawn and Terence Ranger, *The Invention of Tradition* (Cambridge and New York: Cambridge University Press, 1983).
67 William Rogers Brubaker, *Citizenship and Nationhood in France and Germany* (Cambridge, Mass.: Harvard University Press, 1992).

composition of the "founding" population. The importance of migration to the mythic foundations of these "nations of immigration" plays an important role both in silencing and in marking the absence of the voices of indigenous populations. In nations that have well-developed contemporary immigration programs, migration law provides the effective controls on the full membership that is inscribed in citizenship law.[68] In these ways, migration law is essential to creating the population that can become the nation.

Liberal theory, the paradigm within which nation-states came to divide and dominate the world's political landscape, by and large makes the assumption that the borders to the community are, or at least can morally be, closed.[69] Michael Walzer, the dominant theorist to have taken up the issue of the border of the liberal community in detail, argues that the question of membership is of a prior order than those of justice or equality, and that accordingly membership is the primary good that a community bestows.[70] In order for the community to operate against an assumption of closed borders, there must be a way of closing them, of identifying who has a right to cross them, and of providing for enforcement of their closure. Although ultimately the coercive power of the state provides these things, it is the rule of law that legitimates them and makes them part of the liberal state. Again, as was the case in considering the factors that Hirst and Thompson identified as crucial to the nationalization of people, the answers here are, from the jurist's point of view, provided by migration laws.

The role of migration law in giving form to a key assumption of the liberal community points in the direction of the two final features linked to globalization's dilemmas. The first of these is that in questions of migration and citizenship, there is almost no international law. International law leaves it to individual states to determine who may enter their territory – through migration law – and who may become full members – through citizenship law.[71] The three potential qualifications

---

68 This relationship and its implication for illegal migration is discussed fully in Chapter 7.
69 I make this argument in detail in Catherine Dauvergne, "Beyond Justice: The Consequences of Liberalism for Immigration Law," (1997), 10 *Canadian Journal of Law and Jurisprudence* 323; and Catherine Dauvergne, "Amorality and Humanitarianism in Immigration Law," (1999), 37 *Osgoode Hall Law Journal* 597.
70 Michael Walzer, *Spheres of Justice: A Defense of Pluralism and Equality* (New York: Basic Books, 1983), see especially "Chapter 2: Membership." Having argued this point, Walzer moves on to his central argument about justice, leaving the question of membership behind. Thus his argument is similar to other liberals such as Rawls (for whom the community is one which one enters at birth and leaves at death; "Justice as Fairness: Political not Metaphysical," (1985), 14 *Philosophy and Public Affairs* 223 at 233) or Dworkin (for whom communities of principle must settle questions of equality and justice among members; Ronald Dworkin, *Law's Empire* (Cambridge, Mass.: Harvard University Press, 1986) at 208) for whom justice is to be understood within the border rather than across it.
71 *Nottebohm Case (Lichtenstein v. Guatemala) (Second Phase)*, [1955] I.C.J. Rep. 4. There were some discussions in the early years of the twentieth century suggesting that international standards be developed in the areas of citizenship and migration. The idea was raised in international fora and explicitly rejected, largely because of the question of racial exclusion, see Sean Brawley, *The White Peril: Foreign Relations and Asian Immigration to Australasia and North America 1919–1978* (Sydney: UNSW Press, 1995).

to this rule do not dislodge it. I have already argued that the emergence of regional trading alliances is not necessarily hinged to movements of people. The second potential qualification to this rule is that there is an increasing prevalence of provisions for dual citizenships and changing citizenships over a person's lifetime. While this makes citizenship less restrictive than previously, it does not alter its role as the legal signifier of full membership, as I explore in Chapter 7. The third potential qualification to the statement that individual nation-states exercise full control over their membership is the role of international refugee law. This is the most important potential constraint on state control over its border, and I address it in detail in the next chapter. At this point, I note only that refugee law does not explicitly provide a right for any person to enter another state, nor does it confer a right to full membership in a state that provides refuge.

The absence of international law in this area means that in questions of migration outside Europe, legal order at the level of the nation-state overshadows all else. Whereas other legal topics that appear in the globalization script have seen a flourishing of supranational norm development, the as-yet-failed Migrant Workers' Convention is the only significant new law in the migration area. I discuss the European Union separately in Chapter 8 because some do see it as an exception to this rule, a perspective I think is flawed. Because of the persistent predominance of national-level law in migration matters, the question of whether law can become unhinged from the nation – Santos' first step in "unthinking" law – is vital here. Migration law is bound up in the nation's own identity. It is the law that polices the boundary of the community, both on the ground and in theoretical accounts of the liberal nation. Separating migration law from nation would then involve re-imagining the domain of this law in a completely innovative way. An injection of human rights is not sufficient, because shifting the discussion to the plane of rights necessarily invokes the right of the nation itself to control its own borders.

The contemporary crackdown on extralegal migration reveals that in the face of globalizing forces, migration is increasingly being transformed into the last bastion of sovereignty. The basis for this transformation is found in the roles of migration law in the liberal community. These roles mean that migration law itself has traditionally been associated with the core of sovereign power. In states that follow the English common law tradition, control over questions of immigration was originally part of the Royal Prerogative.[72] In the contemporary era, this has evolved into a strong tradition of deference on the part of the courts to executive decision making in questions of immigration,[73] and to leaving key aspects of immigration law in the hands of the executive rather than turning them over to

---

72 Kathryn Cronin, "A Culture of Control: An Overview of Immigration Policy-Making" in James Jupp and Marie Kabala, eds., *The Politics of Australian Immigration* (Canberra: Australian Government Publishing Service, 1993).
73 See Stephen Legomsky's seminal study comparing the immigration law traditions of the United States and Britain and finding strong similarities on this point, *Immigration and the Judiciary: Law and Politics in Britain and America* (Oxford: Clarendon Press, 1987). See also Catherine Dauvergne,

democratic law-making processes.[74] Migration legislation is generally structured so that shifts in political priorities can be quickly implemented. In the United States this is accomplished by having a temporary visa program that overshadows the legal form of the permanent immigration program for all practical intents. In Australia this is achieved through a near incessant amendment of the legislation, with several new bills each year, sometimes as many as a dozen. In Canada, the immigration legislation is touted as "framework legislation." This translates in reality into a law with twenty-seven separate and sometimes conflicting objectives where real numbers and points system priorities are set aside from the legal text. All of these factors contribute a close conceptual association between control over the definition of membership and physical crossings of the border and state sovereignty. The close association of migration law with executive discretion means the ideological commitments of the rule of law are strongly tested in this setting.

To adapt Joseph Carens' image, borders are meaningful because they are ultimately defended by the coercive power of the state.[75] This image of sovereignty parallels Weberian definitions of the state. This is why illegal migration in particular is so important to a consideration of sovereignty and globalization, because the persistence of illegal migration affects the state at precisely this point – the ultimate definition of sovereign power – the border itself is breached. No nation today can hermetically seal its borders. In an ironic challenge to traditional state sovereignty, the uncontested hegemon of the contemporary world hosts perhaps the largest illegal population in the world. At present, prosperous nations are engaged in an increasing competition for the "best and brightest" of the emerging globally mobile class. This competition brings convergence in migration standards and provisions, as some states clearly see themselves as operating on a competitive playing field to attract the most desirable skilled workers.[76] The story of migration and globalization certainly extends to this phenomenon as well. Illegal migration, however, is more compelling for addressing how law operates within globalization. Law is implicated in constructing illegal migration, and is the principal tool thus far deployed to confront it. Illegal migration provokes the sharpest discussion about questions of human rights and citizenship. It leads into the terrain of rule of law, and ultimately to the question of the extent to which sovereignty is, can be, or should be constrained.

Humanitarianism, Identity and Nation: Migration Laws of Australia and Canada (Vancouver: UBC Press, 2005), especially Chapters 4 and 6.

74 For example, the all-important "quotas" that determine how many migrants in which categories will actually be admitted are determined directly by the executive in the United States, Canada, and Australia. Similarly, deportation decisions, which are the aspects of migration law involving the highest levels of state coercion, are generally left to the executive as well.

75 Joseph Carens, "Aliens and Citizens: The Case for Open Borders," (1987), 49 *The Review of Politics* 251, which opens with the statement: "Borders have guards and guards have guns."

76 Ayelet Shachar, "The Race for Talent: Highly Skilled Migrants and Competitive Immigration Regimes," (2006), 81 *NYU Law Review* 148.

In the core sampling chapters that follow, these themes are intertwined. The central notion of a transformation in the nature of sovereignty occurs in each of these settings. The discussion of refugee law addresses human rights and dilemmas of global governance. The exploration of trafficking explores the question of globalization as Americanization, as well as the economic logic of globalization. Attention to the security transformation of migration law focuses attention on rule of law and its emancipatory potential. Citizenship law considers a reading of sovereignty as national identity. Chapter 8 then places these discussions against the narrative of globalization that offers pride of place to the United States and the European Union. Against this analysis, then, the final chapter picks up the questions of precisely how national sovereignty is altered – or not – in this context, and how law itself is weathering globalization's storm.

The "us" and "them" line, so familiarly drawn by migration law to constitute the nation, is shifted in global times to embrace a new "us," and simultaneously redraw the boundaries of exclusion. The seemingly simultaneous arrival of illegal migrants at borders around the world is an effect of the technologies of globalization. We can see three of these stories side by side in the same newspaper, or one after another on the same television program. This fuels the moral panic: "we" the rich are under siege – it is happening everywhere, all the time. Technologies of globalization are also involved in the mechanics of the people-smuggling trade, which supports at least some of this migration. The highly organized snakehead gangs of China's Fujian province make use of the same technologies of communication, finance, and transport to organize "delivery" of paying customers to Britain, Canada, Australia, or the United States.

Yet just as globalization's technologies multiply and rebroadcast to the "us" group images of the threat at "our" doorstep on the other side of the earth, the same technologies present to potential migrants images of alternate lives. Prosperous countries are no longer unimaginably distant or impossible to visualize. Flight is easier to imagine, and choices are more tangible.[77] Those who make perilous illegal journeys, however, encounter the sharp contradiction of globalization mythology: the geographies compressed are metaphorical – traveling in an airtight lorry container each mile counts.

---

77 It was reported at the time of the *Tampa* affair that Australia was the least expensive destination available from people smugglers to Afghans living in refugee camps in Pakistan.

CHAPTER FOUR

Making asylum illegal

This chapter addresses the decreasing availability of asylum in prosperous Western countries. The vital theme here is how international refugee law has become intertwined with the growing global concern about illegal migration. From an advocacy point of view, this is jarring. Refugees are not illegal migrants. Although the Refugee Convention does not specify a right to enter another country, it is widely understood to prohibit turning claimants away from a state party's borders, and it explicitly prevents states from punishing refugees for illegal entry.[1] It seems, therefore, that conditions are in place to prevent refugees from being caught up in the illegal migration panic. This impression is heightened by the observation that international refugee law has been in place for more than half a century, that 147 states are signatories to the key Convention and Protocol, and that this high rate of adherence has prevailed for some time.[2] In addition, the Refugee Convention, as I mentioned in Chapter 3, is the one exception to the principle that international law has very little to say about migration, and that states are by and large free to close – or open – their own borders.

All of these factors mean that it is crucial to understand why refugee law nonetheless fits with the argument I am making. Refugee law's relationship with state sovereignty is my reason for putting this core sample first. Beginning from this point, I argue that globalizing social, political, and legal forces are vital to understanding

---

1 James C. Hathaway, *The Rights of Refugees Under International Law* (Cambridge and New York: Cambridge University Press, 2005) 385–406; Penelope Mathew, "Australian Refugee Protection in the Wake of the *Tampa*," (2002), 96 *American Journal of International Law* 6. Article 31(1) of *Convention Relating to the Status of Refugees,* July 28, 1951, 189 U.N.T.S. 150 (entered into force April 22, 1954) [*Refugee Convention*] states,

> The Contracting States shall not impose penalties, on account of their illegal entry or presence, on refugees who, coming directly from a territory where their life or freedom was threatened in the sense of article 1, enter or are present in their territory without authorization, provided they present themselves without delay to the authorities and show good cause for their illegal entry or presence.

2 *Refugee Convention,* ibid. *Protocol Relating to the Status of Refugees,* December 16, 1966, 606 U.N.T.S. 267 (entered into force October 4, 1967) [*Refugee Protocol*]. UNHCR, "States Parties to the 1951 Convention relating to the Status of Refugees and the 1967 Protocol," on-line: UNHCR: Protecting Refugees, http://www.unhcr.org/protect/PROTECTION/3b73b0d63.pdf.

the increasing illegality of asylum. These forces include the sharp rise in refugee claimant numbers in prosperous Western countries that coincided with increased social importance of globalization in the late 1980s; the spread of legal measures targeting illegal migration; and the increasing vitality of human rights law. These factors each contribute to states resiling from the central commitments of refugee law. This story also contributes insights into the place of economic growth in narrating globalization. Drawing these elements together we also see that refugee law is an important site to observe the potential transformation of the rule of law. This makes it worth considering the emancipatory role of refugee law and how advocates may work to develop this.

The core sample at the heart of this chapter is the story of the MV *Tampa*, a Norwegian flagged container ship that rescued 433 asylum seekers near Australia in August 2001. The *Tampa* story portrays all the key elements of the narration of refugee law in global times. While Australia is a small state in terms of refugee claims and refugee reception, it is not small in terms of refugee mythology. Indeed, following the *Tampa* saga, Australia has been the global leader in the refugee law race to the bottom. Australian advocates have also been extremely creative in pressing the law into service, and its Federal Court and High Court have also been creatively involved in the development of refugee law. I turn first to the *Tampa* story, and then proceed to consider more generally states resiling from refugee law and how a transformation of the rule of law emerges in response.

Threat to the Australian nation

In Australia, the story of the MV *Tampa* is a key marker in the evolution of refugee law and politics. Early in August 2001, a group of asylum seekers, mostly Afghans fleeing the Taliban regime, boarded a barely seaworthy vessel in southern Indonesia. When their vessel began sinking, the Australian coast guard radioed the *Tampa*, which was passing nearby, alerting the captain and crew of the need for rescue on the high seas.[3] After rescuing those on board, the captain sought to disembark them on the Australian territory of Christmas Island. This would seem to be in conformity with international law of the sea, but the Australian government took the unprecedented step of closing its territorial seas in order to prevent the asylum seekers from entering Australia and thus being able to claim refugee status. John Howard's government deployed its strongest rhetorical tools, casting those on board as a threat to the Australian nation.[4] Despite the record that almost 85 percent of all claimants from Afghanistan had been granted refugee status in Australia in

---

3 Don Rothwell has written about the legality at international law of this request and the convention that it be answered. "The Law of the Sea and the MV *Tampa* Incident: Reconciling Maritime Principles with Coastal State Sovereignty," (2002), 13 *Public Law Review* 118.
4 David Marr and Marian Wilkinson, *Dark Victory* (Sydney: Allen and Unwin, 2003). This theme is evident generally in the discussion; see particularly Chapter 3, "Australia v. the boat people" and Chapter 11, "The shadow of the Twin Towers."

this time period, those on board were clearly identified as illegal migrants by the government of the day.

The standoff at sea lasted most of the month of August. Those who had been rescued made it clear to the Norwegian ship's captain that they wanted to seek asylum in Australia. Australia made clear its opinion that the rescuees ought to be returned to Indonesia. At one point the standoff featured elite SAS troops boarding the ship by stealth, ostensibly to deliver requested medical assistance and food. From a legal perspective, one of the key events in the crisis was the attempt by a group of lawyers in Melbourne to "represent" those on board and to bring a habeas corpus motion on their behalf that would require them to be brought into Australia. The application was initially successful, in a decision of the Federal Court of Australia handed down on September 11, 2001.[5] However, within a week the Full Court of the Federal Court had overruled this decision, and also allowed retroactive legislation authorizing some of the government's actions during the crisis.[6] The outcome of the immediate crisis was unforeseeable: the Australian government succeeded in preventing the asylum seekers from reaching Australian territory. In the unfortunately named "Pacific Solution," Australia entered agreements with New Zealand, Papua New Guinea, and Nauru to accept those on board. These agreements featured extensive payments to Papua New Guinea and Nauru, neither of which had an established system for addressing claims. The rescuees were transported to these nearby states by naval ship, which was their closest contact with the Australian state.

By 2004, when the events were drawing to a close with the final decisions regarding those who sought refuge on board that ship,[7] refugee law in Australia was transformed. Shortly after the *Tampa* standoff, a national election was called in Australia, during which the government's response to refugees was high on the agenda, intertwined with the then-new post–September 11 security climate. In the lead-up to the election, the opposition Labour party agreed to several key changes to Australia's migration legislation, which it had been resisting for several years. The centerpiece of this push was to insert a privative clause into the Australian migration legislation that purported to end all judicial oversight.[8] In addition, the government legislated acceptable interpretations of international refugee law, discussed in the next section. The government also quickly passed into law new proposals that determined that some of Australia's sovereign territory would not be considered sovereign for the purposes of making an asylum claim and began more aggressively heading off boats that might possibly reach Australia.[9] The flurry of

---

5 *Victorian Council for Civil Liberties Incorporated v. Minister for Immigration and Multicultural Affairs*, [2001] FCA 1297, 110 FCR 452 (September 11, 2001). The terrorist attacks in the United States began shortly before midnight in Australia, that is, at 23:50 on September 11, 2001.

6 *Ruddock v. Vardalis*, [2001] FCA 1329, 110 FCR 491 (September 18, 2001).

7 "UN Gives Final *Tampa* Boat People Refugee Status," *Agence France-Presse English Wire* (May 20, 2004).

8 *Migration Legislation Amendment (Judicial Review) Act* 2001 (Cth).

9 *Migration Amendment (Excision from Migration Zone) Act* 2001 (Cth).

amendments continued after 2001 and included marking a deeper divide between temporary and permanent refugee protection, and legislatively specifying what procedural fairness could mean in Australian migration law.[10] The legislation that passed in the *Tampa*'s wake has been challenged and has partially survived.[11] The *Tampa* episode is both a local and a global marker,[12] a small but resonant chapter in the story of the decline of refugee law. It is small because in terms of an international legal instrument that is applied to millions around the globe, what Australia chooses to do in response to the arrival of a theoretical maximum of about 8,000 potential refugee claimants per year does not add up to much.[13] It is resonant, however, because the events occupied a high-profile place on the world stage and the Australian uses and abuses of international refugee law at the time are being reflected in Europe, on the international scene, and arguably in North America as well.

We have become inured to the way refugee flows into prosperous Western countries are intertwined with the story of illegal migration, but it is worth pausing nonetheless to consider this acceptance because it reflects key elements of the relationship between globalization and illegal migration. When masses of people flow over the border from Burma to Thailand, from Rwanda to Burundi, or from the Sudan to Chad and the Central African Republic, we are prepared to assume that they are refugees, or even that they should be considered as such despite not fitting within the letter of the law. However, when the border being crossed is closer to home in the prosperous West, and the politics one is fleeing have slipped from the front pages, the assumption is often the inverse. In order to claim refugee status, those seeking it must reach a place where the claim is meaningful. The Refugee Convention does not spell out how this can or should be done. As such, each move over the past fifteen to twenty years that has been aimed at limiting

---

10 *Migration Legislation Amendment Act (No. 6)* 2001 (Cth); *Migration Legislation Amendment (Transitional Movement) Act* 2002 (Cth); *Migration Legislation Amendment (Procedural Fairness) Act* 2002.

11 Following the events of the *Tampa* crisis, the Australian government introduced a number of acts amending the *Migration Act* 1958 (*Cth.*). In addition to the privative clause were measures to confine interpretation of the refugee definition, and rules making it impossible to claim asylum in some Australian territory. In *Plaintiff S157/2002 v. Commonwealth of Australia*, [2003] H.C.A. 2, 211 C.L.R. 476 [*Plaintiff S157*], the High Court of Australia partially upheld the privative clause. Of all the new provisions, this was the one that was easiest to challenge. The decision is a partial victory for asylum seekers and their advocates.

12 In "Making People Illegal" in Peter Fitzpatrick and Patricia Tuitt, eds., *Critical Beings: Law, Nation, and the Global Subject* (Aldershot: Ashgate Press, 2004) 83, I recount the events surrounding the early part of the *Tampa* story as an illustration of globalization narrative.

13 From 1989 to mid-2002, 13,475 people arrived in Australia by unauthorized boats. The highest figures for single years were 1999–2000 when 4,175 people arrived and 2000–2001 when 4,137 people arrived (Department of Immigration Multicultural and Indigenous Affairs, "Fact Sheet 74: Unauthorized Arrivals by Sea and Air 2002," on-line: http://www.immi.gov.au/facts). Since 2001, arrivals have dropped markedly, probably in response to Australian enforcement operations. People arriving in boats are not the only ones who claim asylum in Australia. In 2002–2003, 8,247 asylum claims were finalized, of which 866 were accepted. The following two years saw a similar number of accepted claims. 2005-06, the most recent year for which statistics are available in December 2007, saw 1,272 accepted claims. (Department of Immigration Multicultural and Indigenous Affairs, *Annual Reports*, various years).

extralegal migration has a punitive effect on those seeking refugee status. The effect is more likely to be harmful to potential refugees than to other migrants because their need to flee is by definition acute, and often they lack resources to do so or are cut off from access to their assets. For at least a decade now and perhaps a good while longer, refugee law has officially been in crisis.[14] The endemic sense of crisis should by now push us to the realization that refugee law is about crisis by definition. Crisis should become the standard rather than the exception. Because Western states seek to limit their responsibilities toward refugees, those coming from so-called "refugee-producing" places are often unable to get entry visas. These factors combine to ensure that measures cracking down on illegal migration have especially harsh effects on refugees. Furthermore, the intensification of border-controlling measures also means that the incentive to attempt to exploit refugee law's constraint on sovereignty is heightened. In other words, there are now greater incentives than ever before to attempt to pass oneself off as a refugee seeking protection in a prosperous Western state. For these reasons, refugees and refugee law are now located at the center of concern about illegal migration, despite the *ex post facto*, and sometimes limited, protection extended to their migration.

Resiling from refugee law[15]

What is commonly referred to as international refugee law is set out in the 1951 Convention Relating to the Status of Refugees and its 1967 Protocol.[16] As of November 2007, 144 states were party to the Convention and 141 to both instruments.[17] Although the Universal Declaration of Human Rights also contains a right to seek and enjoy asylum,[18] this has not been successfully articulated as expanding the interpretation of the two refugee-specific documents that followed it. Similarly, while there is now some potential to make an argument that a right to seek asylum has become a principle of customary international law, this argument is not widely recognized nor would such a principle be an advance on the Refugee Convention and Protocol, as a right to seek offers little without a reciprocal right to receive asylum or some other form of protection.

14 James Hathaway and Alexander Neve, "Making International Refugee Law Relevant Again: A Proposal for Collectivized and Solution-Oriented Protection," (1997), 10 *Harvard Human Rights Journal* 115.

15 I published an earlier version of the argument in this section as "Refugee Law and the Measure of Globalization" (2005), 22:2 *Law in Context* 62.

16 *Refugee Convention, supra* note 1; *Refugee Protocol, supra* note 2.

17 UNHCR, "States Parties to the 1951 Convention Relating to the Status of Refugees and the 1967 Protocol," on-line: UNHCR: Protecting Refugees, http://www.unhcr.org/protect/PROTECTION/3b73b0d63.pdf.

18 Article 14 of the *Universal Declaration of Human Rights*, GA Res. 217 (III), UN GAOR, 3d Sess., Supp. No. 13, UN Doc. A/810 (1948) states:

(1) Everyone has the right to seek and to enjoy in other countries asylum from persecution.

(2) This right may not be invoked in the case of prosecution genuinely arising from the nonpolitical crimes or from acts contrary to the purposes and principles of the United Nations.

The key features of international refugee law are the definition of a refugee and the non-refoulement commitment.[19] In tandem these mean that signatory states have committed to determining whether a person is a refugee, and, if she is, to not sending her back to a place where she is likely to face certain types of persecution. In most circumstances, this commitment means that refugees acquire indirectly a right to remain in the state where they have claimed refugee status for the simple reason that nowhere other than their state of nationality is required to welcome them back, and usually the persecution they have fled occurred at home. Two other aspects of the international refugee regime that have received some attention are the exclusions provisions (Article 1F) – setting out that some people who would otherwise be refugees have done something so reprehensible that protection is not available to them – and the commitment not to penalize refugees for illegally entering a state of refuge (Article 31). What this means is that most parts of the Refugee Convention get very little attention. These include many provisions securing basic human rights for refugees, and treatment standards equal to those for other foreigners, or in some cases, nationals.

My argument that key wealthy Western parties to the Convention are now resiling from refugee law addresses these core aspects of the Convention – the parts that have gotten the most attention. These prosperous states are vital to the robust good health of refugee law because they are the most sought-after destinations, and because they come closest to having the capacity to close their borders to refugee claimants should they choose to do so. Although these states hold only a relatively small portion of the world's refugees, they have for better or worse been leaders in establishing the international regime and the extent to which they treat the Refugee Convention as a constraint on their sovereignty is therefore significant.[20] The array of measures Australia has deployed following the *Tampa* events has contributed to reducing asylum flows to a mere trickle.[21] This border closing success makes Australia the envy of many Western states. For poorer states, where most of the world's refugees are currently waiting in camps, the movement of masses of people over their borders is what constrains sovereignty. The abstract

19 Article 1A(2) of the *Refugee Convention, supra* note 1, as amended by the *Refugee Protocol, supra* note 2, states that the term "refugee" shall apply to any person who:

owing to a well-founded fear of being persecuted for reasons of race, religion, nationality, membership of a particular social group, or political opinion is outside the country of his nationality and is unable or, owing to such fear, is unwilling to avail himself of the protection of that country; or who, not having a nationality and being outside the country of his former habitual residence as a result of such events, is unable or, owing to such fear, is unwilling to return to it.

Article 33(1) states: "No contracting state shall expel or return ("refouler") a refugee in any manner whatsoever to the frontiers of territories where his life or freedom would be threatened on account of his race, religion, nationality, membership of a particular social group, or political opinion."

20 At the close of 2006, approximately 3 million of the 32.9 million persons of concern to the UNHCR were in Europe or the Americas; see UNHCR, "2006 Global Trends" Geneva: Division of Operational Services, revised 16 July 2007.

21 In 2000–2001, 5,577 protection visas were granted to asylum seekers in Australia. By 2003–2004, this number was reduced to 869. In 2005–2006, 1,272 protection visas were granted inside Australia. See www.immi.gov.au/media/fact-sheets/60refugee.htm.

constraint represented by the law is a luxury. The formal equality of sovereignty is at odds with the reality of some nations having more sovereignty than others, and thus conforming more closely to the ideal of "nation." Thus, while refugee populations are predominantly located in Africa and Asia, prosperous Western nations have led the development of refugee law from the outset, and continue to do so.

The hidden or silenced parts of the Refugee Convention are a curious phenomenon, worth noting here because of my attention in this argument to questions of access to human rights. In many instances, the silenced articles address points that are well covered in other human rights instruments, such as freedom of religion (Article 4), nondiscrimination (Article 3),[22] rights of association (Article 15), access to courts (Article 16), employment rights (Article 17–19), and freedom of movement equal to that of other foreigners (Article 26). Others of the overlooked provisions address refugee-specific matters such as state duty to issue identity papers and travel documents (Article 27–8)[23] and to facilitate assimilation and naturalization (Article 34). Whichever way one chooses to interpret these provisions, a potentially disturbing human rights discourse arises. Either the presence of these provisions is to underscore that refugees have human rights *too*, and therefore to suggest that states might otherwise choose to ignore this; or it suggests that other human rights instruments are insufficient to guarantee the human rights of refugees, despite their application to all people. Both possibilities are disturbing. Although the Convention was drafted before *some* of these rights were set down universally elsewhere, it is curious that these provisions have not received more attention in the ongoing struggles to establish human rights protections for refugees.[24] This is beginning to change, but slowly and belatedly. An important marker in bringing more attention to the human rights of refugees is James C. Hathaway's 2005 book *The Rights of Refugees Under International Law*, which has the potential to influence refugee jurisprudence significantly.[25] At this point, however, these observations about the Refugee Convention parallel the Chapter 2 discussion of the Migrant Workers' Convention. The all-important difference is that the Refugee Convention is a widely respected treaty that constrains sovereignty, while the Migrant Workers' Convention is as yet an unfulfilled promise skirting sovereignty.

The fact that the majority of these provisions are rarely controversial underscores that the most important content of the Refugee Convention is the awkwardly

---

22 Nondiscrimination in the application of the *Refugee Convention, supra* note 1, on the bases of race, religion, or country of origin.
23 The duty to issue travel documents is qualified in cases of national security or public order risks.
24 For example, these provisions have not featured in recent arguments in Australia, (*Plaintiff S157/2002 v. Commonwealth of Australia*, [2003] H.C.A. 2, 211 C.L.R. 476), in the United Kingdom (*"Q" and Others v. Secretary State for Home Department*, [2003] EWHC 195, [2003] EWJ No. 718 (Admin.)), or in Canada (*Suresh v. Canada (Minister of Citizenship and Immigration)*, 2002 SCC 1, [2002] 1 S.C.R. 3, 208 D.L.R. (4th) 1) where they plausibly could have been put forward.
25 *Supra* note 1.

formulated and inversely constructed right to remain. This right is constructed from the central Article 33 non-refoulement provision and the backdrop of the international legal regime's provision that states are not obligated to admit anyone who is not their own national. Non-refoulement means that refugees cannot be returned to a place where they risk persecution. This is most usually home, and there is most often nowhere else obligated to admit them.[26] The Refugee Convention does not establish a right to remain permanently, and contemplates that protection will end when the conditions at home that lead to risk are resolved.[27] In practice, many Western states with established refugee reception programs either grant refugees permanent status at the outset, or allow them to apply for it.[28] The importance of this right mirrors Walzer's distributive justice model in which membership is to be distributed as a prior good, to be allocated before questions of just distribution are addressed.[29] In refugee law, this prior good is the center of debate, a predicate for contestation over other rights that follow.

Australia's response to asylum seekers on the *Tampa* offers at least three key examples of departures from the Refugee Convention. These have been canvassed by a number of scholars, particularly within Australia, and I will review them here only briefly.[30] The initial act of preventing refugees from entering sovereign territory is not addressed by the Convention directly, but is implicitly covered by the Article 33 prohibition against refoulement in " . . . any manner whatsoever."[31] Thus, the initial step of refusing to allow the boat to land because of the asylum seekers on board was arguably itself a breach. The next step in the Australian plan was to use state resources to transport the asylum seekers to New Zealand, Nauru, and Papua New Guinea. As New Zealand is a party to the Convention, no refoulement is involved in this case. Nauru, however, is not a party and Papua New Guinea has entered important reservations to the Convention.[32] It is unlikely that either Nauru or Papua New Guinea could meet the requirement of offering adequate protection

---

26 This accounts for the importance of dual citizenship to refugee law, refugee status will only be granted to people at risk in each country where they are a citizen. Refugee jurisprudence has therefore spent considerable effort in deciding what constitutes a citizenship right. See for example, *Katkova v. Canada* [1997] F.C.J. No. 549; *Bouianova v. Canada* [1993] F.C.J. No. 576.

27 Article 1C(5).

28 In this regard as well, Australia has been an innovator. Until 1999 all those granted refugee status in Australia were given permanent residency. In late 1999, however, this was altered so that anyone who entered the country without a visa is only eligible for a temporary status.

29 Michael Walzer, *Spheres of Justice* (New York: Basic Books, 1983) at Ch. 2.

30 This discussion draws on arguments put forward by Penelope Mathew, *supra* note 1; Mary Crock, "In the Wake of the *Tampa*: Conflicting Visions of International Refugee Law in the Management of Refugee Flows," (2003), 12 *Pacific Rim Law and Policy Journal* 49; Kim Rubenstein, "Citizenship, Sovereignty and Migration: Australia's Exclusive Approach to Membership of the Community," (2002), 13 *Public Law Review* 102. Each of these authors takes a slightly different approach to the question of Australian noncompliance with the Refugee Convention, and my own analysis varies somewhat from each.

31 Discussed in detail in Mathew, *supra* note 1 at 666–7.

32 UNHCR, "Reservations and Declarations to the 1951 Refugee Convention," on-line: www.unhcr. ch/cgi-bin/texis/vtx/home/+swwBmLeKJSpwwwwrwwwwwwwmFqA72ZR0gRfZNhFqA72ZR0g RfZNtFqrpGdBnqBAFqA72ZR0gRfZNcFqMGn5nGVwBodD5Dzmxwwwwwww/opendoc.pdf.

for refugees, which is an aspect of the non-refoulement commitment.[33] Australia's second significant breach of the Convention was brought in by the legislation declaring that some Australian territory is not in fact Australian territory for the purposes of making a refugee claim.[34] Although such legislation is within Australia's constitutional competence, it is nonsensical from the perspective of international law. To maintain sovereignty for the purposes of, say, asserting resource rights in the Timor Sea, but not for the purposes of receiving asylum applications, is not something contemplated by international law. Finally, in the wave of post-*Tampa* legislation, Australia also moved to "modify" the refugee definition by limiting interpretations of "persecution" of a "particular social group." The legislation also defined serious and nonpolitical crimes.[35] These amendments depart from the accepted international principle that treaties are to be interpreted "in good faith in accordance with the ordinary meaning"[36] by substituting a national parliamentary interpretation of the rules in the place of judicial interpretation and independence. It also ensured that interpretations that had previously been made in Australia and internationally will no longer be possible in Australian courts.

It is possible to point to additional breaches as well. My argument here, however, is not to establish these breaches beyond a point of legal certainty. These arguments have been substantiated by others and in present political circumstances will never be adjudicated. Rather, I want to pick up from this point and consider what the consequences are of resiling from the Refugee Convention in this way and how it fits into the globalization script and my broader argument about globalization and illegal migration. Australia has not suffered any legal consequences. Australia has not at any point suggested that it is moving away from the Refugee Convention, nor has it attempted to make any reservations. Instead, it defends its actions as in keeping with the Convention.[37] No formal challenge to Australia's position is likely to eventuate because with each breach that purports to be in keeping with the Convention, Australia extends the space in which other states may also move away from the Convention's core. Article 38 provides that disputes relating to the Convention, between parties to it, may be taken to the International Court of Justice. This is unlikely to occur as most who would be aggrieved are individuals, not states. To the contrary, most states party would be openly or secretly pleased to assert that Australia's actions fit within the parameters of the Convention.

---

33 Matthew, *supra* note 1 at 667–9.
34 See *Migration Amendment (Excision from Migration Zone) Act, supra* note 9. In 2006, legislation was proposed to extend this principle to cover all of mainland Australia but was defeated.
35 *Migration Act, supra* note 11 at ss. 91R-91U.
36 *Vienna Convention on the Law of Treaties,* May 23, 1969, 1155 U.N.T.S. 331 (entered into force January 27, 1980) at Art. 31.
37 Crock, *supra* note 30 illustrates this well. The Australian government repeatedly emphasizes its adherence to the Convention. For two examples among many, see Minister Amanda Vanstone, Press Release, "Australia's Proud Contribution to World Refugees," (June 21, 2004) and Department of Immigration and Multicultural and Indigenous Affairs, "Fact Sheet 61: Seeking Asylum Within Australia" (2003), on-line: http://www.immi.gov.au/facts.

Since the *Tampa* saga, a number of other states have also made steps away from key components of the Refugee Convention: the United Kingdom has floated proposals for processing asylum claims outside their sovereign territory,[38] the United Nations High Commissioner for Refugees has launched its Convention Plus initiative,[39] Canada has introduced legislation with more stringent exclusions on the basis of criminality than the Refugee Convention contains,[40] and Canada and the United States have entered a Safe Third Country agreement.[41] In April 2004, the member states of the European Union finalized an agreement on asylum seekers that follows the Australian model in mandating interpretations of aspects of the Convention, and that has been criticized extensively, including by the United Nations High Commissioner for Refugees.[42] Each of these initiatives continues the process of chipping away at the Refugee Convention.

It cannot be argued that Australia's actions caused other developments. Indeed, most of these moves were on the drawing table long before the *Tampa* and its legislative aftermath. Similarly, these changes in the law cannot be attributed to the security climate that has prevailed since the terrorist attacks of September 11, 2001. The increased security climate has undoubtedly hastened some moves and lent political support to others, as Chapter 6 addresses directly. For the most part, however, post 9/11 changes in migration law, with their distinct effects on refugee movements, have been consistent with trends observable over the preceding decade among Western nations.

By asserting in each case that their actions maintain compliance with the Refugee Convention, current state practice may, however, demonstrate that the Convention

38 Stephen Castle, "Blair Plans to Go Ahead with Asylum Protection Zones," *The Independent* (June 21, 2003); UK, H.L., European Union Committee, *Handling EU Asylum Claims: New Approaches Examined* (Eleventh Report) (London: The Stationery Office Limited, 2004), on-line: UK Parliament: Publications and Records, http://www.publications.parliament.uk/pa/ld200304/ldselect/ldeucom/74/74.pdf; UK, H.C., Home Affairs Committee, *Asylum Applications* (Second Report) vol.1 (London: The Stationery Office Limited, 2004), online: UK Parliament: Publications and Records, http://www.publications.parliament.uk/pa/cm200304/cmselect/cmhaff/218/218.pdf.

39 UNHCR, "Convention Plus at a Glance (as of May 14, 2004)" (2004), on-line: http://www.unhcr.ch/cgi-bin/texis/vtx/protect/+HwwBmeZxYdewxwwwwnwwwwwwwxFqz6X8n+hv_6mFqA72ZR0gRfZNhFqA72ZR0gRfZNtFqrpGdBnqBzFqmRbZAFqA72ZR0gRfZNDzmxwwwwwww5Fqw1FqmRbZ/opendoc.htm.

40 *Immigration and Refugee Protection Act.* S.C. 2001, c. 27, ss 36–6, 99–101.

41 *Agreement Between the Government of Canada and the Government of the United States of America for Cooperation in the Examination of Refugee Status Claims from Nationals of Third Countries (Safe Third Country Agreement)*, United States and Canada, December 5, 2002 (entered into force December 29, 2004). This agreement was found to be unconstitutional and in breach of international law by the trial division of the Federal Court of Canada in November 2007 (*Canadian Council for Refugees et al. v. Her Majesty the Queen* 2007 FC 1262). This decision is being appealed.

42 EC, *Council Directive 2004/83/EC on Minimum Standards for the Qualification and Status of Third Country Nationals or Stateless Persons as Refugees or as Persons who Otherwise Need International Protection and the Content of the Protection Granted.* "UNHCR Regrets Missed Opportunity to Adopt High EU Asylum Standards" (2004). On-line: http://www.unhcr.ch/cgi-bin/texis/vtx/home/+pwwBmbPe5qnwwwwwxwwwwwwwmFqnN0bIhFqnN0bItFqnDni5AFqnN0bIcFqFw5Oc1MapGdqnm1Gn5amoGnqBoVnDzmowwwwwwwwGFq2uNlg2aelDwq5wppdoDBnmelGmqDa0uaw5Oc1MamoGnqBoVn/opendoc.htm. This is discussed in detail in Chapter 8.

is more important now than ever. This is because in spite of an evident and widespread desire of states to limit their Convention obligations, none of these nations are simply walking away from it. The Refugee Convention is, therefore, being treated as a binding and significant international instrument, worthy of at least rhetorical adherence. This process is part of the transformation from statement of law to rule of law, which is important for advocacy efforts on behalf of refugees from this point forward. There is a long-established critique of refugee law suggesting that it has always been mostly about limiting rather than extending states' obligations.[43] Ironically, it may be that while these recent developments depart from the letter of refugee law, they do not depart from its parsimonious spirit. I will return to this point after sketching some contours of the cluster of phenomena known as globalization that are important for refugee law.

Refugee law and the human rights story

As I outlined in Chapter 3, one of the persistent strands in the story lawyers tell of law and globalization is about the increasing importance of human rights law. It is a trope of contemporary international law analysis that the second half of the twentieth century is marked by the presence of international human rights, which in tandem with the Nuremburg trials, made individuals actors in – or at least subjects of – international law for the first time.[44] There has been a proliferation of agreements concerning human rights negotiated since World War II. Beyond this flurry of negotiations, and more recently, a key part of the story is the increasing reliance on these documents in various international and domestic fora, as well as an increasing number of legal fora that do not fit these categories. There is also tangible evidence of a transformation of classical international law in the area of human rights because it is now possible for individuals to bring complaints, as against the old model where states alone were both the subjects and the objects of international law.[45]

Given all of this, the resiling from refugee law of which Australia is an illustrative but hardly isolated example is oddly placed. Globalization narratives tell us human rights law is stronger than ever before. Refugee law, which is at least related to human rights law, is being contained and curtailed. The explanation for this is that

---

43 Guy Goodwin-Gill, "Refugees: The Functions and Limits of the Existing Protection System" in Alan Nash, ed., *Human Rights and the Protection of Refugees Under International Law* (Halifax: Halifax Institute for Research and Policy, 1988) 149; James Hathaway and Alexander Neve, "Making International Refugee Law Relevant Again: A Proposal for Collectivized and Solution-Oriented Protection" (1997), 10 *Harvard Human Rights Journal* 115; Patricia Tuitt, *False Images: Law's Construction of the Refugee* (London and East Haven, CT: Pluto Press, 1996).

44 John Currie, *Public International Law* (Toronto: Irwin Law, 2001) at 15–16.

45 Individual complaints are possible under the optional protocol to the *International Covenant on Civil and Political Rights*, December 19, 1966, 999 U.N.T.S. 171, Can. T.S. 1976 No. 47, 6 I.L.M. 368 (entered into force March 23, 1976) and the *Convention on the Elimination of all Forms of Discrimination Against Women*, March 1, 1980, 1249 U.N.T.S. 13.

these two developments are interrelated because of the pressures that globalization brings to bear on the state. One does not cause the other (single variable causality is anathema to globalization) but important convergences are observable when the two are placed side by side.

The paradoxical relationship of refugee law and human rights under conditions of globalization raises an important insight suggested in, but not central to, Saskia Sassen's work. As I discussed in Chapter 3, she points to the distinction between those with legal status in a country and those without it. That is, she accepts that without legal status, it is difficult to claim any of the new plethora of rights. Refugee claimants, however, are lost in a middle ground that is invisible in this sketch. Refugee *claimant* is not a status recognized even in the Refugee Convention. By interpretive practice, and to avoid breaching refugee rights, claimants ought to be extended the same rights and protections as refugees. And often they are. In addition to the potential ambiguity of claimant status, the formal structure of refugee law renders the act of refugee determination declarative. This means that one is not a refugee because of the act of a bureaucrat or judicial officer in a host country but, rather, because of one's life circumstances. This raises the possibility that one *is* a refugee but no one knows it, or perhaps worse, no one acknowledges it. This formal distinction is legally precise, but not much help to anyone.

Similarly, amid the blossoming array of human rights, including the rights of refugees to seek employment, to attend public school, to own property and to be naturalized as soon as possible, the explicit right to enter any country is conspicuously absent. Even presuming that states would respect the Refugee Convention bar against penalizing refugees for illegal entry, the Convention does not suggest any other way for those seeking refugee status to enter. It establishes a regime in which states have obligations to those who somehow have crossed the border. Rights follow that crossing; they do not precede it. Those who approach the border claiming asylum enter a grey zone, where liberal good faith treaty interpretation requires that entry be allowed, but the state practice suggests parties do not feel strongly bound to this interpretation. The growing importance and variety of non-entrée policies suggest that, at the very least, states do not respect the requirement to allow entry until some point after geographic entry is already complete, and sometimes not even then.[46] The distinction Sassen draws between having legal status and not having it is foundational for human rights pursuits. It begs the question of getting it. What refugee law interposes into Sassen's scenario is the possibility of obtaining legal status. Ironically, this means that refugee law is either the mother-of-all-human-rights law, or not about human rights at all, as human rights refer to a different kind of thing that everyone can claim on the basis of being human,

---

46 Jens Vedsted-Hansen, "Non-admission Policies and the Right to Protection: Refugees' Choice versus States' Exclusion?" in Frances Nicholson and Patrick Twomey, eds., *Refugee Rights and Realities: Evolving International Concepts and Regimes* (Cambridge and New York: Cambridge University Press, 1999) at 269.

regardless of other circumstances. Refugee status is most explicitly *not* available to everyone, and *not* regardless of other circumstances.

Some of the consequences for refugee law of the worldwide crackdown on illegal migration are straightforward. As states increasingly make migrating outside the law more difficult, it becomes harder for those who are already refugees to make it to places where that status will bring them some measure of protection. The distinction between asylum seeking and illegally migrating becomes harder and harder to discern. Some people will, of course, believe that they are entitled to refugee status and later find out that others do not agree with them. This is not an abuse of the asylum process, but a rational response to any number of difficult or desperate situations. Given that there are no international rights to enter other countries, the inverse "right to remain" created by international refugee law stands as a beacon for all, as well as a potential incentive for deception. Some people will knowingly set out to deceive. Others may do so out of fear or despair or on the instructions of smugglers or traffickers to whom they are beholden. Each of these incentives to lie is heightened by the crackdown atmosphere. These incentives increase the level of difficulty for refugee decision makers, as lying does not exclude anyone from refugee status – it is often a necessary precursor to putting oneself in the position to claim such status.

Beyond these evident points, however, is the puzzle of figuring out how the spread of international human rights law, especially among prosperous Western nations, and withdrawal from core principles of refugee law, especially among prosperous Western nations, occur simultaneously. Putting these divergent trends together requires attention to the nature of globalization. One of the markers of globalization is paradox.[47] This paradox calls to mind Santos' image of contemporary law being poised at a moment of paradigm shift. The tension between states resiling from refugee law and the growth of human rights norms creates an opening for change. It is not yet clear which path this change will take, but let me consider the potential for an emancipatory way forward.

Refugee law is an exception to the general rule that sovereign states are free to decide who crosses their borders. While states have an obligation to admit their own nationals, all other admission decisions are discretionary, save when someone claims refugee status. The scope of the exception is limited and awkwardly expressed, but it is a constraint nevertheless. It stands to reason, then, at a time when nations are reasserting their powers over the migration realm and transforming it into the last bastion of sovereignty, that they would also move to minimize and control the extent of the one exception to state power that is established in this area.

The incentive for states to narrow the constraint that refugee law represents is even greater in the face of an expanded role for international human rights. This

---

47 Anthony Giddens, *Runaway World: How Globalization is Reshaping Our Lives* (New York: Routledge, 2000) at 31; Mark Findlay, *The Globalization of Crime: Understanding Transnational Relationships in Context* (New York and Cambridge: Cambridge University Press, 1999).

argument works in two directions. One part of the immigration and globalization story is that executive branches of government are finding it increasingly difficult to carry out policies to remove migrants or to limit their rights because the courts are blocking actions that infringe human rights principles that have been expressed either internationally or domestically.[48] This is as true of refugees and asylum seekers as of other migrants. Prosperous Western states now have considerable experience with both practical and legal barriers to deporting people – even people who have arrived seeking asylum and who have been found not to be refugees.[49] One of Australia's specific objectives in the post-*Tampa* legislative flurry was to limit access to Australian courts. Canada's new immigration legislation reduced appeal rights in a number of areas and the United Kingdom's recent push against illegal migration contains similar provisions.[50] These moves all fit within globalization's contours: As states are increasingly compelled to accept human rights norms as meaningful constraints on their actions, control over their borders means curtailing the rights of those who would cross them without authorization. One way to achieve control is by limiting the extent to which refugees' rights are perceived as *human* rights.

The second way the expansion of human rights operates within refugee law is in the persistence of the argument that the objective of refugee law is not to remedy all human rights abuses, but only to provide surrogate protection in the case of some extreme abuses, when state protection is inadequate. Several ideas are at play here. First is the principle that states are responsible for protecting their nationals from human rights breaches. Second is the presumption that states are able to do this.[51] Third is the notion that not all human rights abuses will meet the standard of "persecution" required by the refugee definition. This is problematic as it requires refugee decision makers to engage in an analysis that says some human rights abuses are things that people are expected to tolerate. Even James Hathaway's strong advocacy of a human rights reading for refugee law is linked to his careful articulation of a hierarchical human rights structure: some breaches are always persecutory, others are not.[52] Decision makers usually are clever enough to stop short of saying that certain human rights abuses are simply okay, but this

---

48 See above, Chapter 2, at pp. 20–22.
49 Matthew Gibney and Randall Hansen, "Deportation and the Liberal State: The Forcible Return of Asylum Seekers and Unlawful Migrants in Canada, Germany, and the United Kingdom," UNHCR Working Paper No. 77, 2003.
50 Canada's *Immigration and Refugee Protection Act*, S.C. 2001, c. 27 reduces appeal rights for permanent residents facing deportation and for persons deemed to be serious criminals or security risks. The United Kingdom has reduced a range of appeal rights for those in the asylum stream (David Blunkett, "I am not King Herod," *The Guardian* (November 27, 2003)).
51 *Canada (Attorney General) v. Ward,* [1993] 2 S.C.R. 689, 103 D.L.R. (4th) 1. [*Ward*] sets that standard that a state must be presumed capable of protecting its citizens unless other evidence is available to demonstrate that this is not possible. The refugee claimant thus bears the burden of demonstrating absence of state capacity, if this is part of their claim, in most cases. In *Ward* the burden was met because the Irish government stated that it could not protect Mr. Ward from the actions of paramilitary groups.
52 James Hathaway, *The Law of Refugee Status* (Toronto and Vancouver: Butterworths, 1991) at 105–24.

structure of analysis invites an invidious line of reasoning nevertheless. One often-used formula is to draw a line of distinction between "mere discrimination" and "persecution."[53]

The cumulative effect of each of these interpretive points is to make a distinction between refugee law and human rights law. This is a distinction that does not serve refugees well, and which is to be strenuously argued against, but that is fostered by the conditions of globalization. If international human rights law is becoming stronger and courts are more willing to use it to halt the migrant-related policies of their own governments, and states are increasingly inclined to treat their control of people crossing borders as the essence of their sovereignty, then states will have every reason to ensure that refugee law remains akin to *but not fully* about human rights. In this way, the growth of human rights norms is paradoxically linked to states pulling away from refugee law commitments. I am not suggesting a clearly articulated policy framing this move in any nation, but the opposing trends are clearly visible and one-half of the movement is a matter of states' policies.

This argument, therefore, calls for a careful consideration of the role of courts and of the rule of law. Courts are clearly a part of the state. They are, however, theoretically independent from government policy imperatives. The extent to which this is true in practice varies enormously, but in Western refugee-receiving nations judicial independence is a widely accepted value that governments do not overtly attack. The spread of international human rights norms and the ideology of the rule of law are, in tandem, important tools for the judiciaries of Western nations to counter government policies, when they choose to do so. This has been particularly evident in Australia, where the aggressive moves by the executive have been countered by courageous creativity on the part of the judiciary. In the case of the *Tampa* claimants themselves, the original habeas corpus ruling of the Federal Court was overturned during the 9/11 body count.[54] However, in the general transformation of refugee law, the Federal Court of Australia, and sometimes the High Court itself, have been engaged in every step of the government's movements to make asylum illegal.[55] In the absence of constitutionally entrenched individual rights statements in Australia, this engagement has had more to do with rule of law principles than it may have, had it taken place elsewhere.

The challenge that courts pose to government control over policy direction within the state is heightened by the increasing interconnectedness of the globe.

---

53 This is a common distinction in refugee jurisprudence (Guy Goodwin-Gill, *The Refugee in International Law* (Oxford: Clarendon Press, 1996) at 66–8). Jenni Millbank, "The Role of Rights in Asylum Claims on the Basis of Sexual Orientation" (2004), 4 *Human Rights Law Review* 193, makes a compelling analysis of how advances in human rights for lesbians and gay men have not been reflected in refugee jurisprudence in the United Kingdom and Australia.

54 *Ruddock v. Vardalis, supra* note 6.

55 See full discussion in Catherine Dauvergne, *Humanitarianism, Identity, and Nation: Migration Laws of Australia and Canada* (Toronto and Vancouver: UBC Press, 2005) at Chapter 7. The High Court of Australia's decision in *Plaintiff S157, supra* note 11 was a notable capstone to a decade of to-ing and fro-ing regarding procedural rights for asylum seekers.

The traditional rule of law has always been hinged to the parameters of a nation, but recent indications are that it may be, slowly and yet slightly, moving to having a global existence. This, then, forms part of the "threat" to the nation-state that is central to accounts of globalization: If rule of law and nation are traditionally the boundary for each other, a growth of rule of law that spans national borders is part of globalization's threat to nation itself. Such growth raises both problems and possibilities, which I consider in Chapter 9. In terms of refugee law, ensuring that refugee law remains a species of migration control rather than a terrain of human rights is one way to counter this perceived threat of law beyond the nation. In this way, the backdrop of globalization brings a new twist to the old tension between refugee protection and border control.

While globalization has permeated all realms of human endeavor, its core logic rests in economic discourse. Economic rationale is also embedded in the history of global migrations – people move to work.[56] It is, therefore, significant that the most reviled of asylum seekers of the global era is the "economic refugee," under suspicion of fleeing poverty and poor prospects in search of a better life. There is evidence that one aspect of economic globalization is an increase in the gap between the richest and the poorest individuals and the richest and the poorest nations.[57] The technologies of globalization also serve, ironically, to make this gap more obvious by broadcasting, beaming, transmitting, and bouncing images of Western prosperity around the globe, available for anyone with a television, broadband link, or photophone to capture. It is perhaps here that the threat of the spread of human rights looms the largest from the perspective of a prosperous nation seeking to carefully monitor immigration. Just beyond the horizon of the civil and political rights that we in the West are now prepared to accept as essential to our humanity, lie the economic and social rights that are already enumerated in international human rights instruments. Arguments about breaches of these rights are not typically able to ground refugee claims at this point in time, but given the recent and rapid growth of human rights law, this may become possible.[58] Globalizing forces contribute to the creation of "mere economic refugees" and to the legal arguments on their behalf. States baulk.

States resiling from refugee law at precisely the time when human rights jurisprudence is gathering force may simply be further evidence of refugee law's facility for excluding people. This would fit a rendition in which globalization is merely akin to legalization. This is consonant with many theoretical accounts of globalization as well, which suggest that one of its central features is an intensification of effects that have been observable all along. On the other hand, it is also evidence of the

---

56 Saskia Sassen, *Globalization and its Discontents* (New York: New York Press, 1998).
57 United Nations Development Program, *Human Development Report 2003 Millennium Development Goals: A Compact Among Nations to End Human Poverty* (New York and Oxford: Oxford University Press, 2003).
58 See the argument made by Michelle Foster, *International Refugee Law and Socio-Economic Rights: Refuge From Deprivation* (Cambridge and New York: Cambridge University Press, 2007).

paradoxical nature of globalization: its effects move in opposing directions, and in sometimes unpredictable ways. This unpredictability holds out a promise of emancipatory potential embedded within this shift. This potential is linked to the ways in which refugee law is increasingly taking on a rule of law character.

Illegal asylum and the rule of law

The present move to limit refugee law is also evidence that refugee protection is accepted as a binding international obligation, or else under these pressures it would be abandoned rather than contained. At this juncture, then, as states race to the bottom to harmonize refugee law at its least common denominator, important avenues for new and continued advocacy suggest themselves. Australian public discourse following the *Tampa* incident was starkly polarized. While opinion polls suggested that a majority of Australians supported the government, a vocal minority – possibly as much as 40 percent of the population – clearly did not. Although Prime Minister Howard was quick to dismiss his detractors as the intellectual "chardonnay set" who had long opposed his government, it is only in Australia that individuals have publicly signed up to host asylum seekers in their homes rather than have them in detention.[59] The publication and popular success of *Dark Victory* chronicling the government's response to the *Tampa* is another indicator of the widening gulf in Australian opinion.[60] Just as executive action in Australia has led the world in resiling from the Refugee Convention, refugee advocates in Australia have attempted to lead the resistance.[61] This resistance is grounded in the Refugee Convention itself, and makes strong appeals to the international realm and the importance of Australia's reputation there.

A diagnosis suggesting that governments are resistant to human rights assertions on behalf of refugees does not equate to a prescription to stop making these arguments. The inverse is true. Governments are resistant to these arguments because they have been successful, especially in the courts of prosperous states that have sought to restrict various rights of migrants, of whom some are refugees and asylum seekers. The challenge is to find ways to extend the arguments, to persist with them, to reinvent them. It is certainly true that the protective reach of refugee law extends further today than it did when the Convention was drafted in 1951. This has been achieved partially by agreement, and partially by interpretive expansion. Courts work within a discourse of rights, and rights arguments are therefore best suited to these fora. They do not work equally well everywhere. Western governments work within a discourse of democratic politics, where the arena that matters has clear boundaries, marked by the right to vote. The present recoil from refugee law is marked by this right more than others, and therefore

59 "Spare Rooms for Refugees," on-line: http://www.spareroomsforrefugees.com/main.htm.
60 See *supra* note 4.
61 Mary Crock and Ben Saul, *Future Seekers: Refugee and the Law in Australia* (Sydney: Federation Press, 2002) provides an example of the overlap between the academy and advocacy circles in Australia.

popular advocacy is particularly important. In the midst of the *Tampa* events, Australian news reported "views on the street" in the hometown of Arne Rinnan, the Norwegian captain of the ship. Similarly, news reports about the *Tampa* in the *New York Times* made Australian headlines. Both the technology that makes this possible and the mindset that makes these stories newsworthy mark the events as belonging to the global era.

The current state of refugee law encapsulated in the *Tampa* saga stands as an illustration of globalization's flash points. As the gap between the richest and the poorest nations and people increases, refugee law is increasingly put under pressure. As national sovereignty is challenged, refugee law is becoming a key point of response. As globalization multiplies both inclusions and exclusions, refugee law is a key terrain over which this is negotiated, accomplished, and challenged. The paradoxical nature of globalization is mirrored in the paradox of refugee law's current relationship with human rights law. Contemporary moves away from some key commitments of refugee law are also a move toward harmonization of standards among Western nations, a predictable globalization effect. Refugee law also contributes something important to a normative assessment of globalization. The question of whether globalization is a benevolent force or whether it is principally destructive and therefore to be resisted is an important one. Measuring globalization through the lens of refugee law points up the potential for improvement of the human condition that globalizing forces can offer, and the ongoing resistance that is generated and regenerated by the same forces. The result is not equilibrium, but rather an intensification of the sense of crisis that has, from the outset, been foundational for refugee law.

The relationship between human rights norms and the emancipatory potential of refugee law is complex. While human rights norms are increasingly an interpretive source for refugee decision makers, the settings for those decisions are constrained by the crackdown on illegal migration. In this sense, the right to argue about rights is itself framed in very different terms. At the threshold, states are asserting themselves through a full range of initiatives. Emancipatory potential in this setting comes not from human rights norms alone, but from the willingness of states and courts to treat refugee law as rule of law. I believe this is fostered by the human rights backdrop, and the elision of refugee law and human rights law. But it is the space to argue about the right to remain and assert other rights that is provided by rule of law arguments. This space to argue often takes procedural forms, as in the Australian High Court ruling in *S157*[62] or in a series of cases in the United Kingdom in 2002 and 2003 that provided procedural rights for asylum seekers that I return to in Chapter 9.[63] There is evidence here that courts are reaching for a rule of law beyond their own borders. This may signal the beginning of unhinging law

---

62 *Plainiff S157, supra* note 11.
63 *The Queen on the Application of 'Q' v. Secretary of State for the Home Department,* [2003] EWHC 195, [2003] EWJ No. 718 (Admin); *The Queen on the Application of S, The Queen on the Application of D, and The Queen on the Application of T v. The Secretary of State for the Home Department* [2003] EWHC 1941, 100(36) L.S.G. 39 (Admin).

and nation. Whereas most of the story of making asylum illegal is dark indeed, this is a glimmer of a new way of thinking of refugee law.

The next step in the argument is to turn to other areas of migration law and explore what other arguments might possibly be made for the unhinging that is necessary to conceptualize migration law in new ways. The greatest potential for this was, of course, in refugee law itself because here sovereignty is already, albeit minimally, constrained. The following cases of human trafficking, security, and citizenship are a progressively steeper climb.

CHAPTER FIVE

Trafficking in hegemony

The phenomenon of human trafficking stands out as the starkest example of illegal border crossing. Illegal migration with a difference – trafficking has "victims." As victims, those who are trafficked fit differently into the imagination than many of those who are rendered illegal by the migration laws of prosperous nations. The label "illegal" will hardly stick, as the victims are innocent. This makes it more difficult for states to rhetorically cast the victims of trafficking as transgressors, thus altering the familiar illegal migration discourse. It is even problematic to equate the victims of human trafficking with those who suffer from the trafficking of drugs. Drug addicts are discursively more blameworthy than human trafficking victims are; they somehow are associated with some initial choice, a lack of willpower, or at the very least, a deep weakness. Trafficked humans have none of these markers. Although people trafficked are not only women and children, they are overwhelmingly so. In addition, while they do not exclusively serve the sex trade of the prosperous, sex work and sexual exploitation predominate as explanations for the success, in market terms, of trafficking in human beings.

The importance of human trafficking to globalized migration laws is all about victims: what it means to be a victim, how victims are constructed and named, how victims shape criminals, and how victims call forth remedy, or lack the power to do so. More than refugees, the victims of trafficking trouble the insider-outsider dichotomy of migration law. Faced with the victims of trafficking, some of the righteous indignation that defends prosperous borders crumbles away. Because of the importance of victims to legal developments in this area, I focus here on the United States' annual Trafficking in Persons (TIP) Report, which makes trafficking victims central to its story as well.

The moral panic about illegal migration is heightened in the case of human trafficking. In this one instance, I almost hesitate to use the moral panic label because it could be read to suggest that I have my doubts about the importance of the concern about trafficking. Moral panic, as I said at the outset, is a half made up concern that serves powerful interests and reaches beyond any observable account of the phenomenon itself. Is it even possible to be *too* concerned about selling children into sexual slavery? What amount of outrage here would ever be enough, let alone too much? Outrage, even vicious, screaming condemnation, is called up by these facts. This is an appropriate response, or at least the beginnings of one. The reasons why I persist in capturing trafficking within the moral panic about illegal migration are key to understanding state and legal responses to trafficking at this point in time. The idea of moral panic helps to understand why the outrage of buying and selling mostly women and children, and mostly for sex, attracts the particular legal responses that it does. By examining human trafficking as part of the globalized moral panic about illegal migration, key features of contemporary legal responses to trafficking are brought into sharper focus. For example, it becomes clearer why the United States has largely been given the room to assume moral authority in this area, at a time when other hegemonic initiatives are attracting rigorous critique.[1] Paying attention to the moral panic dimensions of trafficking also calls attention to the inability of the law to construct "remedies" for this harm, and the importance of refugee law in this juncture. Finally, the moral panic factor also helps us understand why it has been persistently important to separate human trafficking from human smuggling.

In this chapter, I address each of these elements of the moral panic. I turn first to the importance of victims for fitting trafficking into the migration-globalization narrative. Keeping this in mind, I next explore the American leadership role in this area of the law. This leadership is one key to understanding the unique place of the United States in my analysis, and so this point also links closely with Chapter 8. However, the role that the one remaining superpower has chosen for itself is the bellwether in this subset of illegal migration, hence this chapter's title. I do not mean to suggest that what the United States is doing to confront trafficking is better or more important than initiatives elsewhere, as will become clear.[2] Rather, the TIP Report is a rich core sample for fitting trafficking into the illegal migration analysis. The following section examines the potential of refugee law to provide a remedy and the disappointing conclusion that it may be the best feasible option. This is in spite of everything I have just said about refugee law and the domestication of human rights. Finally, I conclude this chapter by exploring what would be gained – and lost – by giving up the defense of the line between smuggling and trafficking. This line is an all-important front in the battle for sovereignty and the nation–state as traditionally understood, and for maintaining the clear bright line between us and them that keeps the status quo for migration law in place.

---

1 I am thinking here of the Academy's concern, and particularly the concern of international lawyers, about the United States' conduct in Afghanistan and Iraq, as well as in Guantanamo Bay and beyond. See for example, Gerry Simpson, "The War in Iraq and International Law" (2005), 6 *Melbourne Journal of International Law* 167; Michael C. Davis, "Human Rights and the War in Iraq" (2005), 4 *Journal of Human Rights* 37; David Allen Larson, "Understanding the Cost of the War Against Iraq and How that Realization can Affect International Law" (2005), 13 *Cardozo Journal of International and Comparative Law* 387.

2 The EU has taken a number of initiatives in this area, beginning in the mid-1990s. See the Commission Communication of November 20, 1996, to the Council and the European Parliament on trafficking in women for the purpose of sexual exploitation, *COM* (96) 567 final. A detailed discussion of current EU initiatives is provided in Heli Askola, "Violence Against Women, Trafficking, and Migration in the European Union (2007), 13:2 *European Law Journal* 204.

Sketching victims for the human rights cause

In international law terms, the new Conventions regarding human trafficking and human smuggling came into force at lightening speed.[3] The drafting process was coordinated through an ad hoc committee, first convened in the mid-1990s. The Convention against Transnational Organized Crime is a framework document that sets a backdrop for a series of protocols addressing particular criminal enterprises. The first two protocols to be ratified were the Protocol to Prevent, Suppress, and Punish Trafficking in Persons, Especially Women and Children (2003) and the Protocol Against the Smuggling of Migrants by Land, Sea, and Air (2004). A third protocol on the illicit manufacturing and trafficking of firearms came into force in 2005. This trajectory is a stark contrast to the twenty years it took for the Migrant Workers' Convention to cover the same ground.[4]

The quickly emerging consensus about the need for international law to confront human trafficking coincides with the crackdown on illegal migration. Part of the motivation for states to cooperate in this way surely derives from the same sources that fostered the spread of converging domestic regulation beginning in the 1990s. The emergence of these protocols at this point in time reflects directly the transformation in the nation and migration pairing that globalizing conditions fosters, and the threat that migration law evasion represents to sovereignty. In this strand of narrative, trafficking and smuggling are the most sophisticated evasions of migration laws, and therefore the hardest to "crack down" on because they are the best coordinated and the best resourced. The technologies of travel and communication marking globalization serve the trafficking industry well. Some have estimated that human trafficking is now more profitable than its parallels moving drugs or arms. This is another reason that the first protocols of a treaty on international organized crime address migration crimes.

Concern about human trafficking mirrors the phenomenon of globalization itself. Neither trafficking nor regulation of it is new. The first international law regulating trafficking specifically dates to the beginning of the twentieth century.[5]

---

3 *Convention Against Transnational Organized Crime*, GA Res. 217(I), UN GAOR, 55th Sess., Supp. No. 49, UN Doc. A/RES/55/25 (2000) 44; *Protocol to Prevent, Suppress, and Punish Trafficking in Persons, Especially Women and Children, Supplementing the United Nations Convention against Transnational Organized Crime*, GA Res. 25(II), UN GAOR, 55th Sess., Supp. No. 49, UN Doc. A/45/49 (2001) 60 (entered into force December 25, 2003) (*Protocol to Prevent Trafficking in Persons*); *Protocol Against the Smuggling of Migrants by Land, Sea, and Air, Supplementing the United Nations Convention against Transnational Organized Crime*, GA Res. 55/25(III), UN GAOR, 55th Sess., Supp. No. 49, UN Doc. A/45/49 (2001) 65 (entered into force January 28, 2004).
4 Anne Gallagher, "Human Rights and the New UN Protocols on Trafficking and Migrant Smuggling: A Preliminary Analysis" (2001), 23 *Human Rights Quarterly* 975; *International Convention on the Protection of the Rights of all Migrant Workers and Members of their Families*, GA Res. 45/158, UN GAOR, 45th Sess., Supp. No. 49A, UN Doc. A/45/49 (1990) 261 (entered into force July 1, 2003).
5 *International Agreement for the Suppression of the White Slave Traffic*, May 18, 1904, 35 Stat. 1979, 1 L.N.T.S. 83, and *Convention for the Suppression of the Traffic in Persons and the Exploitation of the Prostitution of Others*, December 2, 1949, 96 U.N.T.S., 271.

The particular acts typically involved in a trafficking fact pattern have been criminalized for longer, under the names of kidnapping, forcible confinement, assault, living off the avails of prostitution, and so on. In as much as human trafficking often involves slavery, it has been condemned and legally proscribed for several centuries and stands out as a key example of humanity's progress narrative. It would still be wrong, however, to say that there is nothing new about the way trafficking is now being treated discursively and legally. It is quite likely that there has been a marked increase in trafficking around the globe, facilitated by globalization's technologies. It is certainly the case that the not-really-global crackdown on illegal migration has improved the market for trafficking and smuggling enterprises. Notably, the moral panic about trafficking follows the start of these crackdown measures by about five years. Obviously, legal attention to trafficking has increased, with many countries around the globe now specifying trafficking itself as the harm, not only its embedded elements. Like globalization, there is a cluster of phenomena involving intensification and speed, as well a perception and interpretation, that make the way trafficking now occupies popular, political, and legal discursive landscapes different. This intensification of concern and response is new. Beyond discursive change, states are now starting to devote resources to enforcing these new legal regimes.[6] Trafficking is a rich strand of globalization's narrative: vital concern, seemingly unstoppable, and with individualized victims. Unlike the growing gap between rich and poor, or the knowledge that globalization is enhancing both inclusion and exclusion, in the case of trafficking the victims are among us. In de Sousa Santos' terms, trafficking turns the global South into the inner South.

The fact of victims is another facet of understanding the rapid emergence, response, and shape of trafficking talk in the early twenty-first century. Trafficking, like security in Chapter 6, is a highly gendered phenomenon. Those who are trafficked around the globe are overwhelmingly women. A significant number are children.[7] The gendering of the phenomenon goes beyond the story that the numbers, however disputed or approximate, can tell. Our understanding of trafficking taps into the familiar cultural (Western) elision of women and victimization. It conjures images of helplessness that are bolstered by the prevalence of children in the trade, and which emasculate men who are also trafficked.[8] The gendered facts of trafficking underpin the importance of victimization to its narrative.

6 In addition to the sizable efforts being mounted in the United States and the European Union, there is interesting evidence of less high-profile investment elsewhere. For example, in Vancouver, Canada, by 2005 the national police force had established an anti-trafficking task force with more than twenty full-time members.
7 United Nations Office on Drugs and Crime, *Trafficking in Persons: Global Patterns* (April 2006) at 33 estimates that 77 percent of victims are women, and 60 percent are children. See http://www.unodc.org/unodc/en/trafficking_persons_report_2006-04.html. The American *Trafficking in Persons Report* in 2005, 2006, and 2007 estimated that 80 percent of transnational trafficking victims were women and 50 percent children.
8 The gendering of trafficking affects masculinity in the same way the gendering of rape does. To talk of rape in gender-neutral terms mutes the power that underlies its violence. The acknowledgment that men too are victims of rape is legally but not emotively captured by gender-neutral language.

Two aspects of this narrative are important here. First is the recent insertion of a human rights perspective into an organized crime setting. Anne Gallagher, recounting of the drafting of the Trafficking Protocol, writes that human rights is the "cloak" for the increasing emphasis on security measures in approaches to trafficking.[9] That is, while the security elements of the new international law are written to have some teeth, the human rights statements are much weaker, or purely exhortatory.[10] In this sense, the warm fuzziness of human rights talk justifies and lessens scrutiny of new securitization measures. Joan Fitzpatrick's parallel account offers the insight that human rights advocates worked hastily to introduce accounts of victims into the negotiations in order to ensure that a human rights perspective was reflected in the protocol.[11] Whether human rights talk came first or hastily later, it is linked to victims and central to what we understand about trafficking. One marker of both moral panic and the domestication of human rights is that there is little precision to this story.[12] There are a myriad of potential rights that are breached when someone is trafficked. These could include basic liberty, freedom from exploitation, control over one's own body, the right to be compensated for one's labor, and freedom from slavery. Lurking just behind these rights might be claims like freedom of movement, freedom of choice, right to earn a living, and the right to seek asylum. One moves fairly quickly from a series of rights statements that seem incontrovertible to statements that are bound up with the root causes of trafficking and with the barriers – sovereignty and borders – to effective solutions, in such a way that precision in rights discourse is probably a bad thing for the states concerned. Human rights discourse, when talking about trafficking, is the shorthand reminder that people, not only states, are harmed by this practice. Those who are "rights holders" in this scenario are silenced victims, not powerful claimants.

The second facet of the gendered/victimized narrative that is important, and which overlaps with the first, is the intense debate about women's agency, which was present throughout the work on the protocol. At the core of this debate is the old issue of consent and one's opinion of the sex trade.[13] Is prostitution a legitimately chosen occupation or is working in the sex trade always at some level coerced? Is it coerced by patriarchy or just by men? Is it chosen by free market actors or by fallen women who need to be rescued? Most Western states have prostitution laws that reflect varying degrees of ambivalence about these points. The Trafficking

---

9 Gallagher, *supra* note 4 at 976–7.   10 See discussion below at 83–85.

11 Joan Fitzpatrick, "Trafficking as a Human Rights Violation: The Complex Intersection of Legal Frameworks for Conceptualizing and Combating Trafficking" (2003), 24 *Michigan Journal of International Law* 1143.

12 Anne Orford, *Reading Humanitarian Intervention: Human Rights and the Use of Force in International Law* (Cambridge: Cambridge University Press, 2003).

13 For a detailed discussion of this debate in this setting see Kara Abramson, "Beyond Consent, Toward Safeguarding Human Rights: Implementing the United Nations Trafficking Protocol" (2003), 44 *Harvard International Law Journal* 473.

Protocol's definitions stake out a carefully negotiated line, intricately sidestepping most of this debate, but not settling it:

> "Trafficking in persons" shall mean the recruitment, transportation, transfer, harboring or receipt of persons, by means of the threat or use of force or other forms of coercion, of abduction, of fraud, of deception, of the abuse of power or of a position of vulnerability or of the giving or receiving of payments or benefits to achieve the consent of a person having control over another person, for the purpose of exploitation. Exploitation shall include, at a minimum, the exploitation of the prostitution of others or other forms of sexual exploitation, forced labor or services, slavery or practices similar to slavery, servitude or the removal of organs ... [14]

The discourse of victimization erases the possibility of women's agency. Once one is viewed as a victim, consent is compromised at best. It matters little if the law contemplates consent if all the discourse and decision making that surrounds it does not. The subject position of victim robs women of voice. This in turn impoverishes debate by silencing one of the most authentic positions from which to hear. It also paternalizes the issue – creating an "us" group that knows what is best for "them."

It is also notable that the recent upsurge in concern about trafficking coincides with the end of the Cold War, and with it, the opening of new markets in Eastern Europe. Women from Eastern Europe are high-profile trafficking victims, often featuring in pop culture representations of trafficking.[15] The racialization of this fact is inescapable. The "whitening" of trafficking victims since the early 1990s coincides with prioritizing trafficking as an international crime. This is only one factor in many, but it is important given the role of victims and victimization in shaping the trafficking debate. Just as the international community found it easier to act to confront genocide in Yugoslavia than in Rwanda, race tugs at any analysis of global trafficking trends and responses. There are other explanations, of course; there always are. Here too, the moral panic response comes into play. By this I mean that we might conclude that trafficking is getting more attention these days because of the emergence of white women and white children as victims, and still say that any attention to trafficking is good attention, any response is a good response, and that the murky and racist-but-well-meaning origins of such responses are not important, or are at least forgivable, if the results of any actions taken are not similarly racialized. The comfort one can draw from this reasoning depends on one's capacity to believe that racializing origins can be overcome. This is a faith I do not have. Instead I see the racial marking as a troubling of the "us-them" line that was once national but is going global.

---

14 *Protocol to Prevent Trafficking in Persons, supra* note 3, at Article 3(a).
15 Examples include the commercially released 2002 film *Dirty Pretty Things* (Celador Films, 2002), the award-winning file *Lilya 4-ever* directed by Lukas Moodysson (Memfis Film Rights AB, 2002), and the commercially successful book by journalist Victor Malarek *The Natashas: The New Global Sex Trade* (Toronto: Viking Canada, 2003).

The paternalization of trafficking talk points us to children and their special role as trafficking victims. Paternalizing is the role of parents. There may be nothing that is not worth doing to free children from sexual slavery. Legitimate debate about prostitution does not contemplate children giving meaningful consent. Children are the "best" rhetorical victims because their needs are acute, the damage they suffer is lifelong, and there is no troubling frisson of conscience about agency. The stories of children intensify the discourse of victimization. The place of children in this story is so horrific it compels us, as does roadside carnage, to stare mutely or to turn away. Both rob us of analytic capacity. Children, and our reactions to their images, are important to the story of American hegemony among legal responses to trafficking.

American leadership on the frontier

The United States was slow to ratify the Trafficking Protocol,[16] despite having taken an important role in its drafting, and despite American non-governmental organizations (NGOs) shaping the debate about consent that was central to the drafting. This is a familiar story of American involvement with international human rights law, part of what it means to be the globe's undisputed hegemon at the start of the twenty-first century. Despite this reluctance regarding international law, the United States is staking out a leadership role for itself based in domestic legislation aimed at combating trafficking. The central tool being used to construct this role is the annual Trafficking in Persons Report produced by the American State Department. This report is, in the words of the State Department " . . . the primary diplomatic tool through which the U.S. Government encourages partnership and increased determination in the fight against forced labor and sexual exploitation."[17]

The TIP Report is mandated by the 2000 Victims of Trafficking and Violence Protection Act.[18] This law requires, among other things, that the U.S. government report on the activities of *other* governments in combating human trafficking. The legislation is quite specific. The report is to focus on "severe forms of trafficking"[19] exclusively and minimum standards for the elimination of trafficking are

---

16 The United States ratified the Protocol in late 2005.
17 This statement appears on the home page of the Office to Monitor and Combat Trafficking in Persons, on-line: www.state.gov/g/tip/.
18 *Victims of Trafficking and Violence Protection Act*, Pub. L. No. 106–386, 114 Stat. 1464 (2000) (codified at 22 U.S.C. § 7101).
19 Defined as " . . . (a) sex trafficking in which a commercial sex act is induced by force, fraud, or coercion, or in which the person induced to perform such act has not attained 18 years of age; or (b) the recruitment, harboring, transportation, provision, or obtaining of a person for labor or services, through the use of force, fraud, or coercion for the purpose of subjection to involuntary servitude, peonage, debt bondage, or slavery. *Victims of Trafficking and Violence Protection Act*, *supra* note 18 § 103(8) at 1470.

specified.[20] The legislation also specifies indicators to assist in assessing the minimum standards. On the basis of assessments against these minimum standards, countries reported on are then placed in Tier One (in full compliance with minimum standards), Tier Two (not in full compliance but making significant efforts to bring themselves into compliance), or Tier Three (do not fully comply and are not making significant effort to do so).[21] To ensure that the Report does not function merely as an extraterritorial survey exercise, from 2003 onwards, countries that were placed in Tier Three could then be subject to sanctions by the United States through withdrawal of non-humanitarian, non-trade-related assistance and U.S. opposition to assistance coming from the International Monetary Fund and the World Bank and similar organizations.[22] Since 2003, a number of sanctions have in fact been applied.[23] A 2003 reauthorization of the American legislation further specified that from 2006 onwards, countries would have to deliver up specific data about prosecutions and convictions in order to be considered for Tier One status.[24]

In short, the report is a recipe for hegemonic governance through surveillance, aimed at disciplining the globe. Although it may or may not eventually contribute to reducing the numbers of people who are trafficked annually, it certainly does contribute to putting the United States in a prominent position of international leadership on this front. Or perhaps it is more apt to cast this as a frontier, given the elements of frontier mentality embedded in this report.[25] The role of international enforcer is, by 2005, a familiar one for the United States. In the case of trafficking,

---

20 These are: 1) The government should prohibit trafficking and punish acts of trafficking. 2) The government should prescribe punishment commensurate with that for grave crimes, such as forcible sexual assault, for the knowing commission of trafficking in some of its most reprehensible forms (trafficking for sexual purposes, trafficking involving rape or kidnapping, or trafficking that causes a death). 3) For knowing commission of any act of trafficking, the government should prescribe punishment that is sufficiently stringent to deter, and that adequately reflects the offense's heinous nature. 4) The government should make serious and sustained efforts to eliminate trafficking. *Victims of Trafficking and Violence Protection Act, supra* note 18 § 108 at 1480.
21 *Trafficking in Persons Report 2000* at 5.
22 *Victims of Trafficking and Violence Protection Act, supra* note 18 at 1,483.
23 In 2003, full sanctions were imposed on Burma, Cuba, and North Korea, and partial sanctions were imposed on Liberia and the Sudan. In 2004, full sanctions were imposed on Burma, Cuba, and North Korea, and partial sanctions were imposed on Equatorial Guinea, Sudan, and Venezuela. In 2005, full sanctions were again imposed on Burma, Cuba, and North Korea, and partial sanctions were imposed on Cambodia and Venezuela. See U.S., United States Government Accountability Office, *Better Data, Strategy, and Reporting Needed to Enhance U.S. Antitrafficking Efforts Abroad* (GAO-06-825) (Washington D.C.: United States Government Accountability Office, 2006) at 29. In 2006, full sanctions were imposed on Burma, Cuba, and North Korea, and partial sanctions were imposed on Iran, Syria, Venezuela, and Zimbabwe. See U.S., Office of the Press Secretary, White House Press Release, "Presidential Determination with Respect to Foreign Governments' Efforts Regarding Trafficking in Persons" (September 27, 2006), on-line: U.S. Department of State, http://www.state.gov/g/tip/rls/prsrl/73440.htm.
24 *Trafficking Victims Protection Reauthorization Act of 2003*, Pub. L. No. 108–193, 117 Stat. 2875 (2003).
25 See the excellent analysis of law and frontiers by Ruth Buchanan and Rebecca Johnston, "The 'Unforgiven' Sources of International Law: Nation-building, Violence and Gender in the West(ern)" in Doris Buss and Ambreena Manji, eds., *International Law: Modern Feminist Approaches* (Oxford: Hart Publishing, 2005) 131.

there is little opposition to this role.[26] Rough and ready justice has always been more morally satisfying on the frontier than back in civilization. The place of victims in the trafficking narrative is vital to understanding why the strong arm of the law finds such a comfortable fit here. Rather than assuming the classic posture of critique of United States' foreign policy, we in the chattering classes appear close to grateful that the United States is able and willing to commit its resources to doing something – anything – about trafficking.

The Report has grown in reach and stature since it was first issued in 2001. That initial report contained a mere 102 pages and ranked 82 countries on its tiers. The bulk of the report was devoted to the "country narratives" about each of the countries ranked. The other material amounted to nine pages, mostly devoted to describing the requirements and methodology building the report. By 2006 the annual report was 295 pages, but a smaller font and new page format reduced the 2007 report to 236 pages. In 2007, 151 countries were ranked. Significant additions to the report included highlights of international best practices (which began in 2003), regional maps with law enforcement statistics (new for 2005), descriptions of United States' government efforts (which began in 2003), the addition of a Tier Two Watch List (new from 2004),[27] and a matrix of relevant international conventions noting which countries have signed and ratified which treaties (dates from 2003). (The United States was not included on this list until the 2006 Report, by which time it was a state party to the Trafficking Protocol.) Country narratives became considerably longer beginning in 2005, as did the introductory elements of the Report. The special section on anti-trafficking "heroes" began in 2004.

One thing about the Report that has not changed at all over its first seven years is the aggregate estimate of people being trafficked around the globe over international borders. In 2001, the estimate was "at least 700,000" and in 2002 it was "at least 700,000 and possibly as many as 4 million."[28] By 2004 new data had been assembled, leading to an estimate of 600,000 to 800,000, and adding gender (over 80 percent women and girls) and age (up to 50 percent minors).[29] These figures have been repeated in 2006 and 2007, but by 2007 only the upper range of 800,000 was used.[30] Of all the statistical challenges in tracking illegal migration, an accurate count of persons being trafficked is perhaps the biggest. Some people who are trafficked will even appear in legal migration statistics. As the TIP Report is increasingly careful to

---

26 It is, predictably, common for countries that are listed on Tier Three to issue press releases objecting to this classification, but beyond this opposition is sparse.
27 *Trafficking Victims Protection Reauthorization Act of 2003, supra* note 24.
28 The 700,000 figure drew on American data from 1997.
29 The estimates in the TIP Report are similar to those published by the International Organization for Migration (IOM) and considerably lower than estimates by the International Labor Organization (ILO). The IOM, "Counter-Trafficking Brochure," on-line: http://www.iom.int/unitedstates/Fact%20Sheets/factsheets.htm estimates that between 600,000 and 800,000 persons are trafficked worldwide. The ILO, *A Global Alliance Against Forced Labor* (Geneva: International Labor Office, 2005) at 46 estimates that 2.5 million people are currently the victims of trafficking.
30 2007 Report at p. 8; 2006 Report at p. 6.

point out, not all trafficking involves international borders, although my focus in this chapter is primarily on trafficking that also infringes immigration laws.[31] The difficulty of assessing trafficking numerically makes it nearly impossible to track results of initiatives aimed at curbing it. One conclusion from the statistics over the first seven years of the TIP Report could be that the report is not accomplishing anything. Approximately the same number of people, as near as anyone can tell, is being trafficked now as in 2001. On this logic we could look at the new laws around the world and conclude that the spread of targeted legislation is similarly ineffective. This may also be true, although it is probably too soon to draw a conclusion, but at any rate it is only a guess. This points to the important distinction between law itself and an ideological commitment to the idea of law.

The problem of finding a way to measure results is perhaps one reason why the United States is now turning to counting prosecutions and convictions.[32] These are quantifiable and, in most places, easy to publicly verify. Unfortunately, though, these numbers cannot tell us if trafficking in persons is being reduced. Indeed, it is plausible that an increase in numbers of prosecutions and convictions may mean that trafficking itself is on the rise, rather than the reverse. It may also foster laying indefensible charges or entering questionable convictions. In order for a prosecution to commence, someone must have already been trafficked; the battle has to have already been lost. Quantifying at this end does not seem any more likely to contribute to a solution than attempting precision at the level of broadest statistics. These statistics are nonetheless interesting to sociolegal scholars attuned to globalization's machinations. They provide a succinct picture of the hegemonic sway of American regulation. Who will chose to conform to this imperative and what will the consequences be of not doing so? Prosecution and conviction statistics also tell us something about the functioning of the law. In combination with other approaches to assessment, therefore, they can help interpret the usefulness of law in responding to human trafficking.

There is probably no accurate numerical response to the question of whether trafficking is being reduced, but there are important qualitative ways to approach an answer to this question. These involve asking community workers, sex trade workers, and frontline law enforcers. These assessments involve listening to those who have been trafficked, and to others they have encountered in their home communities, en route, and where they have arrived. It mandates a level of inquiry that is best described as sublocal, giving voice to those who are marginalized and hidden even from what is usually taken to constitute the local community. Not only

---

31 This is because of my broader focus on illegal migration. The horrors of trafficking are not altered by the occurrence of a border, although trafficking that does not involve border crossing is probably easier to remedy (for the reasons I discuss in the upcoming remedies section) and does not infringe migration laws.

32 Both the 2006 and 2007 Reports include a highlight box entitled "Global Law Enforcement Data" that contains a chart showing prosecutions, convictions, and new legislation (at p. 36 in both cases).

is such an accounting the only way to understand if trafficking can be reduced, it is also the beginning of understanding how to remedy the abuses that trafficking entails. This type of research is difficult to conduct and ethically intricate, but it offers a way forward in an area where other avenues are bleak. This potential fits within the dynamic of globalization as well, where attention to measures at the national level is less likely to yield results. Trafficking by its nature calls up a response that both spans borders and goes beneath them.

While the TIP Report has grown, one element has disappeared. The 2001 and 2002 reports contained laudatory references to the Trafficking Protocol. These ended in 2003, presumably as it became clear that the United States was not going to be quick to ratify the agreement. The 2006 and 2007 "post-ratification" reports do mention the Protocol but it is not highlighted, as it originally was, as a key means of combating trafficking. This stance is typical of the American approach to international human rights law in general. The United States has one of the lowest rates of ratification of major human rights treaties among prosperous Western states.[33] What differs here is that the United States is still pursuing and achieving a position of international leadership in this area. Furthermore, this differs from the pattern of human rights instruments under conditions of globalization, but conforms to the patterns of globalized migration laws. Whereas migration is by definition a global phenomenon, most laws confronting it are national. The observable legal convergence, especially in crackdown measures, is related to globalizing forces, but not primarily to international law. This is another indicator that states are reacting to trafficking as a migration issue rather than as a human rights issue, rhetorical assertions aside.

As the TIP Report has evolved it has become an increasingly compelling document. One key aspect of its draw is the addition, since 2003, of victim profiles and of photos. Victim profiles, like the individualized hero stories, humanize the story, drawing the reader closer to the horror of human trafficking, fostering compassion that is so difficult to engender at a statistical level. It is well understood that "the names may be changed to protect the innocent." In this setting our expectations of "truth telling" are culturally conditioned by our habits of confidentiality. But the photos are different. Indeed, photos occupy a different space in our understanding of veracity. A picture is worth a thousand words. The camera never lies. The photos transform the report into a visual medium as well as textual, and give a form to what we imagine while reading it.

The 2003 edition contained ten photos, counting the cover composite as one.[34] Eight of the photos are captioned in the report with a snippet of the story about the trafficked person or persons they portray. The cover composite, like those of

---

33 Oona Hathaway, "Do Human Rights Treaties Make a Difference?" (2002), 11 *Yale Law Journal* 1935.
34 From 2003 to 2007 the cover of the Report has featured a composite photograph showing parts of four faces. The photos are cropped so that only the eyes, eyebrows, and part of each nose appear, and then arranged as a band across the cover.

subsequent years, shows the eyes of four individuals, presumably also victims. The only photo that is not situated in some way is the frontispiece image, half obscured, of a young child's face. The one visible eye looks steadily out from the page. Brown skin and neatly trimmed dark hair – I guess this child to be young by the smoothness of the skin and the shape of the nose, but as I step back from this, I realize I might be wrong. I might see youth here only because of my own fears, my own horror, of what trafficking imports. I guess my conclusion from this must be that the image has what I presume to be the desired effect on me: It stops me in my rhetorical tracks; it makes me afraid. I can find no commentary on this photo in the report. Aside from this arresting image, all the photos here show us "real" victims. They provide a glimpse into a type of truth.

The following year, this approach to illustration was altered; there were many more photographs, and the following statement:

> The photographs on this Report's cover and most uncaptioned photographs in the Report are not images of confirmed trafficking victims, but are provided to show the myriad forms of exploitation that help define trafficking and the variety of cultures in which trafficking victims can be found.[35]

In this version of the report, about half of the photos are not of trafficking victims but of people who look like they could in some way be involved in trafficking. Some photos are captioned ambiguously, they could be "true" or "posed" or merely "coincidental." For example, the caption "Sex tourism draws men from wealthy countries to less developed countries where they can take advantage of economically vulnerable women and children and weak criminal justice systems" is set between two photos. One shows a grey-haired, white-skinned man in a beach chair beside an Asian-looking young woman, also reclining. Their eyes are obscured so that they cannot be identified. The other photo is of two young Asian-looking women dressed in bikini tops and short shorts, viewed from behind, talking to two white-skinned men whose eyes are obscured.[36] The caption does not tell us that anyone in these photos is involved in sex tourism. The photos could be posed as illustrative examples of what sex tourism *might* look like. However, hiding the identities of those in the photos does suggest that these images are "true," or at least that the people who have posed for the photos do not want to be identified. This may tell us another kind of truth.

Not all of the uncaptioned photos obscure identity. There are many instances where photos without specific captions are set beside text, with the suggestion that they are related to the text. For example, the caption stating, "This Vietnamese woman was sentenced to 15 years for sex trafficking of underage girls in Cambodia"

---

35 *Trafficking in Persons Report 2004* at 4; *Trafficking in Persons Report 2005* at 4. This is repeated in an almost identical form in subsequent years, see 2007 Report where the final "can be" is altered to read "are" at p. 4.

36 *Trafficking in Persons Report 2005* at 8.

is set between two photos. One is of a woman, eyes downcast, whom an arrow identifies as the convicted trafficker of the caption. The other photo is a headshot of an Asian-looking child wearing a singlet.[37] The child stares seriously at the camera. It is difficult to look at this page and *not* link the child to the girls trafficked by the person in the companion photo. Was she? Is this photo even of a girl?

The use of photos, and especially of photos that are not of trafficking victims, brings our attention sharply to the role of victims and exploitation in the trafficking narrative. The photo selection in subsequent years is dominated by "real" or posed victims, or images somewhere in between. Consider the example of the photo that I am most disturbed by. (It is admittedly hard to choose.) A tall, obese, middle-aged white man is sitting at a restaurant table. We see his back. Across from him is a young, probably Asian, woman and a child leaning into her arm. This is a posture my six year old often takes when we sit in a restaurant. This child could be six. The eyes of the woman and child are obscured by blurry patches, suggesting they are "real." The caption reads, "A Western man negotiated for the young Thai girl, while she clutched the arm of her trafficker. After settling on a price, the man left with the young girl and the trafficker left with the payment."[38] How can anyone know this? This is not really enough precision for authenticity in a caption. Alternatively, how could anyone know this and still let the narrative of the caption unfold?

Some photos are not of victims or survivors but of anti-trafficking heroes and significant sites such as the Thai government's central shelter for trafficking victims,[39] or a Beijing sign advertising fresh, clean foreign women.[40] Whatever their content, the photos work. They make the TIP Report more compelling, they add a human face, and they give us pause. But the way they work is disturbing. It is easy to understand why the State Department has moved to using photos that are in some way inauthentic. It is understandably hard to obtain photos, and permission to use them, of people who have actually experienced trafficking, in whatever form.[41] The "true" photos pose the further problem of replicating exploitation. To have one's image used in a publication with a potentially immense audience as someone who has been forced into prostitution, raped, sold, owned, bartered, and enslaved requires personal fortitude. To stand before the camera and say, "Yes, this is what happened to me and I am still here" is an enormous thing. Stated like this, it sounds like a moment of empowerment. It could be. However, there is always the risk that it may make someone feel exposed, or marked, or simply known in a way that obscures knowing anything individual or personal.

37 *Trafficking in Persons Report 2004* at 15.   38 2007 Report at p. 10
39 2004 Report at 85.   40 *Trafficking in Persons Report 2005* at 10.
41 Photo credits appear at the end of each report. The majority of the photos are credited to individuals or private companies. Some are credited to the State Department itself or other government sources. It is not clear whether consent for the photos or their publication was obtained and in a telephone call in the summer of 2005 to the State Department, neither my research assistant nor I could not clarify this. We also attempted to follow up our requests through the U.S. Consulate in Vancouver, which hosts an annual launch of the report, but did not receive any further information.

The inauthentic photos seem to solve this problem, but they raise others. I am not sure how these photos were obtained, but I am curious. Were these children paid models? Would I allow one of my children to pose as a trafficking victim? Would I want my daughter's face staring out from beside the image of the identified child trafficker? Is the cause of making this report engaging vital enough to justify this? Or perhaps the pay was exceptionally good, and how good would it have to be for me to overcome my uneasiness at this? What is the victimization of posing as a victim? Can children too young to understand this reasonably be asked to do it? I am not sure how to answer any of these questions, but they disturb me. There is also the question of inauthenticity itself. If standing in such a photo as one who has survived trafficking can be a moment of empowerment – of self-proclamation – does allowing others who have not experienced this horror to stand in the same position, on the same page, diminish the courage of the survivors? Does it make "victims" even more invisible and socially constructed for myriad purposes to select others to stand in their places, as though their actual identities are not the most important thing? How do we ask others to act as representative examples of "forms of exploitation" and "varieties of cultures" as the disclaimer suggests? Can one represent a form of exploitation? Moreover, can one do so without that in itself being exploitative? How can a photo of a person standing in for a trafficking victim represent a culture? The dilemmas of the inauthentic photos have a kaleidoscopic complexity. They may negate what is best about the "true" photos, without offering anything of unproblematic value in return.

Understanding our reactions to these photos requires examining why they achieve their objectives and at what cost. It is not wrong to work to humanize and individualize the TIP Report. It is unrealistic to deny the power of images as tools. The photos help convey the message that trafficking is such a hideous blight that all measures should be used to stop it. They fuel the moral panic that fosters the moral authority of the United States in this area. They help build that case that perhaps this is so bad that we, whether as Americans or as others, should simply be grateful that the one remaining superpower is capable of deploying its resources in this way and chooses to do so.[42] Trafficking provokes the same sense of outrage that Anne Orford writes of in her eloquent discussion of Australian demonstrations in support of armed intervention in East Timor.[43] That is, there are some things so horrifying, some cases where we so desperately want to do something that our usual rational objections to turning things over to military decision making or

---

42 In 2006, the U.S. government spent $74 million on anti-trafficking in persons' projects in seventy countries. See U.S., Office to Monitor and Combat Trafficking in Persons, *Fact Sheet: U.S. Government Anti-Trafficking in Persons FY 2006 Project Obligations: Questions and Answers* (April 23, 2007), on-line: U.S. Department of State, http://www.state.gov/g/tip/rls/fs/07/83372.htm. This number represents a decrease from the $95 million spent in 2005 and the $82 million spent in 2004. See U.S., Office to Monitor and Combat Trafficking in Persons, *Fact Sheet: U.S. Government Anti-Trafficking in Persons FY 2005 Project Obligations: Questions and Answers* (April 24, 2006), on-line: U.S. Department of State http://www.state.gov/g/tip/rls/fs/2006/65042.htm.
43 *Supra* note 12 at ch. 6.

international leadership dissipate. Orford reflected on the image of children being thrown over the barbed-wire fence into the UN compound in Dili. In the end she urged upon us a re-visioning of that image that focused on the agency of everyone involved, and on the portraits of caring and rescue contained in that moment. The problem, she concluded, with the image as a still photo was the helplessness it imposed upon the observer.[44]

The photos in the TIP Report have the same effect. They reduce those who have been victims to their victimization. The inauthentic pictures further reduce the capacity of the "true" to stand as survivors, marking with their image their very existence. They belie any discourse in which agency can be attributed.[45] They render hegemony a blessing. There are ways to move beyond the "stop and stare" effect of these images, but as yet the so-called "remedies" available to those who are trafficked have by and large not done so. It is to this issue that I turn next.

Remedies: sovereignty, law, and refuge

People who have been trafficked are victims of human rights abuses, but there are few human rights remedies available to them. State sovereignty and the migration laws that define and defend it get in the way of providing remedies for trafficking that could have the potential to shift its global dynamics. Sovereignty here leads to failure of the imagination, and thus of law reform, and the worldwide crackdown on extralegal migration expands the trafficking market.

When the question of remedies is raised, the idea that trafficking is a generalized problem, which does not always involve borders, quickly fades into the background. A key problem in meeting the needs of people who have been trafficked across borders has been states' tendency to treat them as migration law transgressors and to simply send them home. I am interested in looking at the alternatives to this, in the border-crossing context only. Of course, I do not mean to suggest that appropriate remedies are always available for people who are trafficked "domestically," but rather that the barriers to appropriate remedies are different, and often lesser, in domestic legal settings.

The Trafficking Protocol plainly shows that it was difficult for negotiating parties to address the needs of victims, especially in the migration law context. States party are obligated to enact legislation criminalizing all aspects of trafficking (Article 5)

---

44 Ibid. at 21.
45 The 2005 Report, which had a focus on sexual exploitation, took an unambiguous position in the consent debate that plagues the international law. The Report states:

> The vast majority of women in prostitution do not want to be there. Few seek it out or choose it, and most are desperate to leave it. A study in the scientific journal *Journal of Trauma Practice* found that 89 percent of women in prostitution want to escape prostitution. Children are also trapped in prostitution – despite the fact that a number of international covenants and protocols impose upon state parties an obligation to criminalize the commercial exploitation of children.

Trafficking in Persons Report 2005 at 19.

and are obliged to cooperate with other signatories (Article 10). States are specifically required to facilitate the return of their own nationals who have been trafficked
(Article 8), and to " . . . strengthen, to the extent possible, such border controls as
may be necessary to prevent and detect trafficking in persons" (Article 11). Requirements for preventative actions are also strongly worded (Article 9). On the other
hand, measures regarding those who have already been trafficked are cast in more
open terms. For example, the privacy and identity of victims is to be protected
" . . . in appropriate cases and to the extent possible" (Article 6). Similarly, states
party "shall consider" implementing measures aimed at assisting the social, physical, and psychological recovery of victims and "shall consider" providing support
such as housing, counseling, and education (Article 6). Signatories are also to
consider temporary or permanent visa status for those who have been trafficked
(Article 7). Thus while an array of mechanisms are canvassed in the Protocol, none
are mandatory. I turn now to considering the array of potential remedies, within
and beyond the parameters of the treaty.

Offering secure immigration status for trafficking victims is a remedy that takes
a variety of forms. Not surprisingly, the most high profile of these has been the
temporary visa regime created by the United States in the same legislation that
grounds the TIP Report.[46] Under this scheme, trafficking victims who comply with
" . . . any reasonable request for assistance in the investigation or prosecution of
acts of trafficking"[47] are permitted to remain in the United States for three years.
At the end of this period, they may apply for permanent residency.[48] To date, very
few of these "T-visas" have been issued; even fewer former victims have become
permanent residents in the United States.[49] There are a number of other countries
where similar temporary residency, specifically linked to trafficking prosecutions,
is available.[50]

The T-visa program is one of the most frequently praised features of the American approach to trafficking. There are good reasons to laud this program. It provides
targeted support to trafficking victims. It makes prosecutions possible, and prosecution is part of a comprehensive response to trafficking. It also provides a bridge
to permanent immigration status, which is one reason why the trafficking matrix
often contains an element of choice. For all these reasons, the T-visa and parallel
programs elsewhere are good remedies for trafficking. This formulation does not,

---

46 *Victims of Trafficking and Violence Protection Act, supra* note 18.
47 *Victims of Trafficking and Violence Protection Act, supra* note 18 § 107(e)(1)(C)(iii)(a–b) at 1478.
    Victims under fifteen years of age can also benefit from this provision.
48 *Victims of Trafficking and Violence Protection Act, supra* note 18 at § 107(c)(3) at 1477.
49 Over the fiscal 2000 to 2006 (fiscal year ending March 2007), the United States issued 729 of the
    "T-visas" to trafficking victims and another 645 to their family members, *2007 Report* at 49. This
    averages assistance to just over 100 trafficked persons each year.
50 This route has been followed in several EU jurisdictions, implementing the 2004 Council Directive
    on the residence permit issued to third-country nationals who are victims of trafficking in human
    beings or who have been the subject of an action to facilitate illegal immigration, who cooperate
    with competent authorities. *O.J.L.* 261, August 6, 2004.

and cannot, go far enough to alter the fundamental globalized dynamics of the problem. In Santos' terms, trafficking is a modern problem for which there is no modern solution.[51] The T-visa is a solution that comes from within the modern paradigm – established migration laws – rather than challenging it. It therefore reinforces the features of globalized migration laws that protect the market for trafficking.

Offering a temporary visa to those who participate in prosecutions reinforces the present and modern structure of migration laws – and their problems – in three ways. First, it retains the focus on prosecution rather than on ending trafficking or even on assisting victims. Prosecution certainly has a role to play, but ought not be an end in itself and it cannot measure anything but itself. Second, this remedy retains an incentive to choose the trafficking-as-migration path. We know that the initial "choice" to engage with a smuggler or a trafficker is often complicated down the line by unscrupulous traders changing the terms of the bargain. Still, if the golden prize of American (for which we can almost fully substitute Canadian, British, French, Australian, and so on) citizenship remains at the end point, and other access to that prize is strictly limited (especially to those we stereotype as potential trafficking victims – poor and uneducated women and children), then the incentive to choose to become a trafficking subject is a meaningful one. Finally, and perhaps most importantly, this kind of remedy is not a human rights remedy. It scarcely addresses the human rights dimensions of trafficking at all because it hinges the remedy – migration status – to participating in prosecution rather than to the harm of being trafficked. In order to be an effective remedy, it must attach and relate to the harm, not to assisting the state in enforcing its migration laws. These final two points are at odds with each other, but they both contribute something to our understanding of the current law and politics of sovereignty. States are willing to tolerate, even to create, an incentive to subject oneself to gross abuse in order to gain a slim chance of becoming a permanent resident, when numbers are very low. States remain in control of this number by decisions about prosecution, because eventual permission to remain is strictly tied to assisting the state. This control gives states the sense that what they are controlling is in fact their borders, and sovereignty is saved.

Another potential remedy would be to give victims of trafficking permanent migration status in destination countries. This is dismissed out of hand as an impossible surrender of sovereignty. An excellent articulation of permanent residency as a human rights remedy is written by Audrey Macklin.[52] When Professor Macklin made this suggestion during a June 2005 meeting convened to discuss the 2005 TIP Report, American and Canadian officials laughed out loud and rolled their eyes. This kind of reaction was possible because the meeting was being held

---

51 See discussion in Chapter 3 at 36–38.
52 Audrey Macklin, "Dancing Across Borders: Exotic Dancers, Trafficking, and Immigration Policy" (2003), 37 *International Migration Review* 464.

by videoconference in four locations and Professor Macklin could not see what was going on in my location. Despite this reaction, however, this remedy would respond precisely to the desire of the United States and others to increase prosecution rates, as well as to actually end trafficking. If trafficking victims could become permanent residents, a key aspect of the trafficking market would disappear. Traffickers would lose the threat that comes of turning people with no secure immigration status over to the authorities, which in most cases means being sent home. Some individuals would want this; for others home is a place of danger or disgrace. We do know that many people are trafficked more than once. Giving all trafficking victims permanent resident status would increase the incentive to allow oneself to be trafficked. However, this is not why state officials laugh out loud at it. They react that way because granting permanent residency to all trafficking victims would be a surrender of control and therefore sovereignty. The fact of trafficking is a loss of control; all politically feasible remedies at this juncture are aimed at re-inscribing that control, at least at a rhetorical level.

There are two other important factors to consider about permanent residency as a remedy to human rights abuse. First, it would lead indirectly, but not directly, to somewhat greater rates of prosecution. Some people would participate as witnesses because of their desire to see their tormentors brought to justice, just as some women participate in sexual assault prosecutions or domestic violence prosecutions. States pursuing higher prosecution rates would therefore have incentives to ensure that trafficking victims were well supported in the community and quickly reunited with family members because these would then be the factors that would make them able to participate in prosecutions. People with robust psychological support also make better witnesses.

The other factor is to consider what would happen to the trafficking matrix with this remedy firmly in place. Some people might be more willing to be trafficked, but perhaps not so many more than those who already become involved with some degree of volition. Trafficking is horrific. Much is not voluntary. One must be careful not to make too much of the incentive idea. But this alone is not enough to end trafficking, just to deflate the market somewhat. Permanent residency would actually function as a "remedy" in a way that the T-visa does not. However, I do not want to tarry too long here, as I think the possibility of such a remedy being adopted anywhere, let alone widely, is politically remote.

There is, however, a legal framework that is already widely applied which can function as a limited remedy for some victims of trafficking, and that is refugee law. For all the reasons that refugee law is not perfect, it is not a perfect remedy for the victims of trafficking. However, because of its limited constraint on sovereignty and its uneasy relationship with human rights law, refugee law has already surmounted some of the barriers to states accepting it as a remedy for trafficking. In addition, many Western states grant permanent residency to refugees even though they are often not strictly required to do so and thus refugee law provides this type of security as well, usually with concomitant family reunion rights. All of these points fit squarely into the discussion in Chapter 4.

It is easy to envision that trafficking itself will meet the threshold of harm to qualify as "being persecuted" under the Refugee Convention. While "persons who have been trafficked" per se may not meet the current criteria for a "particular social group" under the Convention, there are many ways that trafficking victims can meet the nexus requirement of the refugee definition.[53] There are two aspects of refugee protection, however, which are potentially problematic for individuals who have been trafficked: the role of the home state and the requirement that assessment be future looking. Refugee law stands as surrogate protection when a citizen's home state is not able or willing to protect her from particular risks for particular reasons. The "state protection" requirement is a formidable hurdle to obtaining protection of another state because states are generally assumed to be able to protect their own nationals,[54] and because the protection provided need not be a perfect guarantee of safety.[55] So if a state were making efforts, in a nondiscriminatory fashion, and with some success, to protect trafficking victims upon their return, the argument for refugee status would be weak. Similarly, although *having been trafficked* probably constitutes persecution, the question in refugee determination is whether one is at risk of being persecuted upon return. This is the case for many trafficking victims. We know that some people are trafficked repeatedly. We also know that those who are trafficked are often threatened with reprisals against them or against family members. These threats are realistic given that trafficking is often a sophisticated organized criminal activity. Finally, refugee determination is individualized. This means that small differences in circumstances between similarly situated people may mean that one is a refugee and the other is not. Despite these hurdles, some victims of trafficking have made successful refugee claims.[56]

Refugee law is not a panacea for trafficking. In addition to the fact that it only provides a remedy for some individual victims, it also does nothing to reduce the market for trafficking. Given the structure of refugee law as a limited constraint on sovereignty with an uneasy relationship with human rights, it provides support for features of the protected "market" for trafficking. As there is no right to enter another country within refugee law, border crossing itself retains its place as a core feature of the market. To the extent that refugee law can provide a "remedy" it is no more than that. The remedy arises only after someone has been trafficked.

---

53 Writing a sentence like this brushes over extensive jurisprudential nuance and advocate aspiration and almost calls forth an entire paper rather than a footnote. A useful summary of what would be required is outlined in the UNHCR's *Guidelines on International Protection No.7: The Application of Article 1A(2) of the 1951 Convention and/or 1967 Protocol Relating to the Status of Refugees to Victims of Trafficking and Persons at Risk of Being Trafficked*, April 7, 2006. HCR/GIP/06/07. On-line: UNHCR Refworld, http://www.unhcr.org/cgi-bin/texis/vtx/refworld/rwmain?docid=443679fa4.
54 *Canada (Attorney General) v. Ward*, [1993] 2 S.C.R. 689, 103 D.L.R. (4th) 1.
55 Audrey Macklin discusses the tensions in current analysis of the state protection standard in "State Protection Jurisprudence" prepared for the Canadian Federal Court Immigration Education Seminar, September 2006. See also Guy Goodwin-Gill, *The Refugee in International Law* (Oxford: Clarendon Press, 1996) at 77–9; James Hathaway, *The Law of Refugee Status* (Toronto and Vancouver: Butterworths, 1991) at 124–34.
56 Successful claims in Australia have included: RRT Reference NO3/47757 (May 11, 2004), NO3/45573 (February 24, 2003), N02/42226 (June 30, 2003).

It does not have a preventive effect. The current crackdown on asylum seeking supports the trafficking market by making border crossing harder. Some activists have argued that traffickers use refugee law in support of their criminal activities. In this scenario, trafficking victims, who might have legitimate refugee claims, are supported in making spurious claims for refugee status. When they are successful, they attain a secured immigration status and can then work more openly in the host state. Their "market value" to the trafficker changes. Secure immigration status also provides greater avenues for escaping trafficking's enslavement, but it does not guarantee anything. The backdrop of immigration law enforcement is only one feature of the trafficking matrix.

For all these reasons, the hope offered by refugee law to confront trafficking is slim. But on balance, it is an important and politically feasible route. This desultory conclusion reflects the conditions of globalized migration laws. Refugee status offers permanent immigration status, family reunification, and some types of protection. It has two vital features for this setting. First, refugee law focuses on the individual rather than the interests of the state. Second, under current pressures, refugee law is taking on increasingly law-like characteristics as I discussed in Chapter 4. States motivated to limit their obligations are working within the Refugee Convention rather than withdrawing from it. In the trafficking matrix, sovereign assertions at the border contribute to problems rather than solutions. In present globalizing times where the movement of people over borders is increasingly the center of sovereignty, further compromises seem unlikely. Refugee law has proven resilient and has interpretive flexibility. Advocacy within it for people who are trafficked is an important pragmatic avenue.

The array of legal remedies currently available to confront trafficking make a weak arsenal: prosecution of traffickers, temporary or even permanent immigration status for witnesses, and refugee status. Even the possibility of permanent immigration status as a human rights remedy, which respects the structure of contemporary immigration laws, is presently viewed as fanciful. The social conditions that fuel trafficking certainly have sophisticated features, but their broad outlines are not difficult to discern.[57] This human exploitation is fostered by vast disparities in wealth between individuals and between nations, by prosperous and impoverished societies alike demeaning women and tolerating their position as subordinate citizens, by a transactional ideology in which value is always and ever market value, and by the global system of border enforcement. These are conveniently called "root causes." Measures aimed at addressing these causes are not counted for the

---

57 Some sophisticated work on root causes includes Nora V. Demleitner, "The Law at a Cross-roads: The Construction of Migrant Women Trafficked into Prostitution" in David Kyle and Rey Koslowski, eds., *Global Human Smuggling: Comparative Perspectives* (Baltimore: John Hopkins University Press, 2001); Ratna Kapur, "The 'Other' Side of Globalization: The Legal Regulation of Cross-Border Movements" (2003), 22:3–4 *Canadian Woman Studies* 6–16; Kamala Kempadoo, "Victims and Agents: The New Crusade against Trafficking," in Julia Sudbury, ed., *Global Lockdown: Race, Gender, and the Prison-Industrial Complex* (New York: Routledge, 2005).

purposes of the TIP Report. There are many reasons why addressing the root causes cannot count. One is certainly that trafficking is fostered by key elements of the comfortable status quo; chief among these is the entrenched gulf between rich and poor people and nations, and the sovereignty of borders that ensure this. The moral panic about human trafficking shields these factors from attention. Trafficking is about children with smooth skin and serious eyes, about sullen-looking women in handcuffs and silver-haired men on tropical beaches. These images are the immediate face of trafficking. These are the things that call out for us to do something, anything, to stop this horror. And so we should. This moral panic is a shrill call to action, to rescue the good and lock up the bad; to focus on individuals, both as victims and as perpetrators. The slavery of the eighteenth century was once viewed as a necessary if unseemly aspect of the way the world worked. In time, however, "civilized" people came to believe that race-based slavery was inhuman, beyond unacceptable, something worth sacrificing parts of life-as-we-knew-it to end, even if it supported, and was supported by, the status quo. We have not reached this point in our understanding of trafficking. It replicates that older slavery, using international borders and domestic illegality to make it invisible to us. It runs on systems of social organization that secure our privilege as citizens of prosperous Western states.

Our reactions of horror to the human face of trafficking support remedies that legitimate and extend that privilege, but that cannot ever address the root causes. The ongoing development of law and more law cannot shift the parameters of the trafficking matrix, as modern law is itself bound up with securing the way-things-are. Something more far-reaching is needed. It is yet beyond our imaginations. This need for "something beyond" calls up Peter Fitzpatrick's argument about the need for "gods" to shift the shape of international law, and his concomitant analysis that the outlines of this faith are already discernable. I return to this point shortly.

Smuggling, undrawing lines, and concluding

Nearly every discussion of trafficking turns, at some point, to the distinction between human trafficking and human smuggling. A key feature of the new international law initiatives has been analytically separating these phenomena and structuring separate legal responses to each. The distinction is based on exploitation: trafficking has it and smuggling does not.[58] Drawing a clear line between trafficking and smuggling is almost universally regarded as a considerable achievement. Given the evident overlaps and similarities, it is easy to imagine why this is so. Yet a vital insight into the place of trafficking in the global cluster of migration laws comes

58 Article 3(a) of the *Protocol Against the Smuggling of Migrants by Land, Sea, and Air, supra* note 3 defines the "smuggling of migrants" as the "procurement, in order to obtain, directly or indirectly, a financial or other material benefit, of the illegal entry of a person into a State Party of which the person is not a national or a permanent resident." This is to be compared with the definition of trafficking in the *Protocol to Prevent the Trafficking of Persons, supra* note 3.

from querying this line-drawing exercise. The distinction between the two brings us back to the centrality of victims to every aspect of this analysis: trafficking has victims and smuggling does not. The problem with the line-drawing exercise also comes back to this point: a victim identity silences and obscures.

There are good reasons why separating trafficking and smuggling is difficult. Central among these is that the experience of clandestine migration is not neatly categorized. Moha, a young man from XXX, may pay a sum for his journey to the United States and put himself in the hands of people he thinks he is buying a service from. He may know little about the journey, and find himself in dangerous circumstances. He hands over his passport for safekeeping. The journey becomes so dangerous that he wants to back out. He asks to go back and is denied. At the border, he is given a different passport, not his own, and told to tell a different story to border agents. On arrival, he is told he owes an additional $5,000. He has no more money. He is told he must work washing dishes until it is paid off. His passport is not returned to him. He is locked up in the restaurant at night. Has he been trafficked or smuggled? Hard to tell. Has he been exploited? Have his human rights been abused? Is he in danger? In his eyes does The Law look like a way out? The answers to these questions are easier.

Consider Clara from YYY. She learns of an opportunity to work in England. She has been out of work for months and life is pretty tough anyway. She has heard stories of women getting into difficulty working in the West, but the guy she has been talking to seems honest. And the money she could earn each month is more than a year's salary at the factory. She knows there is a risk but decides to take it. She pays $1,000 as an employment search fee. When she arrives she is told she must work in a brothel for three months or pay an additional $5,000. She chooses the sex trade. At the end of this time, she is given a falsified passport and visa. She finds a job clerking in a grocery store and an apartment to share with another young woman whom she met at the brothel. From time to time she turns tricks on the weekend for extra cash. She saves her money and sends it back to YYY. Her younger sister uses this money to complete high school. Has she been trafficked or smuggled? Hard to tell. Has she been exploited? Have her human rights been abused? Has she consented? Will The Law help her or narrow her life choices? Is she a victim of a crime or a criminal?

Eighteen-year-old Mario from ZZZ pays someone to bring him to Canada. He spends six days in the back of a long haul truck. He arrives in Toronto tired, bruised, and hungry, but otherwise without incident. He is dropped off at a house that serves as an overcrowded home for many young men from his home country. Following their advice, he shows up for work at a day-labor construction site. Work is easy to find. He works up to sixteen hours a day at half the minimum wage, without adequate safety equipment. He is paid cash. After food and rent, he hardly has anything left to send home to his family. He certainly doesn't have enough money to return home. He works mostly building luxurious home and offices for upper middle-class Canadians. His conditions of work in Canada are illegal, but so is his presence. He has no medical insurance, no time off, no recourse if he is injured on the job, no way to know if he will work next week, no hope of promotion. He puts up with the racial slurs. Has he been trafficked or smuggled? Is he being exploited? Are his human rights being abused? Is he a victim? A criminal?

Drawing a line between trafficking and smuggling is about assigning guilt. People who are smuggled are culpable; "they" have broken "our" laws. People who have been trafficked never had a choice. They are removed from culpability by removing their agency. This helps explain reluctance to conceptualize trafficking as something to which women can consent. If it is her choice, how can she be absolved of the migration law transgression that follows? The distinction between trafficking and smuggling serves the interests of some of those who cross borders clandestinely. It ensures that some of these people are "victims" and thus have some access to the remedies that come with this label. The distinction does better service to state interests by creating clarity about who is to be excluded and who cannot be. Primarily, however, drawing a clear bright line between smuggling and trafficking makes it harder to interpret the shades of grey where the two ideas are intertwined. In the area of criminally assisted migration, people suffer tremendous abuse, hardship, and unyielding legal consequences. Separating smuggling and trafficking turns our focus to the polarized limits of the phenomenon: the children in the TIP Report photos and the wealthy passport purchasers.

What would we lose if we gave up defense of this line? The distinction between trafficking and smuggling stands as an easily read shorthand, telling us who to blame. Without this distinction, we would have to think harder about victimization; examine its elements, weigh its degrees. Without this line, it is harder to use victim as a simple catchall, a silenced, one-size-fits-all space. We would need to understand the differences and the similarities among Mario, Clara, and Moha. We would have to give up the still-life approach to trafficking images, allowing for moving pictures, interactions, and agency. This is not easy for the law. Law specializes in drawing clear bright lines. The distinction facilitates a legal response. Such a response is limited by the capacity of the law. It is only as useful as the legal remedy it can support. Without distinction we are left with a muddle; with overlapping layers of inclusion and exclusion; with degrees of agency and consent that tell us more about the array of choices available to different individuals than about the culpability of traffickers.

The line between trafficking and smuggling bolsters the state with a reinforcement of the insider-outsider dichotomy. Globalization's dynamics are shifting the location of this line from the border of the nation–state, but that does not render it any less important nor any less vital to state interests. As with other instances of extralegal migration, states are moving to ensure they can continue to tell "us" from "them." Defending the trafficking-smuggling border defends this border as well. It serves the interests of not-yet-post-modern law, and impairs our imagination of solutions that look beyond. In this area it is vital to unthink the law, and there are few signs for optimism. The contemporary approaches to trafficking show globalization pinned to an unshakable economic logic and captured by hegemonic Americanization. While the United States looks to other states to halt trafficking, there is little discussion of the role played by the massive American domestic market for trafficked persons of all types, and the effect of this economy on illegal migration generally, which I return to in Chapter 8. Peter Fitzpatrick's vision of a new future for international law is also grounded in a deep concern about American super-power in the international realm. Trafficking is perhaps one of the most pointed examples of this trend that can be brought, precisely because of the absence of critique. It is possible to be vitally concerned about the horrors of human trafficking and also concerned about transforming this horror into straightforward support of American initiatives. Voicing critique at this juncture must also mean calling for a community of ethics worthy of fledgling faith; hoping that the space opened for a change in the rule of law can be transformed in profound ways. Human trafficking also forces us to understand that some problems are beyond the reach of the law; that law's capacity is limited even in these hyper-legalized global times.

The pictures illustrating the TIP Report are an important beacon. The emancipatory potential of law is difficult to discern in the trafficking matrix. This is because an obsession with victims obscures the space in which new law might arise. In moving to confront human trafficking, we have images of exploitation but no truth. Confronted by a lack of knowledge and a global scale, we must listen to sublocal secrets, told in whispers. We must go to ground. If law can be a tool here, it must be grounded in the talk that is silenced by victimization. We need the thousands of words that the pictures replace. Hegemonic power cannot solve a problem for which sovereignty is an insurmountable barrier, even in the imagination. Although victimization replaces illegality in this migration context, it does not replace it with the empowered, rights-bearing individuals that Western law is tooled to protect. This contrast between rights-bearing individuals and victims is clarified by considering the difference between the moral panic surrounding trafficking with that surrounding security concerns in the migration realm. I turn to the matter of security in the next chapter, and consider how migration laws are responding to the new politics of terror.

CHAPTER SIX

The less brave new world

I started writing this chapter in July 2005 as the forensic sifting following the first coordinated bombing of London's public transit system was beginning. Within days, the investigators had discovered that the suicide bombers had been "home-grown" Britons, citizens, full members of the society they had attacked.[1] Three of the four had been born in the United Kingdom, and all had grown up there. This detail was repeated in news reports, even when the report was clearly focused not on place of birth as a potential determinant for terrorist predilection, but as a detail that somehow had relevance nonetheless. This news, presented as "shocking," was quickly followed by a story originally carried by the *New York Times*, but soon syndicated to the corners of the globe, arguing that Britain had allowed itself to become a haven for Muslim extremists and that the attacks were a complicated consequence of having been "too tolerant."[2] Later it emerged that at least one of the bombers had trained in Pakistan. These events, and this coverage of them, encapsulate the new notes in the migration law – security fugue. They point to diverse aspects of the urgency that security issues have taken on for those concerned with migration, and to the reasons that security, a marginal concern at most in a statistical panoply of migration, now clamors for attention at the center of the discursive stage.

The news that the bombers were British was noteworthy for two reasons. First, it challenges the idea that our borders can protect us; that threats come from "out there" and that when they reach us it is because our borders and their guards have somehow failed. Second, it calls for a re-reading of the public and political discourse of migration and security that has predominated since the emblematic events of September 11, 2001. This chapter opens by addressing these points. The way this finding was immediately followed by other news aimed at making these attackers somehow less British – by social isolation, ties to Pakistan, or training elsewhere – is a security setting manifestation of the global shift in the line between "us" and

---

1 Don Van Natta, David Johnston, and Stephen Grey, "Bombings in London: Physical Evidence" (July 9, 2005) *New York Times*, A1. The focus on a "homegrown sleeper cell" occurred almost immediately after the bombing despite admissions by a senior British investigator that there was insufficient evidence then to make "even a sensible guess" about those who were responsible.
2 Irshad Manji, "Why Tolerate the Hate?" *New York Times* (August 9, 2005) A19. Manji writes, "And ultimate paradox may be that in order to defend our diversity, we'll need to be less tolerant."

"them." The notion that Britain has been too tolerant is central to understanding how security and migration are linked for a liberal democratic community. This linkage is an intricate balancing act calling upon us to decide anew at each instant whether our greatest fears are of our own governments, or of the unknown other. Like any fine balance, this act is characterized by incessant shifting. This discussion is at the center of this piece, with core sampling attention to how courts are responding to exceptional detention provisions for noncitizens. Finally, the second bombing attempts two weeks after the first burst the small bubble of hope that the terrorism in London might be an isolated event. After all, nothing *really* big had happened to a *really* big Western power since September 11 (provided we work very hard to ignore Madrid, and, no, Bali does not count either. Let's leave CNN in charge of arbitrating importance). These attempts confirmed our unease that what we are instead experiencing is a new normal. This chapter concludes by examining this "normal" and situating it within the story of globalizing migration laws.

This analysis takes as its starting point the notion of migration as a "security issue." Without falling headlong into international relations theory, it is useful to say something about what this means. A classic analysis of security finds security issues only in military and strategic matters, with an emphasis on war itself. This picture has been challenged in international relations for some time,[3] and may have been cut off at the knees by the advent of the "war on terror" and the challenge it presents to state-based understandings of war and threat. In the migration realm, security is more easily understood in the terms of newer constructivist and critical scholarship that tell us that when something is a security issue, both threat and exceptional politics are to be expected. These newer understandings of security focus on how states, nations, peoples, or others come to understand something as an important threat to their existence or way of being.[4] In response to this threat, they are then prepared to take actions that are in some way extraordinary, suspending, or circumventing what counts as "normal" decision making. "Normal" involves the rule of law; when one is jettisoned, the other often goes with it. This way of understanding security issues helps us make sense of reactions that would seem nonsensical without the elements of both threat and exception. Examples include the idea that 433 asylum seekers aboard the *Tampa* were a threat to the Australian nation, or in the case of the London bombing, the idea that four bombs killing fifty-six people were a threat to British society. Those who argue that these threats *are* nonsense are contesting the politics of security – and the tantalizing "reality" of threats. I will return to these points in discussing the new normal later. I turn first to mapping the contemporary migration security agenda and considering where law fits within it.

---

3 The so-called "Copenhagen School" is one central locus of this critique. This is usefully discussed in Barry Buzan, Ole Waever, and Jaap de Wilde, *Security: A New Framework for Analysis* (London: Boulder, 1998).
4 Ibid. at 5.

The importance and unimportance of September 11, 2001

The monumental terrorist attacks that leveled the World Trade Center and damaged the Pentagon are a key marker for the global security agenda. They jolted the sense of personal security of many citizens of Western countries, and changed the threat perspective of many Western states. Although the point has frequently been made that many around the globe have long lived with this level of insecurity, the capacity of these events to nonetheless shift the global agenda affirms the role of prosperous Western states in setting that agenda. Like other aspects of globalization, it is not that a linking of migration and security is new, but rather that attention to this linkage has heightened and its politics have shifted. There are new elements to the migration-security intertwining since September 11, 2001, but they are not those one would anticipate on the basis of global headlines.

Migration regulation has had a security element since its inception.[5] Whether the arriving hordes have constituted a true threat, and what exactly has been threatened have been contested, but the linkage to security has not. Even in liberal theoretical accounts of migration, the notion of a national security threat as an impetus for making exceptions to established principles has been a common denominator.[6] Similarly, the events of September 11 did not mark the beginning of the crackdown on extralegal migration. This had been ongoing throughout the 1990s. At most, it can be said that the events of September 11 served as a tidal wave clearing away political opposition to the advance of increasingly strict crackdown provisions, or at least rendering mute this opposition. This was clearly the case in Australia, where the terrorist attacks in the United States coincided with both the *Tampa* crisis and subsequent national election, as discussed in Chapter 4. Similarly in Canada, new immigration legislation featuring more far-reaching governmental powers and a further restriction of appeal and review rights, passed with subdued opposition in November 2001. While it is true that both Canada and Australia have significant new elements to their migration laws that postdate September 11, 2001, the provisions were drafted well in advance of this date. In 2002, the Center for Migration Law at the University of Nijmegen undertook a study of changes in migration law measures in Europe since September 11, 2001, examining both changes at the European Union (EU) level and at the national level. Both Germany and the United Kingdom had introduced some migration law changes as an aspect of omnibus anti-terrorism legislation (i.e., not specifically migration legislation). At

---

5 This is outlined in Buzan et al., *supra* note 3 at Chapter 6. See also Audrey Macklin, "Borderline Security" in Ronald J. Daniels, Patrick Macklem, and Kent Roach, eds., *The Security of Freedom: Essays on Canada's Anti-Terrorism Bill* (Toronto: University of Toronto Press, 2001).
6 Catherine Dauvergne, "Amorality and Humanitarianism in Immigration Law" (1999), 37 *Osgoode Hall L. J.* 597; Michael Walzer, *Spheres of Justice: A Defense of Pluralism and Equality* (New York: Basic Books, 1983); Donald Galloway, *Essentials of Canadian Law: Immigration Law* (Concord, Ont.: Irwin Law, 1997); Joseph Carens, "Aliens and Citizens: The Case for Open Borders" (1987), 49 *The Review of Politics* 251.

the EU level, the analysis showed a very similar pattern as in Canada and Australia: "EU Member States reached, in a few months, agreement on subjects which used to be highly controversial among them, and for which without the terrorist attacks years of negotiation would have been necessary."[7]

Despite the general statement that the events of September 11 have not led to major changes in migration legislation, there are three ways in which these events have shifted the legal context. Migration laws contain an exceptional breadth of discretionary provisions as a matter of routine. This takes different forms in different states, but the laws are generally designed to quickly and efficiently reflect changes in governmental policy. This feature of migration law means that its application and enforcement can and do change quickly in response to changes in the perception of security issues. There have clearly been changes in the enforcement and application of immigration provisions in many Western countries, which make a significant difference to those affected by the law, even in the absence of any change to legal texts. One example of this is reflected in the drop in numbers of people seeking asylum in prosperous Western states.[8] This probably does reflect some measure of increased safety and a reduced collective desire for asylum, but it also gives testament to the effect of an array of measures such as directing people back to the United States at Canadian land borders,[9] turning boats away from Australian territorial waters, and putting the EU's newest members on "migration probation" and thereby turning them into buffer zones.[10] Other discretionary migration law provisions where the post-9/11 climate is imprinted include the lists of countries whose citizens require visas to travel, the use of immigration detention, and the rates at which people who are considered "removable" from prosperous states are actually removed.

A second and closely related change reflecting the new security climate can be discerned in the creation of new agencies. Didier Bigo made compelling arguments in the 1990s about the European security agenda by examining police practice.[11] Similarly sobering conclusions are suggested even by simply noting that the United States' Immigration and Naturalization Service was swallowed whole by the

---

7 Evelien Brouwer, "Immigration, Asylum, and Terrorism: A Changing Dynamic Legal and Practical Developments in the EU in Response to the Terrorist Attacks of 11.09" (2003), 4 *European Journal of Migration and Law* 399 at 402.

8 The UNHCR reports that asylum applications submitted to industrialized countries last increased in the three quarters prior to the September 11 attacks. Following 9/11, there has been a steady and uninterrupted decline in the numbers of asylum applications made to industrialized countries. Since 2001, asylum requests to industrialized countries have dropped 40 percent. This figure is compiled from data available at UNHCR, on-line: http://www.unhcr.org/cgi-bin/texis/vtx/home.

9 *Agreement Between the Government Of Canada and The Government of the United States of America for Cooperation in the Examination of Refugee Status Claims from Nationals of Third Countries*, United States and Canada, December 5, 2002 (entered into force December 29, 2004), on-line: Citizenship and Immigration Canada, http://www.cic.gc.ca/english/policy/safe-third.html.

10 This is examined in Chapter 8.

11 Didier Bigo, *Polices en réseaux: l'expérience européenne* (Paris: Presses de la Fondation Nationale des Sciences Politiques, 1996).

Department of Homeland Security in March 2003.[12] This has the effect of moving migration issues into an organizational structure with a differing governing ethos. A similar shift happened in Canada. In late 2003, the enforcement roles that had belonged to the Department of Citizenship and Immigration were moved to the newly created Canadian Border Services Agency (CBSA), housed within the similarly new Department of Public Safety and Emergency Preparedness. The CBSA was created by Order in Council within days of Prime Minister Paul Martin taking power in December 2003.[13] In October 2004, legislation supporting the CBSA was introduced into the House of Commons and passed into law in November 2005, after the agency had been operating for nearly two years.[14] The CBSA is now responsible for security screening of potential immigrants and of asylum seekers (drawing on information provided by police and the national security agency), and for "removals." Thus the most draconian aspects of immigration policy and politics are now managed and delivered by an agency that has a control and enforcement mandate, housed in a department addressing emergencies and safety. The functions of immigrant selection, integration, overseas recruitment, and naturalization remain together in Citizenship and Immigration. The law that the CBSA applies and enforces has not changed, nor was a legal change necessary to bring the CBSA to life.

A third post-9/11 effect has been an increase in cooperation between states on security matters – at least, an increase in the cooperation of prosperous Western states with the United States. This is another shift that requires no change in law but that affects how people experience the law. In questions of cooperation, hegemony is vitally important. In the new and less brave world, states and the citizens feel increasingly vulnerable to terrorist attacks, with some good reason. There is a sense, and we hope it is right, that some attacks, at least some of the time, can be thwarted by finding out about them in advance. This idea is clearly challengeable. The failure of intelligence agencies to act in advance of September 11 has been well reported.[15] In the case of the London bombings, the immediate analysis was that attacks by citizens with backpacks on mass transit systems are almost impossible to prevent through advance warnings. Despite evidence that this may not work, however, we want to believe that there are things that can be done to reduce the risk that attacks of this nature will continue unabated. In short, the case for more and better information is usually an easy one to make, and to make

---

12 "INS History," online: Transactional Records Access Clearinghouse, Syracuse University, http://trac.syr.edu/tracins/findings/aboutINS/insHistory.html.

13 Paul Martin took over as leader of the Canadian Liberal Party from Jean Chretien on December 12, 2003, and became Prime Minister immediately because the Liberal Party was in a majority position in the Canadian House of Commons. The umbrella department, Public Safety and Emergency Preparedness, was created on the day the new Prime Minister took office.

14 *Canada Border Services Agency Act*, S.C. 2005, c. 38.

15 "The 9/11 Commission Report," on-line: National Commission on Terrorist Attacks Upon the United States, http://www.gpoaccess.gov/911/.

politically appealing.[16] The capacity to gather intelligence around the globe is very unevenly spread. The United States has a well-developed intelligence capacity, as do the United Kingdom and France, but many fellow traveler states do not maintain much intelligence apparatus; Canada and New Zealand come to mind here, and to some extent Australia.

If we want the safety that comes with more knowledge (provided we are sold on the importance of this safety in the first place, which Western states certainly seem to be even if their citizens are not uniformly so), we need to cooperate. At least cooperate with those who gather the information. This has been the Canadian response to the Mahar Arar debacle.[17] Officials felt it was necessary to give information to the United States to ensure an ongoing reciprocal flow. It is clearly a motivating factor behind the Smart Border Accord,[18] which sets various standards for the passage of goods and people over the lengthy U.S.-Canada land border. One aspect of this Accord is the Safe Third Country Agreement for asylum seekers.[19] There had been talk of an agreement of this nature between Canada and the United States since at least the early 1990s. The likely effect will be to dramatically reduce the number of refugee claims in Canada, with a corresponding increase in the United States.[20] Although Canadian officials had been interested in such an agreement for this obvious reason, the numeric disparity made it clear why this would be of less interest for the United States. The numbers have not shifted, but the security agenda has. The benefit to Canada of this agreement is still a drop in

16 This corresponds well with the Copenhagen School's analysis of the "grammar" of a security speech act: a plot with an external threat, a point of no return, a possible way out. It is the notion of a way out that makes the speech act a call for securitization. This way out means that there is something that can address the threat provided the actors involved are willing to move beyond the limits of normal politics. Without the possibility of a way out, there is no securitization because there is no call to action (Buzan et al., *supra* note 3 at 33).

17 Mahar Arar, a Canadian and Syrian citizen, was sent to Syria by the United States in September 2002, where he was detained for thirteen months and tortured. A public inquiry was held into how this could have happened, during which it came out that Canadian officials had supplied erroneous information about Arar to the U.S. authorities. See *Commission of Inquiry into the Actions of Canadian Officials in Relation to Maher Arar*, on-line: http://www.ararcommission.ca/eng/. See also Commission of Inquiry into the Actions of Canadian Officials in Relation to Maher Arar, *Report of the Events Relating to Maher Arar: Analysis and Recommendations* (Ottawa: Public Works and Government Services Canada, 2006).

18 "Smart Border Declaration: Building a Smart Border for the 21st Century on the Foundation of a North American Zone of Confidence," on-line: Department of Foreign Affairs and International Trade, http://www.dfait.gc.ca/can-am/main/border/smart_border_declaration-en.asp. The Smart Border Declaration was signed by Canadian Foreign Affairs Minister John Manley and U.S. Homeland Security Director Tom Ridge on December 12, 2001.

19 *Supra* note 9. The agreement only applies to those crossing at land borders, and has exemptions for people with relatives who are already established in either Canada or the United States. It is currently being challenged in Canadian courts, see Chapter 4, note 41.

20 The increase will not correspond exactly as there are great classes of excluded claims in the United States. The first year of operation confirms a massive drop in refugee claims made in Canada, from 6,444 from December 29, 2003 – March 30, 2004, to 4,639 in December 29, 2004 – March 30, 2005. See Citizenship and Immigration Canada, *First Statistics Under Canada-U.S. Safe Third Country Agreement Show Decline in Refugee Claimants*, on-line: http://www.cic.gc.ca/english/policy/safe-third-stats.html.

claimant numbers. The benefit to the United States is now an increase in control of the asylum process in a North America context. In the present security climate, greater border control is read as greater security and an additional 10,000 asylum seekers per annum is now an affordable price to pay.

This leads directly to the vital unimportance of the September 11 events to the migration-security pairing, and to what I term "fact resistance." In the immediate aftermath of the September 11 events, there were a number of news reports suggesting that the attackers had entered the United States through Canada and that this was attributable to less stringent Canadian laws, particularly pertaining to refugee claimants. These stories were part of a trend in reporting following September 11 that linked refugee claimants with the events or with a risk of terrorist attacks generally. As anyone who works in the area of migration law is now very tired of repeating, these stories were not true. The standard response to this concern, raised in various ways in public, political, and academic gatherings, goes something like this. The September 11 terrorists were not asylum seekers. They were much smarter than to take on a vulnerable and highly scrutinized status. Most of them had student, tourist, or business visas that ensured that they could remain in the United States for a predictable period of time. Asylum seekers in the United States, as elsewhere, face an unpredictable decision-making process that involves detailed scrutiny of their backgrounds and inquiry into their present circumstances. They have limited ways of supporting themselves, and limited access to education. They can be detained for any number of reasons. None of this is conducive to the clandestine planning of a major attack; quite the opposite. In short, asylum seekers are highly vulnerable individuals. They lack security themselves – a point that has been lost in the recent security turn in migration discourses. The September 11 attackers did not enter the United States from Canada, despite Canada's arguably more generous refugee determination system.[21] Sixteen of the nineteen terrorists had some sort of U.S. visa, including student visas, tourist visas, and visas obtained through the "Visa-Express" program then in operation for Saudi citizens. None of the attackers entered the United States as asylum seekers. Although the visa status for three of them is not known, the majority had received immigration clearance from the United States' government. They had been screened and approved.

I have myself made this response to the query many times now. While my audiences are generally respectful, there is always at least one person who does not believe me. They do not know much about the area, they have not done any research, they cannot remember what newspaper they read, but they are just certain I must have my facts wrong. This is "fact resistance." It is a security effect, a sign that a particular issue has moved to the unquestionable plane of exceptional security measures. It does not matter how expert I am or how large my podium, I must

---

21 One person who had claimed refugee status in Canada and been denied it was apprehended at the U.S. border in December 1999 on his way to bomb the L.A. airport. Ahmed Ressam has been sentenced to twenty-two years in prison, plus five years of supervision after his release.

surely be missing the point, because refugee flows *are dangerous*. Fact resistance is important because there is no obvious way to counter it and it is so widespread that it demands a political response. In some cases, it is political leaders themselves who resist the facts. Indeed, since the 2001 events, Canadian government policy has explicitly linked asylum flows and security concerns – so it is not a phenomenon that can be dragged to the doorstep of the media and deposited there.[22] Six years after September 11, 2001, I am not convinced that any quantity of factual reiteration will dissuade a serious number of people from this view about those particular terrorists, or about refugees in general, at least in the short term. The challenge for anyone who is concerned about the harms of portraying refugee claimants as a security issue is how to move beyond the simple reiteration-of-the-facts response.

This quality of fact resistance is a key link to theorizing security. Security scholars recognize that security is a " . . . self-referential practice, because it is in this practice that the issue becomes a security issue – not necessarily because a real existential threat exists but because the issue is presented as such a threat."[23] At the core of any successful securitization – of any movement of an issue into the realm of exceptional politics demanding extraordinary action – is the acceptance of an issue as a threat. It is not important, or even possible, to discover whether a threat is "real."[24] The logical corollary of this is to understand that once an issue has broad currency as a security issue, asserting that the threat is not "real" will have little effect. Setting refugee flows up as a security issue depends on the authority of those actors who establish the linkage and the receptivity of their audiences to this message. The "reality" of the threat is in the stream of policy and politics that treat it as such. There is, of course, still a place for advocacy based on correcting the facts. But this cannot be the entire strategy. Countering this linkage must also involve interrogating the conditions under which these security politics flourish; in this instance the intertwining of globalization and illegal migration.

Ironically, given the erroneous linking of refugee flows to the 9/11 plot, it was the "homegrown" London bombers who had refugees in their number. Several of the successful and unsuccessful July 2005 attackers came to Britain as refugee children. Their stories tell of families who arrived from troubled parts of the globe, with no question of their "legitimacy" as refugees and no hint of insidious motivations, to find their own security in Britain. The parents who made the decision to remake their lives have done so in ways that all evidence suggests are blameless. One of the bombers was even identified to the authorities by his parents.[25] In this story,

---

22 Government of Canada, *Securing an Open Society: Canada's National Security Policy* (Ottawa: Privy Council Office, April 2004).

23 Buzan et al., *supra* note 3 at 24.

24 Buzan et al., *supra* note 3 at 30 further explain: "It is not easy to judge the securitization of an issue against some measure of whether that issue is 'really' a threat; doing so would demand an objective measure of security that no security theory has yet provided."

25 Daniel McGrory, Richard Ford, and Stewart Tendler, "Ready to Strike Again" *The Times [London]* (July 27, 2005) Home News 1.

there is a link between being a refugee and being a terrorist, but it is not a causal one, and it counters rather than reaffirms the public panic. We accept as a given the innocence of children; they did not cross the globe at nine years old intent on planting a bomb on the Tube. These children are another counterfactual, but fact resistance renders them invisible.

One way into this analysis is to consider what the moral panic narrative and the reiterated facts response have in common. The common elements are part of the explanation for fact resistance. The terrorists who have made these attacks on prosperous Western nations are all "outsiders" of one sort or another. They can all be portrayed as migrants with ties elsewhere. They are members of "ethnic minority," or "visible minority" communities (depending on which nation's *patois* one uses). There is not a Timothy McVeigh in this group (although this may be just around the corner). The British citizenship of some of the London bombers can be read as reinforcing the point that it is migration laws rather than citizenship laws that truly constitute the community.[26] Nonetheless, the persistent othering of security discourse underscores the limits of the law in constituting a community. The law can produce citizens; it cannot erase distinctions among them in any more than a formalistic sense. It is startlingly easy to see the "us-them" line running through the security discourse. Reports more sympathetic toward the London bombers have focused on the racism and cultural insularity that one would have experienced growing up as a Somali refugee in Leeds;[27] that is, being never really one-of-us, citizenship or legal legitimacy notwithstanding. Muslim communities are acutely aware of how religious difference is used in this othering process. Racialization is deeply implicated. All of these modes of othering can be applied to any category of migrant.

The forces of othering and insidious climate of fear that provide fertile ground for security politics are also assisted by the commonalities between those who have committed, and from afar supported, these attacks: young, brown men with attachments to Islamic fundamentalist sects. An image of "foreign-ness" makes it easier to understand why the attacks occur (for surely there is no rational reason, no reason that "we" understand) and harder to perceive meaningful differences between degrees of youngness, brownness, maleness, and religiosity. The facts foster fact resistance. Fact resistance means that we know whom to fear. The current security panic harkens back to a time when the borders of the state coincided more closely with the "us-them" line. There is clearly an "us" group in the current security matrix, but it does not fit neatly within national boundaries. We may feel that the United States or Britain is more vulnerable to a terrorist attack than Canada, Australia, Spain, or Bali, but we do not feel "safe" by virtue of being in the outer circle of the in-group. The new security agenda reflects globalization's redrawing of the "us-them" line in a way that has some correspondence with the borders of the prosperous West, but that marks other distinctions as well. This redrawing

26 This is elaborated in Chapter 7.
27 Robert Little, "For Many in Leeds, Radicalism No Shock," *The Baltimore Sun* (July 14, 2005) A1.

corresponds with the global convergence in migration laws, at least among desirable destination states.

The othering at the center of security politics is linked directly to migration laws, and to the desire to crack down, to hermetically seal borders against all possible attack, passage, or infiltration. Indeed, in the first few hours following the September 11 attacks, American borders were closed. However, for prosperous nations, closing the borders would be as much of an existential threat as terrorist bombs. Hermetically sealing prosperous nations would end our "way of life," that central value that is under threat. At a most basic level, it would lead to dramatic changes in what "we" in the prosperous West eat and the temperature inside our homes. Turning borders into walls – as in the Israeli security perimeter and the fortification of the U.S.-Mexico border – has some security value, but the costs on many fronts are exceptionally high. In the former case, the International Court of Justice struggled to even name the wall, and ultimately found it contravened international law because, in order to meet security objectives, it does not follow the legal border.[28] This is a stark illustration that security and the border no longer fit neatly together. In the latter instance, the body count along the border has risen markedly with fortification, but extralegal crossings have not been significantly reduced.[29] The way people in the prosperous West now live depends extensively on economic flows, including economic flows of people. What the shift in the security climate does, however, is call up a reexamination of whether we have the balance right between letting people in and keeping people out. It is this question of balancing that the idea of Britain having been "too tolerant" of diversity evokes.

The post-9/11 world has provided fertile grounds for security politics flourishing. Fear is pervasive. Politicians, pressed for a response, are quick to vilify. British Prime Minister Tony Blair provides an easy example. Following close on the heels of the news that the London bombers were British citizens, he announced new crackdown measures targeted at foreigners as a direct response to the attacks.[30] This was not an isolated measure; it was accompanied by increased targeting of mosques and investigation of known activists. Nonetheless, it shows the precise disconnect at the heart of the present immigration security politics. Citizens have committed terror attacks, and the government moves to crack down on foreigners. Moving beyond pointing this out, however, requires giving careful thought to what states ought to do to enhance security. Exceptions and extremes are the core of security politics. They will not be assuaged by a counteroffensive that says, "Do nothing because

---

28 *Legal Consequences of the Construction of a Wall in the Occupied Palestinian Territory* (2004), Advisory Opinion, on-line: International Court of Justice, http://www.icj-cij.org/icjwww/ idecisions.htm. At paragraph 67 of the joint judgment, the Court states: " ... the 'wall' in question is a complex construction, so that term cannot be understood in a limited physical sense. However, the other terms used, either by Israel ("fence") or by the Secretary-General ("barrier"), are no more accurate if understood in the physical sense."

29 See Chapter 8.

30 Alan Cowell, "Blair is Seeking to Curb Radicals Who Preach Hate," *The New York Times* (August 6, 2005) A1.

nothing has changed." Nor will many states be satisfied by mounting a campaign advertising that most risk indicators show little change. Urging that governments be more strategic in their security measures, that their targeting affect those who are potential threats rather than merely noncitizens contains the corollary that we are willing to accept more surveillance, more police work, more information sharing across borders. Whether this is really the new compromise is the point I will return to after considering the key site where immigration law and security intersect at present – indefinite detention of foreigners.

Bargaining and balancing

The classic bargain of the liberal state is that between the perils of individuated life without the protection of a collectivity on the one hand and loss of individual liberty to the state on the other. Whether this balance involves an abject state of nature and a Leviathan, a social contract, or an original position, its basic structure is the same. The fulcrum of this balance is security – staying safe is the reason for the trade, constituting a community is the result. As a central construct of the liberal state, this balancing act is replicated in diverse settings. Contemporary contestation of security and migration is a key illustration.

I have already mentioned that since September 11, 2001, there have been shifts in a wide range of discretionary practices under migration laws. Arguably the most contentious discretionary security procedure is the indefinite detention of non-nationals who are considered to be security risks. A typical feature of this procedure is that information that cannot be made public because of national security concerns is relied upon.[31] In Canada, as elsewhere, these and similar provisions have been found constitutionally valid on the basis that the detention is not for a criminal purpose, but for an immigration purpose.[32] Another way of expressing this is to say that the detention is not punitive. This context means that an individual can

---

31 The "national security" qualifier is most frequently used to keep information secret. See Craig Forcese, "Through a Glass Darkly: The Role and Review of 'National Security' Concepts in Canadian Law" (2006), 43 *Alberta Law Review* 963.

32 In Canada, indefinite security detention for non-nationals worked this way until 2007. Once the Minister for Immigration and the Solicitor General have reviewed the secret evidence and decided that a person ought to be detained as a security risk, they issue a certificate of inadmissibility and refer this document to the Federal Court of Canada for a determination regarding whether it is reasonable. Designated judges of the Federal Court can review the secret intelligence information that is part of the basis of the certificate. The person named in a certificate can also put their case to the court, but neither they nor their lawyers have access to the secret information. They receive instead an approved summary of the information. If the certificate is found to be reasonable it becomes a nonreviewable and non-appealable removal order and the person is detained until they are removed from Canada. As this process can take some time, a person held under a security certificate can be detained at length. This detention is subject to periodic reviews, once every six months. There is a presumption that if the person cannot be removed in a "reasonable" period of time, they will be released, provided such release will not pose a "danger to national security or to the safety of any person." Release is rare, which is not surprising given that security risk is most often the reason for the certificate in the first place. The procedure is set out in the *Immigration and Refugee Protection Act*, S.C. 2001, c.27, Part 1 Division 9.

be detained as a matter of executive rather than judicial action. While there is an element of sleight of hand in this reasoning, it has proven resilient.[33]

Civil liberties groups hate these provisions. I must confess to participating in a protest letter to Canada's solicitor general regarding the Canadian procedure to make plain that I agree with much of the critique.[34] The features of the process generally found to be objectionable are the secrecy of key evidence and the possibility of indefinite detention. Secret evidence is an anathema to common lawyers.[35] The possibility of indefinite detention, although not present on the face of the legislation, arises in these cases because some people are, in immigration parlance, "unremovable." This can arise for a number of reasons, but in the case of national security risks it would usually be because either the individual's home state refuses to take them back (or to acknowledge them) or because there is a risk that if they are returned they will be tortured or killed. It is a breach of international law to return people to circumstances where they face these risks; such a significant breach, in fact, that most Western states take it reasonably seriously.[36] If someone cannot be returned, the Western state is then faced with deciding what to do with him. This may be a "Not In My Backyard" effect – better to protect ourselves by just having terrorists go somewhere else. It may be because the secret evidence would not stand up to the higher evidentiary standards of a criminal trial. For example, some have speculated that the reason the United States has deported some people to Syria is *because* they will be tortured and perhaps reveal evidence, not in spite of this risk.[37] It could also be a combination of these two factors in that in criminal prosecution there is a higher standard of proof than in immigration security matters, and therefore a greater risk, from the state's perspective, that the person will be released.

33 See *Canada (Minister of Employment and Immigration) v. Chiarelli*, [1992] 1 S.C.R. 711; *Chu Kheng Lim and Ors v. Minister for Immigration Local Government and Ethnic Affairs and Anor* (1992), 176 C.L.R. 1 (High Court of Australia); *R v. Governor of Durham Prison, ex parte Hardial Singh*, [1984] 1 W.L.R. 704 (Q.B.); *Clark v. Martinez* 125 S.Ct. 716 (2005) is a recent consideration by the U.S. Supreme Court.
34 Letter to Hon. Anne McClellan, October 14, 2004, signed by sixty members of the legal community in Canada. I am grateful to Professor Sharry Aiken for organizing this public appeal.
35 In the midst of one recent security certificate proceeding, Canadian lawyer Rocco Galati dramatically resigned, stating that the secrecy of the proceeding brought him into breach of his sworn duties. *Jaballah v. Canada (Minister of Citizenship and Immigration)* 2004 FC 299.
36 In *Suresh v. Canada (Minister of Citizenship and Immigration)*, 2002 SCC 1, [2002] 1 S.C.R. 3, 208 D.L.R. (4th) 1 [*Suresh*], the Supreme Court of Canada stated that the risk of deportation to torture needed to be balanced against the risk to national security of allowing the person to remain, and that in most cases the balance would tilt in favor of allowing a person to remain in Canada. The Court further stated that this balancing should be left to the Minister's discretion, and it declined to conclude that international law's absolute prohibition on deportation to face torture was part of Canadian domestic law.
37 See Stephen Grey, "United States: Trade in Torture" (April 2005) *Le Monde Diplomatique* 4. December 2005 news reports suggested this practice is particularly widespread. In a public address, Condoleezza Rice defended the process known as rendition saying it was a "lawful weapon" in the war on terrorism. See Anne Gearan, "Rice Defends U.S. Terrorism Policy," (December 5, 2005) *Globe and Mail*. For the text of her address, see Condoleezza Rice, "Full text: Rice defends US policy," on-line: BBC News, http://news.bbc.co.uk/2/hi/americas/4500630.stm.

What we think of these procedures lies at the center of the classic liberal balance, and the core question of how much we are willing to trust our governments. Alternatively, to cast the balance in the language of security threat, it calls on each of us to consider what we fear most, terrorism or unchecked executive power. I am just as afraid as the next person of my plane being hijacked or my train being bombed. I like to think that faced with a serious threat to one of my children I would act with utter disregard to the law. Some insight into the rule of law, to which I return later, is gained by understanding that these reactions are commonplace, a contemporary casting of the state of nature. My objection to these procedures comes because I do not trust that this much secrecy is necessary, and I am skeptical about the much-touted value of sharing secrets with other nations. I think liberty could be less infringed, even while acknowledging that national security concerns call up some space for exception, and that if this exception is not found within the law, it will be made outside it. I have also come to think that this question of degree of trust is fundamentally political, not legal. That is, there is no right or even "just" answer to how this balance should be weighted for the liberal democratic society. There is instead an ongoing renegotiation of the balance. As we do not have access to the evidence in national security certificate cases, we cannot decide whether we agree with the outcomes or not, only whether we trust those who have made the decisions to do the right thing. In the Canadian case, both the executive and the judiciary have a role to play in the process, but the judicial role is so closely aligned to the executive that the scene does not play out like a traditional separation of powers narrative. Instead, given the close alliance of all three branches of government, the state here functions as state in a monolithic sense. The question of trust is about the whole enterprise.

Not surprisingly given the rise in use of these procedures and whom they most recently have targeted, this balance has come under increased scrutiny of late. The case that most fully canvasses these issues is *A v. Secretary of State for the Home Department*[38] in which the House of Lords reviewed the legal basis for the detention of nine foreign nationals who had been "certified" under the 2001 Anti-Terrorism, Crime, and Security Act.[39] None of the detainees were facing any criminal charges. Their detention was potentially indefinite because they could not be deported due to a binding European Court of Human Rights ruling creating an absolute prohibition against deportation to face torture or inhuman or degrading treatment or punishment.[40] In addition, the government was constrained by an influential 1984 ruling that non-nationals could be detained for the purpose of deportation only for such time as reasonably necessary to achieve the deportation.[41] Faced with

---

38 *A v. Secretary of State for the Home Department* (2004), [2005] 2 A.C. 68 (H.L.) [*A*], decided December 16, 2004.
39 *Anti-terrorism, Crime, and Security Act 2001* (U.K.), 2001, c. 24, s. 21.
40 *Chahal v. United Kingdom* (1996), V Eur. Ct. H.R. Rep. Judgments & Dec. 1831, 23 E.H.R.R. 413.
41 *R v. Governor of Durham Prison, ex parte Hardial Singh*, [1984] 1 W.L.R. 704 (Q.B.) per Woolf J (now Woolf LCJ). This decision has never been questioned and was followed by the Privy Council

these constraints, the government had taken steps to formally derogate from the liberty provisions of the European Convention on Human Rights (ECHR) and the International Covenant on Civil and Political Rights, which set out rights of liberty and permissible constraints upon them.[42] The case revolved around the ECHR provisions as they are binding in United Kingdom law under the Human Rights Act.[43] Under the ECHR, derogation is permissible "in time of war or other public emergency threatening the life of the nation."[44] Derogations are limited to "the extent strictly required by the exigencies of the situation" and must not breach other international law obligations.

The House of Lords ruled in favor of the appellants, reigning in the government, even while acknowledging in strong terms the security setting of the decision. Lord Bingham of Cornhill, who penned the lead judgment for the majority, describes the September 11 events as having been " . . . committed by terrorists fired by ideological hatred of the United States and willing to sacrifice their own lives in order to injure the leading nation of the western world."[45] Seven of the eight Lords who comprise the majority found that there was indeed a public emergency threatening the life of the nation.[46] However, they quashed the derogation order and ruled that the indefinite detention provisions were in breach of the European Convention on Human Rights because they were disproportionate and they discriminated impermissibly on the grounds of nationality or immigration status.

in *Tan Te Lam v. Superintendent of Tai A Chau Detention Center* (1996), [1997] A.C. 97. It is also implicitly affirmed by the House of Lords in the present decision.

42 Article 5(1) of the *Convention for the Protection of Human Rights and Fundamental Freedoms*, November 4, 1950, 213 U.N.T.S. 221, Eur. T.S. 5 [*ECHR*] states:

Everyone has the right to liberty and security of person. No one shall be deprived of his liberty save in the following cases and in accordance with a procedure prescribed by law:

. . .

(f) the lawful arrest or detention of . . . a person against whom action is being taking with a view to deportation.

The parallel provisions of the ICCPR are contained in Article 9.

43 *Human Rights Act* (U.K.), 1998, c. 42. This is why Prime Minister Tony Blair included the possibility of amending the *Human Rights Act* in his August 5, 2005, announcement of a more aggressive posture toward deporting dangerous foreigners. See Tony Blair, "PM's Press Conference – August 5, 2005 (Monthly Downing Street Press Conference)" on-line: Latest News from Downing Street, http://www.number-10.gov.uk/output/Page8041.asp.

44 *Convention for the Protection of Human Rights and Fundamental Freedoms, supra* note 42 at Article 15(1).

45 *Supra* note 38 at para. 6.

46 Ibid. at para. 218. Lord Walker of Gestingthorpe would have dismissed the appeals. In concluding his reasons he stated:

I think it is also significant that in a period of nearly three years no more than seventeen individuals have been certified under section 21. Of course, every single detention without trial is a matter of concern, but in the context of national security the number of persons actually detained (now significantly fewer than seventeen) is to my mind relevant to the issue of proportionality. Liberty [a U.K. nongovernmental organization that made oral and written submissions] in its written submissions appears to rely on the small number of certificates as evidence that there is not a sufficiently grave emergency. That is, I think, a striking illustration of the dilemma facing a democratic government in protecting national security." (*Supra* note 38 at para. 218).

This is an important decision, which has been the subject of significant commentary.[47] I want to highlight aspects of the decision that situate it within the migration-globalization-security matrix. First among these is that the reasoning turns on unmasking the fiction that this detention of non-nationals is an immigration matter. Lord Bingham of Cornhill stated, "The comparison [between nationals and non-nationals] contended for by the Attorney General might be reasonable and justified in an immigration context, but cannot in my opinion be so in a security context, since the threat presented by suspected international terrorists did not depend on their nationality or immigration status."[48] Lord Hope of Craighead used a sharper form of words: " . . . it would be a serious error, in my opinion, to regard this case as about the right to control immigration."[49] Lord Rodger of Earlsferry makes reference to how the September 11, 2001, events shifted discretionary practices, and with them the analysis of this detention. He states, " . . . so far as the need for detention is concerned, the critical factor is not the suspects' immigration status but the threat that they are suspected of posing to the life of the nation: that is why, although the Secretary of State had previously wanted to deport the appellants, it was only after 9/11 that steps were taken to provide for their detention."[50] Casting her reasons as a summation of the ruling, Baroness Hale of Richmond said, "These people are not detained under article 5(1)(f) 'with a view to deportation or extradition' because they cannot be deported and no other country has asked for their extradition. They are being detained on suspicion of being international terrorists. . . . "[51] The crucial fact supporting this rejection of the previously intact sleight of hand was that British citizen terrorist suspects were not subject to indefinite detention: "The foreigners who can be deported are not like the foreigners who cannot. These foreigners are only being detained because they cannot be deported. They are just like a British national who cannot be deported."[52]

This shift in reasoning regarding the nature of the immigration security context signals a globalized understanding of the perceived threat. The Law Lords, perhaps ironically given the events of 2005, rest their ruling on an understanding that terrorist threat may arise inside or outside the nation. It is not dependent on immigration status. There is a line between us and them in this discourse, but it does not map onto the border of the nation. As with the Israeli security fence, protection does not come at the border line. Lord Rodger of Earlsferry goes further

---

47 See Tom R. Hickman, "Between Human Rights and the Rule of Law: Indefinite Detention and the Derogation Model of Constitutionalism" (2005), 63.4 *Modern Law Review* 655; Alexandra Chirinos, "Finding the Balance Between Liberty and Security: The Lords' Decision on Britain's Anti-Terrorism Act" (2005), 18 *Harvard Human Rights Journal* 265; Adam Tomkins, "Readings of *A v. Secretary of State for Home Department*" (2005), *Public Law* 259.

48 *Supra* note 38 at para. 54.

49 Ibid. at para. 103. He continued, "This is because the issue which the Derogation Order was designed to address was not at its heart an immigration issue at all. It was an issue about the aliens' right to liberty."

50 Ibid. at para. 171.   51 Ibid. at para. 222.

52 Ibid. at para. 235 per Baroness Hale of Richmond.

and rejects the submission that foreigners may be the controlling forces of terrorism and the British citizens mere minions: "There is nothing in the open material which gives the slightest basis for inferring that the foreign suspects made up the generals and chiefs of staff, while the British suspects provided the foot-soldiers."[53]

Resolutely rejecting the notion that removing non-national terror suspects serves an immigration purpose is a marked departure from earlier immigration and security discourse. It is remarkable in the context of this decision that confirmed that the question of whether a threat to the life of the nation exists is an essentially political decision. Arguments that an emergency must be imminent, or temporary, were rejected. Only Lord Hoffman rejected the government's classification of the security climate in the United Kingdom in late 2004 as an emergency threatening the life of the nation. In language that resonates with rage and national pride, he casts the issue thus:

> This is a nation which has been tested in adversity, which has survived physical destruction and catastrophic loss of life. I do not underestimate the ability of fanatical groups of terrorists to kill and destroy, but they do not threaten the life of the nation. Whether we would survive Hitler hung in the balance, but there is no doubt we shall survive Al-Qaeda. The Spanish people have not said that what happened in Madrid, hideous crime as it was, threatened the life of their nation. Their legendary pride would not allow it. Terrorist violence, serious as it is, does not threaten our institutions of government or our existence as a civil community. . . .
>
> The real threat to the life of the nation, in the sense of a people living in accordance with its traditional laws and political values, comes not from terrorism but from laws such as these. That is the true measure of what terrorism may achieve. It is for Parliament to decide whether to give the terrorists such a victory.[54]

Lord Hoffman's powerful language, while it did not persuade his colleagues, points to the vital balance between individual freedom and state power that, in times of security threat, is renegotiated in a reflection of how much we trust our governments. Lord Hoffman sees the case as a battle over national values. He says, "The question in this case is whether the United Kingdom should be a country where the police can come to such a person's house and take him away to be detained indefinitely without trial."[55] He ultimately reaches the same conclusion as the others in the majority, but he rests the battle line here, rather than looking within the monolith of state power and finding, as the other majoritarians do, a judicial expertise regarding liberty rights. Of course, outcomes have an effect that mere reasoning does not, so perhaps this distinction is trivial. But it calls upon us to reflect on what we fear. Lord Hoffman calls upon us to deconstruct the political rhetoric of securitization. I will return to this point presently, after considering parallel decisions in other Western liberal democracies.

53 Ibid. at para. 185   54 Ibid. at paras. 96–97.   55 Ibid. at para. 87.

Several weeks before the House of Lords ruling, the Supreme Court of New Zealand tackled a case with close parallels in *Zaoui v. The Attorney-General and Ors*.[56] Ahmed Zaoui, an Algerian citizen found to be a refugee in New Zealand, had been detained for close to two years pending a review of a security risk certificate. Zaoui was associated with the Algerian terrorist group Islamic Salvation Front. The principal legal issue in the case was whether the High Court's inherent jurisdiction to grant bail had been ousted by Part 4A of the Immigration Act 1987.[57] In its analysis the unanimous Supreme Court considered both the requirement under the Refugee Convention that contracting states not restrict the movement of refugees unnecessarily[58] and the fact that all detention powers under the act are related to the possibility of removing detained individuals from New Zealand.[59] Ultimately concluding that Zaoui could be bailed by the High Court, the court stated, " . . . it is of prime importance that any powers of detention be approached in light of the fundamental right, long recognized under the common law, of liberty for all persons subject only to such limits as are imposed by law. The Supreme Court rejected the argument, which had proven persuasive below, that the secrecy-protected nature of the national security evidence would render bail impractical. The legislation contemplated a speedy review of the certificate; in cases where this requirement was not met, bail could be considered. In concluding its reasons, the Court stated:

> This is a case where national security issues arise. It is also a case about the liberty of someone who has refugee status in New Zealand and who is entitled to the benefit of the Refugee Convention requirement that only such restrictions upon his liberty as are necessary should be imposed upon him. The applications fall to be considered against the background of concern for liberty recognized by the Bill of Rights Act and the common law. Accordingly the case raises significant matters of public concern which require careful balance.[60]

Zaoui differed factually from the *A* decision in two ways. First, he had not yet been found to be unremovable. Second, he had refugee status. The tenor of the reasoning suggests that refugee status is of considerable importance here. The question of unremovability is dealt with in the legislation.[61] Despite these differences, the decision draws on the identical vital principle that indefinite detention is an anathema to the basic liberty values of the common law and that concerns of security and secrecy do not trump these. While *Zaoui* does not expressly address the

---

56 *Zaoui v. The Attorney-General and Ors* (2004), [2005] 1 N.Z.L.R. 577 (S.C.) [*Zaoui*].
57 Immigration Act 1987 NZ 074 (commenced April 21, 1987).
58 *Convention Relating to the Status of Refugees,* July 28, 1951, 189 U.N.T.S. 150 (entered into force April 22, 1954) at article 31(2). See *supra* note 56 at paras. 44, 51, 59 for references in the decision.
59 *Zaoui, supra* note 56 at para. 46.
60 Ibid. at para. 101.
61 Ibid. at para. 60. The Court states, "A person who is the subject of a security risk certificate but who cannot be deported is released without conditions." at para. 60. This provision may possibly be one reason why the executive branch had delayed the security certificate review in this case.

question of anti-terrorism measures disguising themselves as immigration regulation, the reasoning never suggests that noncitizens may have inferior rights to liberty. On the contrary, a rarely invoked provision of the Refugee Convention is used to bolster the rights claims of a nonmember.[62] Both *Zaoui* and *A* address the post-9/11 turn in migration-security discourse and directly name the balancing of rights and security that grounds this.

Other jurisdictions are approaching the question of indefinite detention for noncitizen terror suspects. In the United States, where immigration crackdown measures have perhaps been the sharpest, recent decisions have also narrowed the issues for judicial consideration. The January 2005 ruling in *Clark v. Martinez*[63] established that indefinite detention could not be justified under immigration legislation in the case of those considered to be a "risk to the community."[64] Martinez, along with Benitez whose case was joined, had arrived in the United States from Cuba as part of the 1980 Mariel boatlift. Although many Cubans in the United States were allowed to regularize their status in 1996, both Martinez and Benitez had been convicted of several criminal offenses by that time and thus were barred from attaining immigration status. Removal to Cuba is not possible. While they are now criminally inadmissible, they had in fact never been formally admitted, only paroled into the country as part of the admission procedure. The majority opinion, penned by Justice Scalia, held that the statute could only authorize detention that was related to its basic purpose of removing aliens.[65] This consideration of the legislation's context was bolstered by separate analysis that liberty interests must have the same consideration that they would receive in a criminal context.[66] In reasoning paralleling that of the House of Lords, a key portion of the analysis required that the same provisions of a statute could not be read differently when different categories of people were being considered. The government had raised border security issues in argument. The Court's response on this issue was that Congress has separate recourse to address security concerns, but that it had not done so in this instance. This point makes reference to provisions introduced as part of the USA PATRIOT Act[67] providing for indefinitely renewable detention for unremovable terror suspects. This provision has not been fully tested yet.

The issues considered by the House of Lords and the Supreme Court of New Zealand may be circumvented in the United States by the post-9/11 case law relating to enemy combatants. In these cases, the question of indefinite right to detain

---

62 Article 31(2) of the *Convention Relating to the Status of Refugees*, July 28, 1951, 189 U.N.T.S. 150 states:

> The Contracting States shall not apply to the movements of such refugees restrictions other than those which are necessary and such restrictions shall only be applied until their status in the country is regularized or they obtain admission into another country. The Contracting States shall allow such refugees a reasonable period and all the necessary facilities to obtain admission into another country.

63 125 S.Ct. 716 (2005), decided on January 12, 2005.   64 Title 8 U.S.C. at para 1231(a)(6).
65 *Supra* note 63 at 722.   66 Ibid. at 724.
67 *Uniting and Strengthening America by Providing Appropriate Tools Required to Intercept and Obstruct Terrorism Act of 2001*, Pub. L. No. 107–56, 115 Stat. 272.

has been resolved as a matter distinguishing between domestic criminal law and military law, rather than as raising immigration law issues. The question of indefinite detention of non-nationals has been most prominently associated with the Guantanamo Bay detainees. In *Rasul v. Bush*[68] the Supreme Court held, paralleling the House of Lords' reasoning, that a distinction based on citizenship was an indefensible basis for denying the application of the habeas corpus statute.[69] Tribunals established in response to this judgment were found in June 2006 to be unjustified in American law and also in contravention of international law.[70] Parallel challenges relating to American citizens in military detention in relation to the war on terror have been resolved on the basis of designating them as "enemy combatants."[71] While the criteria for determining citizens to be enemy combatants are narrow (presence on the battlefield at some point in time and actual taking up of weapons against the United States),[72] it is conceivable that more flexibility would be found in the case of individuals who are noncitizens. Thus military law rather than immigration law could well be the solution when the executive seeks recourse to indefinite detention. This would have the result of clarifying the purpose of the detention, which is precisely what the House of Lords ultimately required of the British executive.

In February 2007, the Supreme Court of Canada ruled that the Canadian national security certificate procedure infringed the constitutional guarantee that individuals can only be deprived of liberty in accordance with the principles of fundamental justice.[73] The case considered the immigration detention of three men: Adil Charkaoui, a Moroccan citizen and permanent resident of Canada, detained in May 2003; Hassan Almrei, a refugee from Syria first detained in October 2001; and Mohamed Harkat, a refugee from Algeria detained since 2002.[74] These appeals brought Canada's security certificate process directly before the Supreme Court for the first time since its predecessor was given constitutional clearance by that Court in 1993.[75] Despite the available precedents of the House of Lords' *A* decision and the importance of international refugee law for *Zaoui*, the ruling in this case has a muted tenor. This is somewhat surprising given extensive public discussion of these

---

68 542 US 466 (2004) decided on June 28, 2004.
69 Ibid. at 479–80, per Justice Stevens for the plurality.
70 *Hamdan v. Rumsfeld* 125 S. Ct. 2749 (2006).
71 *Hamdi v. Rumsfeld* 542 US 507 (2004); *Padilla v. Hanft* 423 F.3d 386 (4th Cir. 2005), decided on September 9, 2005, penned by Justice Luttig with Justices Michael and Traxler concurring.
72 In the case of Jose Padilla, who was not taken into custody on the battlefield, one might add that being on an enemy mission and having previously been on the battlefield are the criteria.
73 *Charkaoui v. Canada (Citizenship and Immigration)* 2007 SCC 9 (February 23, 2007) [2007] 1 S.C.R. 350. Section 7 of the *Canadian Charter of Rights and Freedoms* states: "Everyone has the right to life, liberty and security of the person and the right not to be deprived thereof except in accordance with the principles of fundamental justice."
74 See *supra* note 32. Two others were subject to security certificates at the time. Their cases were not joined in this appeal but they will be affected by its result.
75 The Supreme Court approved this process in *Canada (Minister of Employment and Immigration) v. Chiarelli*, [1992] 1 S.C.R. 711. The procedure was introduced to Canadian law in l991. The *Suresh* decision did involve the security certificate process but those aspects of the case were not at issue before the Supreme Court of Canada.

detentions and the fact that the Court held three days of hearings on the matter, the longest hearing since the *Quebec Secession Reference* in 1998 examining the constitutionality of the Canadian state.[76] It is clear from the Court's unanimous decision in *Charkaoui* that it was not willing to elevate indefinite detention of non-nationals to a similar level of importance.

The court in *Charkaoui* takes a stance that is directly opposite from that of the House of Lords and the New Zealand Supreme Court, as signaled by the opening words of the judgment: "One of the most fundamental responsibilities of a government is to ensure the security of its citizens."[77] The judgment declines to follow the House of Lords in breaking the linkage between this detention and an overall "immigration context" for the detention, and it explicitly rejects the argument that broader rule of law issues are engaged.[78] The Court similarly declined to address rights that might arise from the Refugee Convention. In contrast to the decisions elsewhere, this ruling did not find the potential of indefinite detention to be a problem with the legislative scheme.[79] Instead, the Court held that the secrecy provisions used to protect security-sensitive information do infringe constitutional rights. This aspect of the British and New Zealand provisions had not been viewed as an infringement. The Court suggested that less harmful alternatives were available and gave the government one year to alter its legislation rather than striking it down.[80] Despite the specific invitation provided by the *Canadian Charter of Rights and Freedoms* to consider whether rights' breaches are justified in a free and democratic society, the Court asserted without discussion that "protection of Canada's national security and related intelligence sources undoubtedly constitutes a pressing and substantial objective."[81] This is a concise statement of the securitization of migration law, at least in the eyes of the Supreme Court of Canada.

The coincidence of this group of cases is instructive – there is a reason they all arise at this point in time. They each bring the balancing issues of fear and liberty before the final appellate courts, signaling a desire to adjust the fulcrum. To differing degrees, the reasons call for a rearticulation of the migration-security coupling. For the House of Lords, this comes to the fore in rejecting the fiction that this administrative detention is permissible because of the immigration context. The setting is named a security setting instead. In New Zealand, the Court looks to the Refugee Convention as a source of rights, rather than merely of identity, which is in

---

76 *Reference re Secession of Quebec* [1998] 2 S.C.R. 217. In the case of each of these three men, an NGO has now been formed around the individual, and each has also received endorsement of support from prominent Canadians.
77 *Supra* note 73 at para. 1.   78 Ibid. at para. 133–37.
79 The Court finds that the detention scheme is constitutionally saved by the scheme of periodic review established in the legislation (paras. 108 and 109). It does, however, strike down provisions that set differing schedules for periodic review for foreign nationals as opposed to those with permanent resident status in Canada.
80 As I complete work on this manuscript in December 2007, new legislation is before Parliament. In the event that this does not pass, the security certificates currently in place will be automatically invalidated in February 2008.
81 *Supra* note 73 at para. 68.

itself a significant change. The United States Supreme Court holds out the possibility that indefinite detention for terror suspects might be constitutionally approved, that that object cannot be reached by sleight of hand, and that a generalized fear of wrongdoers will not suffice. The Supreme Court of Canada reasserted citizenship and national security and appealed for political rather than judicial action.

These provisions subjecting migrants to extremes of state power are rarely used, but they are not constructed as exceptions to the law. Instead, they stand out as a key feature of migration law, revealing what values the state will stand by in dangerous times. They operate as executive action, but their legislative framing and occasional judicial involvement forces the stamp of rule of law upon them. As security and migration discourses shift globally, the importance of this feature under conditions of a newly normalized fear is heightened.

Lessons of the new normal

The constant rebalancing between legal and political, between the executive and the courts, is slated to continue even in the short term, with new legislation being drawn up and judicial decisions pending in several states. All of this suggests that the compromise this procedure represents is not holding steady. Migration law is the current setting in which the classic trade-offs of the liberal state are being renegotiated. This fits squarely within the broader story of migration laws under conditions of globalization. Migration law is becoming the last bastion of sovereignty, the key location for contesting the core of both "nation" and "state." Perhaps the most essential element for the liberal state is the way the bargaining between individual freedom and collective safety is struck. This balance is worked out, refined, and transmitted at many sites in the liberal state. In global times where national level control is threatened, and where a small "l" liberal, Western, prosperous "us" group of states align their migration laws to reify a global "us-them" divide, the ability to exclude individuals at the border (and to detain them as a consequence of that power) because they are security risks of some sort, is becoming ever more important. There are evident ironies here. States are seeking to assert control even as the threats and fears are increasingly not bounded by national borders. In this regard, nations are reasserting a traditional "nation-ness" because other options are limited and new ways of doing security have yet to be fully imagined.

Buzan and his colleagues assert that some security issues are "normalized," so that the exceptional politics of securitization need not be put in motion each time a threat in these areas is perceived. They use the example of an established military complex or dikes in the Netherlands. The courts' response to the indefinite detention dilemma suggests that migration is becoming normalized as a security threat at this point in time, and that the present political shift is the consequence of this normalization. This shift means it is more and more normal to treat migration, particularly of asylum seekers, as a policing matter rather than a question of economic redistribution, social composition, or humanitarianism. The long-time twinning of migration and security remains, but its contents have shifted. Fear of migration is no longer predominantly a fear of loss of cultural or linguistic hegemony;[82] it is instead a fear of guns and bombs, of anthrax and sarin. This is key to the normalizing effect, the perceived threat itself now takes a form that we understand in military terms. Fears that migrants will bring crime (in an ordinary sense), contagion, or social dilution remain, but pale beside this new dimension. This shift makes the threat of migration easier to normalize because it is similar to that which is already existing and normalized.

One consequence of this normalization is that the migration-security matrix is highly gendered. Much as discussions of trafficking are constrained by a gendered discourse of the victimization of women, discussions of security are masculinized. Almost all of those who have been targeted by indefinite security detention have been men.[83] This may reflect a reality – more men may be involved in terrorist threats – but it also creates it. Given this, more men will be suspected and scrutinized. In our current climate of fear this may be appropriate, but any governmental practice with such a marked gendered pattern should be investigated for this reason alone. It may be that a focus on men as suspects will make women particularly successful as terrorists. Similarly, it could mean that terrorist organizations will use coercive measures to recruit women because they benefit from lower levels of scrutiny. It may also provide fertile grounds for investigating the essentializing premise that women are less violent than men are, or even less "political."

The gendered nature of security concern also aids in understanding current panic politics of migration security. Although the extent of trafficking is massive, measures to address it are few. On the other hand, the number of even merely suspected border crossing terrorists is tiny, but the political attention they attract is immense. There are, of course, many straightforward reasons for this, but gender ought not to be lost in the explanatory mixture. "Mere" victimization has never been sufficient or unique in terms of "women's issues" grabbing headline attention. Sovereignty itself is a masculinized concept. Masculinized threats to it are intelligible in a way that feminized threats seem not to be.

Another consequence of this normalization is that the law is sidelined. A typical security setting is one in which the routine operation of the law is suspended. This accounts in part for separate systems of military justice as the dominant mode of military discipline. Sudden eruptions of security concern lead predictably to the

---

82 *Supra* note 3. This was the case in the original scheme described by Buzan et al.
83 In Canada, twenty-five of twenty-six people named in security certificates have been men. In Australia all thirteen detainees in 2005 were men. The nine detainees in *A, supra* note 38, were men. Two Afghani journalists released from detention in Guantanamo Bay claim to have seen forms lying on a desk that indicated that some women were detained there (Ashfaq YusuFzai, "Journalists Release Guantanamo Bay Report" Inter Press Service (July 31, 2006), http://us.oneworld.net/article/view/137201/1). This is scant evidence indeed. No women have been among the publicized releases from Guantanamo. There is no doubt it is a male-dominated setting.

suspension of normal operations of law, for example through the device of declaring martial law. Security politics thrive on exception, the defined antithesis of the rule of law. This is why legal arguments in this area are always about the fundamentals. The issues they embody tend not to be about the particular contents of a given regulatory framework, but about the importance (or not) of law existing at all on this plane. The stakes are large. The call that the rule of law is foundational for our understanding of civilized peoples is at the center here, because the compromises – from Guantanamo Bay to secret trials – are beyond what the rule of law (whether spread thick with human rights or thin with process) typically entails.

Migration law has always held open a place for unlaw-like exceptions. From its origins as exclusively a part of the Royal Prerogative, this has been an area of law making where space has been preserved for unquestioned executive action.[84] In this respect, an international relation theorist's understanding of sovereignty crosses paths with more traditional legal theory. Sovereignty itself is bound up with power over exceptions. Exceptional security politics fit easily into the existing framework of migration law, demonstrating again how closely tied to community values and definitions this law is. For these reasons, the question of whether Britain has been too tolerant arises. It demonstrates that tolerance has always been a matter of choice, of discretion, rather than a matter of legal requirement. Whether there remains a choice to be intolerant will perhaps be raised by new legal challenges to the direction Britain strikes from this point onward. Up until now, however, it has been clear that tolerance is not demanded of the law, provided intolerance is applied evenhandedly.

Indefinite detention cases expose being a lawyer as an act of faith. When I protest that indefinite detention is not a compromise worth having, that the costs are simply too high, I am exposed as having a deep and unshakable commitment to at least one version of the rule of law. And to others of my faith, the argument is one of degree: When is an issue sufficiently political, or exceptional, that a departure from the strong line of the law is required in the circumstances? In other words, when should our faith in law be matched by a faith in government? Thus the in-house argument among lawyers unfurls. Meanwhile a broader argument rages. Its challenge is this. Given that you lawyers may have a point, what ought governments to do to counter these new threats? What other compromise would you offer up? Lord Hoffman's response might go like this – sacrificing individual rights and the rule of law in the hopes that some future attack may be thwarted misses the point as it concedes defeat by giving away what is good and true about "our way of life," the thing itself that is threatened here. It is a good response, one I have made myself, though never with his eloquence. But it is insufficiently political for present times.

---

84 This story is presented in detail by Kathryn Cronin, "A Culture of Control: An Overview of Immigration Policy Making" in J. Jupp and M. Kabala, eds., *The Politics of Australian Immigration* (Canberra: Australian Government Publishing Service, 1995). For a recent judicial discussion see *Khadr v. Canada (Attorney General)*, 2006 FC 727, [2006] 142 C.R.R. (2d) 116, 268 D.L.R. (4th) 303.

This argument calls up problems encountered above with fact resistance. Security politics calls upon us to say more than this, to say whether we support Tony Blair's latest foray or not, to identify sources of and remedies for our own fears. In this sense we are, again, called upon to engage with faith in Peter Fitzpatrick's terms: to consider the ethics of equality, freedom, and impartiality he names.

The measures I am willing to accept include things like enhanced security screening in vulnerable public spaces (such as airports, theaters, and stadiums), enhanced police presence in public spaces, front-end security screening of new members of the community (provided this is accompanied with sufficient resources not to slow the process excessively), enhanced community education about asylum (to displace the notion that asylum seekers are a security threat), stricter enforcement of deportation for criminal matters when there is no risk involved on return, sharing of information between security agencies (provided the public is informed of the nature and extent of this sharing) and domestic trials of those suspected of international terrorism or planning offenses. This last point in vital. Since the events of September 11, 2001, many countries have enacted new legislation to try suspects, even with secret evidence provisions.[85] However, these have rarely been used; instead, discretionary use of migration law provisions aimed at getting terror suspects to go elsewhere has increased. This does not solve the problem, nor ultimately can it protect us as it is increasingly clear that terrorists at large elsewhere pose similar risks to those who are at large within our borders. Deporting terror suspects is a lose-lose proposition.

Of course, these measures will not prevent all future attacks. But nor will the indefinite detention measures and racial profiling currently employed. There is a lot that states can do, faced with the current change in fears at the border, that they are not yet doing. Measures grounded in the notion of a generalized fear of future attacks we cannot predict, rather than in stereotyping and discrimination, seem more likely to succeed anyway. If governments want to persuade us otherwise, they must divulge the information required to do so. Secrecy makes us all more afraid and less prepared for whatever it is that we fear.

The contemporary security panic, more than any other issue, suggests that nations' efforts to shore up their sense of self through migration law may be ineffectual. The "us-them" line of the security debate does not fit well onto national borders: we know that the threat comes from "outside," but it is harder to say outside what. Deporting people who pose security risks seems likely to win domestic political points, but unlikely to make Western societies safer. The indefinite detention dilemma is caught at the juncture of the new normal. It arises directly from the constraints of the rule of law. Fulsome principles of the rule of law (the "thick" human rights infused version) require that we not deport people to face torture or worse. This forces the clash with indefinite detention, and what to do

---

85 For example, the new evidentiary provisions brought in by Canada in the omnibus *Anti-Terrorism Act*, S.C. 2001, c. 41.

with people if they are not deported. The new normal of migration security politics puts the spotlight on this dilemma. Tony Blair's proposed solution was to alter the *Human Rights Act*, moving the line of the law back.[86] Canada's current compromise is to permit deportation to torture.[87] Wrapping this exception power within the text of migration law does not alone render it law-like. Instead, it brings attention to the myriad ways in which migration laws serve as a mere conduit for executive priorities. This attention leads to crisis, because exception is a central logic of migration law. As security concerns are increasingly globalized, exceptions based on community difference lose their underpinnings. This reveals one facet of globalization's cultural homogenization. Western states are all pursuing the same thing: they cannot justify it with an appeal to their uniqueness, the appeal that has long been the strongest argument of liberal theorists in this area.[88]

The current framework of migration law cannot withstand this level of scrutiny, and thus the pressure is building for migration laws to be done differently, to become more law-like, to express the "us-them" coupling differently. Although the politics of security is built around exception, the rule of law is not. This is precisely why the increased scrutiny of indefinite detention cases arises at this moment in time – contemporary politics has made this normal. As in the case of refugee law in Chapter 4, the desire of states to move away from rule of law principles proves a test of their resilience. In the case of indefinite detention, the emerging rule of law consensus might be called "thin" rather than "thick." In other words, prohibiting indefinite detention without conviction is scarcely a robust or creative reading of this principle (and the Supreme Court of Canada was unwilling even to go this far). What is, however, potentially emancipatory here is the glimmer of unhinging of law and nation. Perhaps it is predictable that this begin with the originary writ of habeas corpus. Where human rights arguments have failed to travel well across borders, this substantive nub of the rule of law is demonstrating some success. The attention to indefinite detention is dragging migration law to the center of the legal stage. It is indisputable that these are the key cases of our times: they define "us" as "civilized" nations and peoples. The law is backed into a corner here, and new ways forward are certain to be forged. In the process, fact resistance must be broken down, taking up Lord Hoffman's exhortation to reexamine what it is we most fear.

---

86 Patrick Wintour, "Blair Vows to Root Out Extremism," *The [London] Guardian* (August 6, 2005), on-line: http://politics.guardian.co.uk/terrorism/story/0,15935,1543786,00.html.
87 In certain circumstances, which the Supreme Court of Canada in *Suresh, supra* note 36, suggests should be rare but are within executive discretion. The Federal Court of Appeal in *Almrei* read this as simply meaning it is possible to deport to torture. One reading of *Charkaoui* is to see the Supreme Court of Canada as deliberately ruling so as to preserve this possibility.
88 This argument is most eloquently and influentially expressed by Michael Walzer, *Spheres of Justice* (New York: Basic Books, 1983). See especially Chapter 2: Membership. See also Donald Galloway, "Liberalism, Globalism, and Immigration" (1993), 18 *Queen's L.J.* 266. In addition, for a contrasting view, Joseph Carens, "Aliens and Citizens: The Case for Open Borders" (1987), 49 *The Review of Politics* 251.

In our less brave new world, globalization and illegal migration combine as a potent security discourse. This intersection reveals global convergence at the sharpest end of migration law, but also a shift in the position of migration law itself. This new focus on migration law is related to the redrawing of the "us-them" line, as well as to a re-reading of sovereignty under conditions of the global. The "us-them" line is no longer fixed on the border of the nation, as our fear of outsiders within makes clear. In repositioning this "us-them" linkage, citizenship law works in tandem with migration law, a point highlighted by media attention to the citizenships of the London bombers. Contemporary trends in citizenship law itself are the focus of the next chapter, with attention to citizenship law's capacity to refract globalization's central paradox.

CHAPTER SEVEN

Citizenship unhinged

Changes in migration laws, whether formalized or discretionary, reverberate throughout citizenship law. Like migration laws, citizenship laws in prosperous Western states are displaying an increasing similarity at present, with more states permitting dual citizenship and more states opting for citizenship rules that come somewhere between the traditional *jus sanguinis* and *jus soli* principles. Citizenship, as the most privileged form of membership, seems remote from illegal migration. Nonetheless, both popular and scholarly talk of illegal migration introduces citizenship into the discussion in fairly short order. This happens because citizenship is easy shorthand for legitimacy, and because citizenship law and migration law work together in creating the border of the nation.

This chapter considers what citizenship laws mean for illegal migration. Its central assertion is that citizenship as a formal legal status is enjoying a resurgence of authority at present and this is directly linked to the worldwide crackdown on illegal migration. I begin by considering how migration law and citizenship law work in tandem. Given this relationship, I then outline how the pressures of globalization on migration laws are transferred through the migration law "buffer" to citizenship laws. This leads to the conclusion that citizenship law reflects the paradoxical nature of globalization as we see here that inclusions and exclusions are increasing at the same time. Finally, in considering the role that amnesties play in both the politics and the law of illegal migration, the fiction of formal legal citizenship is unmasked.

My focus is on citizenship as a legal status. Furthermore, the broader analysis in the book is about migration and thus I am primarily interested in how citizenship status is transferred to migrants: the process of naturalization. This concern is, of course, at the margins of citizenship analysis in one sense as most people in the world are born into a citizenship and do not change it. Although there has been a resurgence of scholarship about citizenship over the past two decades, its central concerns have not been legal structures and provisions.[1] Instead, a

---

1 A survey of this literature is presented in Will Kymlicka and Wayne Norman, "The Return of the Citizen: A Survey of Recent Work on Citizenship Theory" (1994), 104 *Ethics* 352. The growth in work about citizenship has continued steadily since this survey was published. Some exceptions

sustained conversation has developed about social citizenship and participatory citizenship, citizenship as a measure of inclusion and respect.[2] Most recently, in the context of globalization, there has been considerable analysis of the extent to which citizenship is losing its relevance, or in a related way, becoming "denationalized" or deterritorialized.[3] In these arguments, it is formal legal citizenship that is losing ground, not its more robust counterparts. My argument is at least a partial counter to both of these trends. I argue that formal legal citizenship persists, that it merits its own conversations, and that it is shifting rather than losing ground.

A focus on the bare legal relationship between the individual and the state remains vital because it underlies work considering interpretations of the relationship it asserts, or perspectives that can be added to it. When Alexander Aleinikoff argues for a new legal status of "denizen" to acknowledge the membership of those who are not citizens but not "others," the argument is grounded in the persistence of formal citizenship status.[4] Inquiries into how citizenship is "denationalized," or how it is disaggregated, also set markers against the formal categorization.[5] Citizenship has also retained a role as a bare legal status, the importance of which is being reasserted in the face of the contemporary politics of a global war on terror. From Guantanamo Bay to Syrian jails, the thin line of formal citizenship is asserting itself with crucial consequence.[6] Citizenship in this legal sense is a creature of the law, a formalized categorical designation; but it also attracts the protection of the law and triggers the now somewhat old-fashioned right of the state to act on behalf of its citizens. The original version of the international legal principle of state diplomatic protection is what has been asserted in the Guantanamo Bay and Mahar Arar cases.[7]

to the trend include Kim Rubenstein, *Australian Citizenship Law in Context* (Sydney: Law Book Company, 2002), and T. Alexander Aleinikoff, *Semblances of Sovereignty: The Constitution, The State, and American Citizenship* (Cambridge: Harvard University Press, 2002).

2 Much of this work can be traced to the influence of T. H. Marshall, whose seminal collection of essays, *Citizenship and Social Class* (Cambridge: Cambridge University Press, 1950) is a touchstone for much contemporary work. Other influential books in this area include Will Kymlicka, *Multicultural Citizenship: A Liberal Theory of Minority Rights* (Oxford: Oxford University Press, 1995); Bryan Turner, ed., *Citizenship and Social Theory* (London: Sage Press, 1993); Seyla Benhabib, *The Claims of Culture: Equality and Diversity in a Global Era* (Princeton: Princeton University Press, 2002).

3 Yasemin Soysal, *Limits of Citizenship: Migrants and Postnational Membership in Europe* (Chicago: University of Chicago Press, 1994); David Jacobson, *Rights Across Borders: Immigration and the Decline of Citizenship* (Baltimore: Johns Hopkins University Press, 1996); Linda Bosniak, "Citizenship Denationalized" (2000), 7 *Indiana Journal of Global Law Studies* 447.

4 This is one of the key contributions of Alexander Aleinikoff, *Semblances of Sovereignty: The Constitution, the State, and American Citizenship, supra* note 1.

5 Bosniak, *supra* note 3, inquires into how citizenship is denationalized across a range of discourses, and asks when and why this *should* take place. She notes that denationalization is least likely in legally bounded renditions of citizenship. Seyla Benhabib, *supra* note 2, argues that the elements of citizenship are being disaggregated in a way that separates social membership from political membership and thus creates a space for membership without citizenship.

6 Citizens of prosperous Western states have received attention and some assistance from their governments after being detained at Guantanamo Bay. British citizenship has proven more valuable than Canadian and Australian citizenships for Guantanamo detainees. Regarding Mahar Arar, see Chapter 6 at 98.

7 Ian Brownlie, *Principles of Public International Law* (Oxford and New York: Oxford University Press, 2003) at 391–2.

In both instances, the importance of citizenship formulated as *a right of the state* has prevailed where human rights arguments of individuals have failed. It is true the United Kingdom was more effective in protecting its citizens in Guantanamo than either Canada or Australia, but this reveals more about the power and efforts of respective states than about the legal concept itself.[8]

Legal citizenship remains, as Audrey Macklin has described it, "a thin but unbreakable guard rail."[9] The formal rights associated with legal citizenship make for a short list, far short of the aspects of participation and identity that are the basis of a full participatory engagement in social and political life. In the migration context, citizenship means the right to enter and remain. It typically also permits formal political participation and, often, public service employment. These rights do not add much to legal permanent residency, but the pressures of globalization are affecting even the permanence of permanent residency status.[10] Narrow, formal, legal citizenship has never been irrelevant. Part of my argument here is that it is undergoing a resurgence of importance in globalizing times. Understanding the persistence of citizenship in the thick social, political, and psychological realms beyond formal legality is a compelling enterprise, and citizenship law itself can be reasonably dull. However, the ways that citizenship is legally framed are an important starting point for any analysis that considers citizenship beyond this context. Whatever else citizenship is or is to become, it remains tied to national legal texts. This chapter contributes to understanding these foundations, including how and why they are shifting at present.

The citizenship law–migration law dichotomy

In prosperous Western nations with developed immigration programs, migration law rather than citizenship law is the principal effective hurdle to formal membership.[11] This is especially true in settler societies such as Australia, Canada, the United States, or New Zealand that have built part of their national mythology around being "nations of immigration." In part this is because the distinctions

---

8 Britain successfully negotiated for the repatriation of its nationals to Britain from Guantanamo in early 2005. Australian David Hicks remained in Guantanamo for more than two additional years, until May 2007. Penelope Debelle Smith, "High Security Jail for Taliban Trainee; Guantanamo Bay Prisoner Returns Relieved, Grateful: Hicks on Home Soil" *Newcastle Herald (Australia)* (May 21, 2007), p. 4. Steve Larkin, "Hicks Thrilled To Be Back, Says Father" *Bulletin Wire* (May 26, 2007). Canadian Omar Khadr is still in detention as this manuscript goes to press in December 2007.

9 Audrey Macklin, "Exile on Main Street: Popular Discourse and Legal Manoeuvres around Citizenship," in Law Commission of Canada, ed., *Law and Citizenship* (Vancouver: UBC Press, 2006) 22 at 24.

10 In the United States the scrutiny of permanent residents from the Islamic Middle East was heightened dramatically following the events of September 11, 2001. In Canada recent legislative changes have reduced rights for permanent residents being stripped of their status for residency violations or criminal activity. In Australia, permanent residency rights for some refugee claimants have been sharply curtailed since 2001.

11 I have made this argument in more detail in "Citizenship, Migration Laws, and Women: Gendering Permanent Residency Statistics" (2000), 24 *Melbourne University Law Review* 280.

between those with permanent legal residency status and those with citizenship are small. More important, however, is the fact that once newcomers are accepted as migrants, the hurdle for full membership in the form of citizenship is a low one. Typically, a certain number of years of legal permanent residency must be accumulated,[12] one must have a minimal knowledge of the "national" language,[13] and pledge to defend the nation and respect its laws. Applicants must also be of good character, a hurdle that may become more significant in these ominous times. Australia, Canada, and the United States also require that new citizens have some knowledge of the nation they are joining, but this testing requirement is not onerous for those who have lived in the country for the required number of years.[14] In general, applying for citizenship is cheaper, easier, and quicker, with a far greater likelihood of success, than applying for permanent immigration status.

Applications for permanent residency are more onerous, as well as more expensive. Applicants are subject to medical examinations and to more rigorous character assessments. The nature of state scrutiny of an immigration application varies with the category. For family class applicants the focus of eligibility, and therefore scrutiny, is personal relationships. For economic applicants, scrutiny focuses on financial affairs and on qualifications. In humanitarian categories (the most formalized of which is refugee status[15]), the scrutiny will depend on the particular nature of the claim being made. Refugees must have a story to tell, and must be able to tell it.[16] Other humanitarian migrants are typically required to demonstrate both need and desert. Prospective migrants are confronted with legal regimes where, generally speaking, the state agents have more powers than the police and individuals have fewer rights' protections than criminal accused.

The group of permanent residents that is eligible to become new citizens is a group recruited and constituted by migration law. Migration laws aim to discriminate – to determine who will be admitted and who will be excluded. Significant scholarly work has focused on the overt racism of Western countries' migration

---

12 In the United States the requirement is five years' residency. In Australia the requirement is four years, and in Canada it is three years. In each case some periods of absence are permitted.

13 There is a language component in the United States, Australia, and Canada. In each case the standard is one of basic communication skills.

14 The knowledge requirement is focused on history, politics, and citizenship rights. The United States and Canada both administer a formal written test at approximately a primary school level of difficulty. Some applicants in each country are exempted from this testing. In 2006 and 2007, Australia introduced amendments that would require more extensive citizenship testing. This proposal did not pass along with the new *Australian Citizenship Act* (Cth, No. 20 of 2007) but did so shortly after and took effect on 1 October 2007. (*Australian Citizenship Amendment (Citizenship Testing) Act 2007* No. 142 of 2007).

15 In the United States, status can be granted to both "refugees" and "asylees." Both categories follow the refugee definition set out in the *Convention Relating to the Status of Refugees*, July 28, 1951, 189 U.N.T.S. 150 (entered into force April 22, 1954), see Chapter 4.

16 This point is well made by Audrey Kobayashi, "Challenging the National Dream: Gender Persecution and Canadian Immigration Law" in P. Fitzpatrick, ed., *Nationalism, Racism, and the Rule of Law* (Aldershot and Brookfield: Dartmouth Press, 1995). Kobayashi argues that refugee women are confined by the victimization they must portray to attain their status.

provisions over the course of the twentieth century, and on how racist preferences continue to be communicated through facially neutral law.[17] Much less attention has been drawn to how migration provisions are gendered. In each of the major admission categories – family, economic, and humanitarian – gender is played out in the law. Examining how this genders the effects of citizenship law provides a compelling example of the migration law–citizenship law dichotomy.

This is one juncture where a focus on formal citizenship is directly linked to the concerns of substantive inquiries into citizenship. The underlying assumption of the immigration preferences of prosperous Western nations is that liberal nations are generally morally justified in closing their borders. That is, the discrimination inherent in this law is justified by the need of the liberal community for closure and its right to identity.[18] Racist provisions eventually came to be seen as abhorrent to liberal principle, but the basic logic of a migration law that discriminates between applicants on the basis of choosing those who best meet the needs and values of the nation has not been impugned overall. The criteria that immigration laws enshrine read as a code of national values, determining who some "we" group will accept as potential future members. These messages of acceptance overlap the preoccupations of substantive citizenship: Who do we value and why? Who can contribute to vital social sectors: the economy and the family? Who is deserving of our protection and our humanity? The migration law filter gives legal form to the answers to these questions. The bodies for which these answers are a fit can pass through this filter and become formal legal citizens. This is not the only kind of membership, and is arguably not the most valuable kind of membership, but it is a privileged form of membership nonetheless.

The citizenship law–migration law dichotomy functions to ensure for citizenship law a rhetorical domain of formal equality and liberal ideals. The messy policing of the national boundary by inquiring into debt and disease, criminality and qualifications, is left to migration law. Most prosperous contemporary states would not tolerate a citizenship regime that excluded individuals from naturalizing because of having a child with an intellectual disability, being poor, or dropping out of high school. Migration law specializes in precisely this type of distinction. In the citizenship law–migration law coupling, migration law does this dirty work. This

17 See for example Ghassan Hage, *White Nation: Fantasies of White Supremacy in a Multicultural Society* (Sydney: Pluto Press, 1998); Sherene Razack, *Looking White People in the Eye: Gender, Race, and Culture in Courtrooms and Classrooms* (Toronto: University of Toronto Press, 1998); Sean Brawley, *The White Peril: Foreign Relations and Asian Migration to Australasia and North America 1919–1978* (Sydney, UNSW Press, 1995).
18 Some liberal thinkers have taken an "open borders" position (see for example several articles by Joseph Carens, "Aliens and Citizens: The Case for Open Borders" (1987), 49 *The Review of Politics* 251; "Open Borders and Liberal Limits" (2000), 34 *International Migration Review* 636; "Refugees and the Limits of Obligation" (1992) 6 *Public Affairs Quarterly* 31), but it is less prevalent than a closed borders argument. I have argued that the dispute between open borders liberals and closed borders liberals is not resolvable and is one reason for the intransigence of political debate about migration provisions. See "Amorality and Humanitarianism in Immigration Law" (1999), 37 *Osgoode Hall L.J.* 597.

relationship is important in understanding how current changes in both legal texts take effect.

Considering the citizenship law–migration law pairing in this way also allows a clear view of what it is not. The people with disabilities, poor people, and people with little formal education noted here are often denied full citizenship within a polity, regardless of their citizenship status and of how they obtained it. It is importantly the rhetoric of liberal equality that is reserved to citizenship law through this dichotomy, not a full and unproblematic substantive equality. The two legal texts work together to construct the border of the nation; as such they are both implicated in excluding, and in drawing a line between inclusion and exclusion. Citizenship law perfects the exclusionary mechanism of migration law by cloaking it in a discourse of inclusion. Although the majority of permanent residents can move comparatively easily to citizenship status in the "new world" nations of migration, the final screening of citizenship law still has teeth. Its bite is felt in exclusions of those with criminal convictions, and the surveillance attached to a citizenship application may even imperil immigration status. The point of separating them in this way is to draw attention to the final formal phase for migrants seeking membership in a new polity.

The gender of naturalization[19]

Considering how the citizenship law–migration law coupling positions gender illustrates its operation as a key exclusionary mechanism. Gender has attracted much less attention than race in discussions of immigration rules, but feminist analyses of citizenship are well developed.[20] It is instructive to bring these two threads together. Migration law is typically a site of permissible discrimination designed to meet state objectives. This is called "immigrant selection" rather than discrimination. In each of the major admissions categories, selection is handled differently and thus the role that gender plays is fragmented. It is different in each category, taking varying forms depending on the underlying logic of the particular need the category aims to address. This mechanism is most fully developed in states with well-defined immigrant recruitment schemes and a self-understanding as a nation of immigrants because it is these states that have the most well-established legal mechanisms for converting new arrivals into full citizens. For this reason, I draw on examples from Australia, Canada, and the United States.

19 A chapter based on this section will appear in Seyla Benhabib and Judith Resnick (eds.), *Migrations and Mobilities: Gender, Borders, and Citizenship* (New York: NYU Press) 2008.
20 Examples include Carole Pateman, *The Disorder of Women: Democracy, Feminism, and Political Theory* (Stanford, Calif.: Stanford University Press, 1989); Ruth Lister, *Citizenship: Feminist Perspectives* (Basingstoke: Palgrave Macmillan, 2002); Ayelet Shachar, *Multicultural Jurisdictions: Cultural Differences and Women's Rights* (Cambridge and New York: Cambridge University Press, 2001).

Table 7.1. *Australia: Principal applicants, family class 1994 to 2005*[21]

	Female	Male	Percentage Female
1994–95	17,987	11,153	61.3
1995–96	23,948	14,407	62.4
1996–97	16,929	11,297	60.0
1997–98	12,732	8,410	60.2
1998–99	13,266	8,235	61.7
2000–01	10,633	6,587	61.8
2001–02	12,528	7,184	63.6
2002–03	15,055	8,744	63.3
2003–04	15,266	9,481	61.7
2004–05	16,759	10,377	61.8

Table 7.2. *Canada: Principal applicants, family class: 1995 to 2004*[22]

	Female	Male	Percentage Female
1995	29,084	22,275	56.6
1996	28,625	21,153	57.5
1997	26,360	18,831	58.3
1998	24,022	15,618	60.6
1999	26,479	16,971	60.9
2000	28,727	18,516	60.8
2001	30,574	20,337	60.1
2002	27,627	18,618	59.7
2003	30,677	18,769	62.0
2004	31,349	18,718	62.6

Family reunification is by far the largest admission category in the United States and was the largest category in Canada and Australia until the mid-1990s, when those two nations led the worldwide move to tailoring immigration requirements to fit immediate market need. In the family category, women predominate.

The story told by these numbers is broadly similar in each of the three nations: family reunification immigration includes a significant proportion of what might

21 Australian statistics are reported per fiscal year, which runs July 1 to June 30. These statistics were obtained directly from the Department of Immigration Multicultural and Indigenous Affairs in response to an email query. They are not published.
22 Canadian statistics are drawn from Citizenship and Immigration Canada, *Facts and Figures: Immigration Overview: Permanent and Temporary Residents 2004* (Ottawa: Minister of Public Works and Government Services Canada, 2005).

Table 7.3. *United States: All admissions, family categories: selected available years*[23]

	Female	Male	Percentage Female
1994	262,210	201,389	56.6
1995	261,846	198,519	58.9
1996	340,227	256,025	57
2002	388,810	284,180	57.8
2003	286,038	205,503	58.2
2004	359,425	261,003	57.9

* Publicly available American statistics do not separate principal appli-cants. This is most likely the reason the "percentage female" is smaller in Table 7.3 than in Tables 7.1 and 7.2.

sardonically be called "wife import." A tiny portion of these women fit the stereo-typical descriptor "mail-order bride." The vast majority do not. Nonetheless, it remains the case that under the heading of family reunification immigration, women arrive as migrants on the basis of their legally defined relationship of dependence. Although children and some other family members are in the cat-egory, approximately 80 percent of admissions are under various "partnership" headings.[24] In the Australia, Canada, and United States this dependence is rein-forced through the mechanism of sponsorship agreements, whereby the sponsoring partner must undertake to ensure that the sponsoree will not accept various welfare state payments from the government for a set number of years. The sponsor must demonstrate financial independence from the state.[25] The statistics do not follow the same categorization in the United States, but some preference for women in this category still persists. In addition, the publicly available American statistics are not broken down in the same way (i.e., by gender *and* principal applicant status) and therefore mask these trends.

23 U.S. statistics are drawn from three publications: *Immigration to the U.S. in Fiscal Year 19XX* (for successive years), *Statistical Yearbook of the Immigration and Naturalization Service*, and since 2002 the *Yearbook of Immigration Statistics*. These reports are available at The Office of Immigration Statistics, on-line: uscis.gov/graphics/shared/statistics. From 1997 to 2001 statistics are given for immigrants admitted by age and sex but not cross-referenced with category. The numbers of principal applicants in family categories have been calculated by adding together numbers of principal applicants in the family-sponsored preferences class and those in the immediate relatives of U.S. citizens class. On inquiry to the Office of Immigration Statistics, a further breakdown was not available.
24 Traditional marriage is no longer required in all legal regimes. Canadian migration law recognizes three types of relationships: spouse, common law partner, and conjugal partner.
25 There is generally a minimum income requirement for sponsorship in the United States (s. 213A of the *Immigration and Naturality Act*, U.S.C. tit. 8 § 1183a), Canada, and Australia. In Canada, this requirement is waived when sponsoring a partner or dependent child (*Immigration and Refugee Protection Regulations* S.O.R./ 2002-227, s. 133(4)). However, the prospective sponsor still must not be in receipt of state welfare-type payments (s. 133(1)(k)).

Table 7.4. *Australia: Primary applicants in economic categories 1999–2000 to 2004–05*

	Female	Male	Percentage Female
1999–00	4,213	8,647	32.76
2000–01	5,166	10,342	33.31
2001–02	5,005	10,194	32.92
2002–03	5,596	10,395	35.00
2003–04	7,324	13,672	34.88
2004–05	7,638	14,099	35.14

Table 7.5. *Canada: Primary applicants in economic categories 1995–2004*

	Female	Male	Percentage Female
1995	15,663	28,075	35.81
1996	16,742	34,656	32.57
1997	15,908	36,500	30.35
1998	12,444	29,308	29.80
1999	13,090	34,207	27.68
2000	14,891	43,206	25.63
2001	17,016	48,269	26.06
2002	15,397	42,821	26.45
2003	14,667	36,557	28.63
2004	16,773	38,406	30.40

Table 7.6. *United States: Combined admissions in economic categories*[26]

	Female	Male	Percentage Female
1994	60,413	62,864	49.01
1995	42,265	43,066	49.53
1996	58,634	58,862	49.90
2002	84,678	90,219	48.42
2003	40,362	41,761	49.15
2004	75,025	80,289	48.31

26 The American data are not directly comparable to the Australian and Canadian because publicly available American immigration statistics do not report entry category cross-referenced by gender *and* primary applicant status.

The economic migration categories are tailored in an attempt to ensure that those granted admission will find good jobs immediately and begin contributing to the economy upon arrival. Whether the indicator used is guaranteed job placement, particular skills, experience, education, or personal wealth, the category is tailored to indicate a preference for men. Gendered disparities on these indicators persist in the wealthy nations that are sought after immigration destinations. In migrant-sending nations, such disparities are often more pronounced. The migration provisions therefore serve to import gendered disparity. The economic indicators that are preferred for their "neutrality" of course reflect gendered and racialized dimensions of privilege. Some nations even label these skilled migrants as "independents," signifying overtly the parallel with the citizenship discourse emphasis on individuality and autonomy.

Humanitarian migration is also gendered. In the international population of refugees and other persons of concern to the United Nations High Commissioner for Refugees, the numbers of women and men are approximately equal. Despite this, men outnumber women in the tally of those who receive refugee status.[27] Where figures are available indicating principal applicants separately from family members, the difference between the number of men and number of women is much larger.[28] This demonstrates that men are somewhat more likely than women to benefit from the particular type of "solution" to refugee status that is represented by resettlement in a prosperous nation. It also shows that more women obtain refugee status on the basis of their male partner's status as a refugee than on the basis of their own experience. This demonstrates both that there are more male than female heads of households, and that men's experiences fit more easily into the definition of a refugee.[29]

As migrants in each of these categories, women's and men's experiences are distinct. The distinctions reflect fault lines of privilege and dependence that are familiar to citizenship theorists. Many women arrive as new migrants because of

---

27 These categories contain only some of those admitted permanently on the basis of humanitarian considerations. Others include those who do not fit within the internationally agreed-upon refugee definition but who are in refugee-like situations as well as people admitted under various categories of humanitarian exception to the immigration rules that exist in each of these countries.

28 This is true despite the fact that women are generally more successful as refugee claimants than men. See Catherine Dauvergne, Leonora Angeles, and Agnes Huang, *Gendering Canada's Refugee Process* (Ottawa: Status of Women Canada, 2006).

29 There is a considerable body of scholarship on the gender biases of refugee law. Some examples include Susan Kneebone, "Women Within the Refugee Construct: 'Exclusionary Inclusion' in Policy and Practice – the Australian Experience" (2005), 17 *International Journal of Refugee Law* 7; and Melanie Randall, "Refugee Law and State Accountability for Violence Against Women: A Comparative Analysis of Legal Approaches to Recognizing Asylum Claims Based on Gender Persecution" (2002), 25 *Harvard Women's Law Journal* 281; Thomas Spijkerboer, *Gender and Refugee Status* (Aldershot, England and Burlington, USA: Ashgate, 2000); Audrey Macklin, "A Comparative Analysis of the Canadian, U.S., and Australian Directives on Gender Persecution and Refugee Status" in Doreen Indra, ed., *Engendering Forced Migration: Theory and Practice* (New York and Oxford: Berghan Books, 1999); Audrey Macklin, "Refugee Women and the Imperative of Categories" (May 1995), 17.2 *Human Rights Quarterly* 213.

Table 7.7. *Australia, humanitarian admissions all subclasses, all categories of applicant*

	Female	Male	Percentage Female
1994–95	4,518	7,110	38.85
1995–96	4,742	6,927	40.64
1996–97	3,310	5,087	39.42
1997–98	3,157	4,400	41.78
1998–99	4,364	4,426	49. 65
2000–01	904	1,603	36.06
2001–02	766	1,312	36.86
2002–03	1,072	1,870	36.44
2003–04	1,212	1,868	39.35
2004–05	1,572	2,386	39.72

Table 7.8. *Canada, refugee admissions, principal applicants*[30]

	Female	Male	Percentage Female
1995	5,468	10,186	34.93
1996	5,435	10,216	34.73
1997	4,257	8,893	32.37
1998	4,270	7,856	35.21
1999	4,662	8,441	35.58
2000	5,786	10,195	36.21
2001	5,475	9,367	36.89
2002	5,250	8,129	39.24
2003	5,729	8,951	39.03
2004	7,498	10,561	41.52

their relationships of dependence: either as new marriage partners or as defined dependents of skilled migrants. Although the legal categories that condition their admittance cannot of course determine their personal outcomes, they do convey to these women and others important messages about how and why they are valued by the nation. These migrants are the pool of new citizens. The universal values of membership as citizenship are made available to women on the basis of their gendered experiences as the objects of immigration law. Access to the citizenship debate about participation, representation, and equality is conditioned for these

---

30 It is not possible to identify "all humanitarian" admissions in Canadian statistics, so these data are not identical to the Australian data. The Canadian and American data are more comparable in this regard.

Table 7.9. *Refugee and asylee adjustments, united states*[31]

	Female	Male	Percentage Female
1994	59,633	61,790	49.1
1995	55,630	59,020	48.5
1996	61,178	67,386	47.58
2002	61,616	64,331	48.9
2003	21,950	22,932	48.9
2004	34,315	36,794	48.3

people on their prior acceptance through the much more intimate and personal screening of immigration law.

As Canada and Australia have moved since the mid-1990s to reserving a greater number of places to economically skilled migration over family migration, they have moved to having a greater number of men than women selected as primary applicants. The United States is contemplating similar moves, but it would take massive changes for economically based migration to overtake the size of the United States' family reunification program. The size of the American economy alone creates a draw, which other nations are adjusting their law and policy to imitate. It is also critical to note that immigration statistics concern those who are admitted to remain permanently. In the United States, tens of thousands of people are admitted each year on a temporary basis for work, outstripping the numbers admitted to Canada or Australia. This temporary admission is often a step on the way to later permanent status. Aggregate statistics about economic migration often show approximate gender parity. This is partly because economic migrants bring their families (many women do, of course, qualify as economic migrants).[32] When a woman arrives as a partner of a primary economic applicant, her right to enter (and sometimes her right to remain) is conditioned by her relationship (usually with a man). While this relationship may not personally be experienced as a dependence, it is legally framed that way. A shift in emphasis toward economic migration does not, therefore, remove women from the pool of potential new citizens in a straightforward way, but it does ensure that women enter this pool because of their relationships of legal dependence.

Gender is an important example to add to the analysis of migration law in this way as too little attention is paid to how a "rational" policy preference for skilled migrants is also a preference for men instead of women, and a preference

31 It is probably the case that U.S. statistics are closer to gender parity because these numbers do not disaggregate principal and secondary (dependent) admissions. Without access to this breakdown, I can only guess that the United States follows similar patterns to the other states.

32 This is shown starkly in the tables presented earlier. For Australia and Canada, where the numbers are disaggregated into "principal" and "secondary" (or dependent) entries, men predominate. In the United States, where everyone is lumped together, a veneer of gender parity emerges.

for ensuring that women migrate in defined relationships of dependence. The lofty neutrality of citizenship laws is lost when we consider how naturalization functions in tandem with migration law. The way gendered exclusions function in this pairing is paralleled in any group that is excluded by the economic focus of migration, especially poor people. Similarly, whereas our Western citizenship laws may establish formal equality, their relationship with migration regulation ensures that we import wholesale any inequality that exists around the globe. In the face of globalizing forces, there is evidence that citizenship laws are shifting in ways that have implications for the functioning of the citizenship law–migration law dichotomy.

Shifts in formal legal citizenship

For the privileged subjects of globalization, citizenship is indeed becoming more flexible:[33] more states tolerate dual citizenships (which are especially meaningful for migrants); formal inequalities are being worked out of citizenship laws; and citizenship requirements are more perfunctory.[34] Part of this expansion of formal citizenship can be accounted for as a story about provisions becoming less rigorous. Alongside this story, however, runs a counternarrative: the story of citizenship with a vengeance.

I have been focusing on law as it expresses rules for naturalization because of its role as the final movement in migration. A brief digression, however, is appropriate at this point. Traditionally, citizenship regimes have been divided into two broad categories according to whether the state permits citizenship to be passed down on the basis of parentage (*jus sanguinis*) or whether citizenship is based on birth within national territory (*jus soli*). Most *jus soli* regimes have long had some exceptions for nationals giving birth away from home. More recently, however, the bedrock idea of birthright citizenship represented by the *jus soli* principle is eroding. This is significant because of the bold, migration-embracing logic of a *jus soli* regime. It announces that those who are born here are our members. What comes before does not matter; birth in the new land establishes equal entitlement. In the

---

33 We owe the term "flexible citizenship" to Aihwa Ong, *Flexible Citizenship: The Cultural Logics of Transnationality*, (Durham and London: Duke University Press, 1999). Ong has more recently written a companion study of the most disadvantaged migrants, focusing on refugees from Cambodia arriving in the United States in the 1980s. In *Buddha is Hiding: Refugees, Citizenship, the New America* (Berkeley and Los Angeles: University of California Press, 2003) she makes the argument that economic globalization has contributed to deterritorializing citizenship. Her argument rests in contemporary social theory and a nuanced understanding of the making of citizen-subjects. I hope that my argument parallels the point she is making but with attention instead to the narrower (and drier) realm of formal legal citizenship.

34 Kim Rubenstein, "Citizenship in a Borderless World" in A. Anghie and G. Sturgess, eds., *Legal Visions of the 21st Century: Essays in Honour of Judge Christopher Weeramantry* (The Hague: Kluwer Law International Publishers, 1998); Kim Rubenstein and Daniel Adler, "International Citizenship: The Future of Nationality in a Globalized World" (2000), 7 *Indiana Journal of Global Legal Studies* 519.

United States, birthright citizenship is constitutionalized, signifying an immovable commitment.[35]

In places where *jus soli* is being modified, the change has been motivated by a desire to ensure that the children of undesirable migrants do not "accidentally" obtain citizenship by birth. In Australia this change was made in 1985 in the months following the High Court of Australia's decision in *Kioa v. West*, which suggested that the Australian citizenship of a child whose parent had no migration status might alter the contents of natural justice in deportation proceedings.[36] Despite this constrained reading, and the fact that nothing turned on this aspect of the Court's reasoning, the law was changed soon after to ensure that only the children of citizens and permanent residents are Australian from birth.[37] In Ireland, the central politicking of the 2004 citizenship referendum revolved around a desire to ensure that Irish citizenship (and thus European citizenship) was not available to the children of women willing to travel, pregnant, to Ireland to give birth but who otherwise had no connection to the place.[38] In each of these cases, the legal change ensures that the functioning of the citizenship law–migration law dichotomy is intact: citizenship law may be about formal equality but it is predicated on migration law functioning as an effective prescreening of potential members.

Alongside these developments there is an emerging story of states making membership provisions, through citizenship laws, more meaningful. These changes are more varied, and make a challenge to my sketch of the citizenship law–migration law dichotomy that I will address shortly. The Canadian government, in a variation on the impulse to limit birthright citizenship, has proposed ramping up restrictions on rules for citizens outside Canada passing on their citizenship.[39] In the United States, there have recently been calls for a "national language" to strengthen homogeneity; presumably this would involve making the present language requirement more stringent.[40] The Australian government introduced a more rigorous citizenship test, which took effect on October 1, 2007. Over the same time as this strengthening of traditional citizenship has been debated and implemented, three

---

35 This is provided by the U.S. Const. amend. XIV. See Joseph Carens, "Who Belongs? Theoretical and Legal Questions About Birthright Citizenship in the United States" (1987) 37 U.T. Fac. L. Rev. 413.

36 *Kioa v. West* (1985), 150 C.L.R. 550 (H.C.A.).

37 *Australian Citizenship Act 1948* (Cth.) at section 10.

38 Following approval of the constitutional change, Irish citizenship law was amended to provide that citizenship would be acquired by those born in Ireland whose parents were Irish citizens or entitled to be Irish citizens. See also John Harrington, "Citizenship and the Biopolitics of post-Nationalist Ireland" (2005), 32.3 *Journal of Law and Society* 424. *Chen and Zhu v. Secretary of State for the Home Department*, C-200/02, [2004] E.C.R. I-9925 was also part of the political backdrop to these events. Chen traveled pregnant to Ireland from the United Kingdom to ensure European citizenship for her child.

39 Bill C-18, *The Citizenship of Canada Bill*, 2nd Sess., 37th Parl., 2002 (Second Reading November 8, 2002). This proposal has been floated by several recent governments, most recently in 2007. To date the measure has not passed through Parliament, primarily because it has never been a sufficiently high priority item for the government of the day.

40 Michael Martinez and Aamer Madhani, "English Bill's Meaning Lost in Translation, Experts Say," *Chicago Tribune* (on-line version) (May 20, 2006).

new stories with a common thread have emerged in the home states of three of the most well-established diasporas: Italy, Ireland, and India.

The April 2006 Italian election was the first election following a 2001 change to electoral laws to allow Italian citizens living abroad to elect representatives in four overseas constituencies.[41] It is not unusual for expatriate citizens to have a right to vote in national elections. The Italian electoral reforms, however, go a significant step further in terms of formalizing the relationship between the nation's government and its dispersed citizens. The "Overseas Constituency" is divided into four electoral zones: Europe, South America, North and Central America, and, finally, Africa, Asia, Oceania, and Antarctica.[42] Each zone may elect one member of each the upper and lower houses, with the remaining seats (totaling six in the Senate and twelve in the Chamber of Deputies) divided according to numbers of eligible voters in each zone. Italian citizens are eligible to vote, whether or not they are dual citizens of some other state. Bars to running as a representative of a zone in the Overseas Constituency include holding an elected office in another state. In the closely contested April 2006 election, the Overseas Constituency became an important factor.[43]

The Italian Overseas Constituency gives Italian citizenship important new meaning for those living outside of Italy. The right to elect overseas representatives to parliament has the potential to introduce new issues and new perspectives to "domestic" political discussion. It also changes the gravitas of casting a vote for members of the diaspora, who are now entitled to choose between voting in the Overseas Constituency and voting in the constituency of their former residence. Overseas candidates in the 2006 election were campaigning in reference to both domestic and overseas issues. For example, it is unlikely that any domestic candidate would have raised issues such as the quality of consular services and satellite reception of state broadcasting.[44] This new constituency also portrays the state's recognition that membership does not cease at territorial borders. It is impossible to predict whether Italy will continue with this experiment, in part because of its extraordinary success. The experiment was successful because more than one million expatriates turned out to vote[45] and because prominent expatriates entered the electoral race, prepared to devote their time and energy to the homeland and to

41 *Provisions Governing the Right to Vote of Italian Citizens Abroad,* Law 459 of December 27, 2001, Official Journal No. 4 of January 5, 2002.

42 Ibid. at Article 6.

43 Commentators argue that the overseas votes may have played a critical role in breaking a tie between Prodi and Berlusconi. Prodi won four of the six seats in the Senate, while Berlusconi won only one. The remaining seat went to an independent party. See John Hooper, "A Triumph of Sorts as the Professor Beats the Clown," *The [London] Guardian* (April 12, 2006); "Italy's Berlusconi Demands Election Recount" *CTV News* (April 11, 2006) on-line: CTV News, http://www.ctv.ca/servlet/ArticleNews/story/CTVNews/20060411/italy_election_060411?s_name=&no_ads=.

44 Barbara McMahon, "The Expat Factor" *The [London] Guardian* (March 23, 2006) on-line: Guardian Unlimited. http://www.guardian.co.uk/elsewhere/journalist/story/0,1738183,00.html.

45 "A Million Italians Abroad Vote," *Associated Press* (April 9, 2006). This number represents 42 percent of those eligible to vote.

at least partially "repatriate" to do so. However, the greatest marker of success was that the Overseas Constituency influenced the electoral outcome.[46]

Recent changes in Ireland and India are less dramatic, but they do illustrate a willingness to formally specify membership, if not full citizenship, outside of territory. One aspect of Ireland's 1998 Good Friday agreement was the amendment of key membership provisions of the Irish Constitution.[47] The headline story about the amended Articles 2 and 3 is that they establish a constitutional framework that recognizes both the existing territorial limits of the Irish state and the aspiration of many that the state extend its sovereignty over the entire island.[48] This is, of course, a compromise for relinquishing constitutional claim to the entire territory. In effect, the constitutional reforms formally shift sovereignty from the territory to the people. The Irish "nation" has had a prominent place in the Irish Constitution since 1937. This use of nation clearly draws on an ethnic understanding of nation, rather than a more contemporary constructed or contingent version.[49] In the Irish Constitution, there is a considerable overlap between the nation and its citizens,

---

46 *Supra* note 43.

47 The Good Friday Agreement (formally this is the Belfast Agreement) was signed by the British and Irish governments on April 10, 1998, and was voted on by the people of North Ireland and the Republic of Ireland in a referendum on May 22, 1998. The Agreement recognizes the right to self-determination of the peoples of North and South Ireland, lays out a political framework for this self-determination, and remains committed to a process of reconciliation in Ireland. See Desmond M. Clarke, "Nationalism, The Irish Constitution, and Multicultural Citizenship" (2000), 51.1 *Northern Ireland Legal Quarterly* 100.

48 Article 2 and 3, *Constitution of Ireland*, 1937, read as follows:

Article 2: It is the entitlement and birthright of every person born in the island of Ireland, which includes its islands and seas, to be part of the Irish Nation. That is also the entitlement of all persons otherwise qualified in accordance with law to be citizens of Ireland. Furthermore, the Irish nation cherishes its special affinity with people of Irish ancestry living abroad who share its cultural identity and heritage.

Article 3: (1) It is the firm will of the Irish Nation, in harmony and friendship, to unite all the people who share the territory of the island of Ireland, in all the diversity of their identities and traditions, recognizing that a united Ireland shall be brought about only by peaceful means with the consent of a majority of the people, democratically expressed, in both jurisdictions in the island. Until then, the laws enacted by the Parliament established by this Constitution shall have the like area and extent of application as the laws enacted by the Parliament that existed immediately before the coming into operation of this Constitution.

(2) Institutions with executive powers and functions that are shared between those jurisdictions may be established by their respective responsible authorities for stated purposes and may exercise powers and functions in respect of all or any part of the island.

49 There has been a strong shift in scholarship about "nation" over the past twenty years. While this term was first strongly associated with an ethnic coherence (Anthony Smith, *The Ethnic Origins of Nations* (Oxford: Blackwell Publishers, 1986)), more recent work has argued that this coherence is constructed and not essential to nation (Benedict Anderson, *Imagined Communities: Reflections on the Origin and Spread of Nationalism,* rev ed. (London and New York: Verso, 1991); William Rogers Brubaker, *Nationalism Reframed: Nationhood and the National Question in the New Europe* (Cambridge: Cambridge University Press, 1996); Eric J. Hobsbawn, *Nations and Nationalism since 1780: Programme, Myth, Reality,* 2d ed. (Cambridge: Cambridge University Press, 1992)). What is interesting about this shift is that the parsing of nation and ethnicity that is well established in academic discourses has not effectively penetrated popular or political discourse. It leaves "nation" as a term that is difficult to use with any precision at all, and in this way perhaps contributes to the academic turn toward "citizenship" as a discursive framing of membership.

which speaks directly to concern about the partition. The sidebar story of the 1998 constitutional reforms is, therefore, the constitutional recognition of the Irish diaspora. This results from the compromise language used to make a membership claim to the entire island without a reference to its politically contested geography. In unhinging the Irish nation from its territory, there is a potential to reestablish ties of membership that may have been severed through the inevitable shifting of citizenships that occurs in all diaspora communities. Although the "special affinity" is far from a rights entitlement, it parallels the political impulse of the Italian electoral reform by tugging at ties of distant belonging as a response to domestic political tensions.

In India, amendments late in 2005 created a new legal form of membership known as "overseas citizenship of India."[50] This is a status distinct from dual citizenship, which is not (yet?) permissible in Indian law. Overseas citizenship of India, however, provides members of the India diaspora with the potential of a formal legal linkage with India despite having become citizens elsewhere. The status functions as a lifelong multiple entry visa, and can be used as a transitional step to resuming full citizenship. Despite the inclusion of "citizenship" in the title, most of the core rights usually reserved to citizens are absent. Overseas citizens of India cannot vote or run for office, nor can they hold constitutionally named government posts or indeed most forms of government employment. Instead, this status acts as an exemption to provisions typically found in the text of migration laws, border-crossing rights, and the right to participate in the economy.[51] This fledgling provision is novel in its repackaging of the bundle of citizenship rights. It appears to aim at facilitating economic participation, and thereby fostering a return of wealth to India.

These shifts each show states moving to reestablish membership ties, through the vehicle of formal legal citizenship, with those who have, in the ideologically charged language of migration, *chosen* to establish their lives elsewhere. It is clear that one impetus behind the increase in possibilities for dual citizenship is a desire of states to retain an attachment with members. In combination with an erosion of *jus soli* principles, these moves show a trend toward reasserting citizenship's linkage to a hereditary community. As global migration increases, this trend can be cast as a thinly disguised reassertion of *jus sanguinis*. These changes contribute to showing formal citizenship rules as an assertion of sovereignty, defined as a control over a defined "people," regardless of their geographic location. The most important contemporary example of this trend arises through considering European Union citizenship.

The European Union has, famously, moved citizenship to the supranational level and is most recently committing to make this citizenship more meaningful.[52]

---

50 *Citizenship Act of 1955*, ss.7A, 7B, 7C, 7D.
51 Restrictions on ownership of agricultural and plantation property remain.
52 The *Treaty On European Union (Maastricht)*, February 7, 1992, O.J. 1992 No. 191/1, 31 I.L.M. 247 created European citizenship in 1993. Since that time, commitments to strengthening it have been

European citizenship is important to the story of globalization, and is written about extensively in this context. There are two points about this new form of citizenship that fit into my analysis of citizenship law and globalization. The first is that in the push to harmonize rules about European borders and their crossings (discussed is Chapter 8), citizenship rules in member states are not being harmonized. The second is that the invention of European citizenship has succeeded in reversing the trend identified by Saskia Sassen as devaluing citizenship.[53] Both of these facts tell us something about the importance of the migration law–citizenship law dichotomy, and I will consider each in turn.

Since the Treaty of Amsterdam (1997, taking effect in 1999) and the Tampere Conclusions (1999), Europe has embarked on the creation of an Area of Freedom Security and Justice. A central focus of this is harmonization of the most stringent aspects of migration regulation.[54] Extensive work has been done to harmonize both substantive and procedural aspects of refugee law, and progress has also been made in coordinating responses to illegal migration. At the same time, however, it has been made plain that member states will retain discretion in selecting temporary and permanent migrants in the area of economic migration.[55] The push to build the Area of Freedom Security and Justice includes commitments to European citizenship. Now as ever, European citizenship is derivative. No one is solely a citizen of the European Union; this citizenship is based on first having citizenship in a member state.

Citizenship in a member state is still determined on the basis of national rules and there has not been any sustained discussion regarding coordinating these rules. It is of course true that some converging trends among the citizenship rules of prosperous Western states pertain in Europe as well, so it would be incorrect to say there is no harmonization. It is instead the case that harmonization is viewed as coincidental rather than being a key plank in building European citizenship or even the area of freedom security and justice. The result of this is that as European citizenship becomes an increasingly valuable prize, the states that control access to this privileged status have increased power. The functioning of the migration law-citizenship law dichotomy is important here because the very terms of the harmonization texts put control over desirable migration explicitly in the hands of member states, thus member states are the gatekeepers not only to their own citizenship but also to citizenship of the entire Union. Each move to make the supra-national phenomenon of European citizenship more meaningful thereby inscribes increased sovereign power to the states.

---

repeated, most recently in EC, *The Hague Programme: Strengthening Freedom, Security and Justice in the European Union*, [2005] O.J.L. 53/01 [the Hague Programme] agreed upon in 2004.

53 Saskia Sassen, *Losing Control?: Sovereignty in an Age of Globalization* (New York: Columbia University Press, 1996).

54 This harmonization is one of the core samples in Chapter 8.

55 This is probably also true in the area of family reunification migration, however the European Court of Human Rights is developing some constraints in this area.

One result of privileging European citizenship is to make the distinction between citizens and permanent residents more important than it was in the 1980s or early 1990s. This is, in turn, a way of reasserting the importance of national citizenship against the trend described by Sassen and others. That is, that the most meaningful distinction is now between those with legal status in any state and those without it, rather than citizenship itself. Despite permanent residents acquiring the same rights as citizens across a range of areas, and human rights protections being extended with increasing regularity to temporary residents, the increasing importance of European citizenship means there is now more difference between national citizens and permanent residents than there was previously. Citizens have free passage across Europe's borders and can vote (and run) in local and European elections,[56] creating new distinctions between citizens and permanent residents. While permanent residents have generally not been qualified voters, the significance of governance at a supranational level means that some non-nationals are still subject to governance by a body that represents them in some way and has some measure of accountability to them. This makes the right to vote more significant than it was formerly. Looking at the European citizenship law–migration law dichotomy, migration law remains the key mechanism for policing membership, even while in this new configuration citizenship law recovers importance. This evidence is not enough to invert Sassen's assertion, but it does temper the argument and signal that formal legal citizenship is a key site to monitor in future evaluations of rights entitlements.

Changes to citizenship laws including curtailing birthright citizenship, extending membership beyond territory, and the European innovation of making nations the arbiters of supranational citizenship each reinforce the citizenship law–migration law dichotomy. Each of these changes is aimed at making citizenship a more valuable prize; none aims at reducing the role of migration law in controlling access to citizenship for new members of the polity. In each case, we can also trace migration shifts as a motivator of the citizenship law change. While most people only ever have one citizenship, contemporary changes in citizenship laws are being driven by migration. For Ireland, India, and Italy, the new provisions extend the reach of membership to emigrants, as the nation-state seeks to define itself in defiance of geography. The other Irish reform, as well as the Australian changes and the U.S. and

56 EC, *Council Directive of 2004/38 of the European Parliament and of the Council of 29 April 2004 on the right of citizens of the Union and their family members to move and reside freely within the territory of the Member States amending Regulation (EEC) No. 1612/68 and repealing Directives 64/221/EEC, 68/360/EEC, 72/194/EEC, 73/148/EEC, 75/34/EEC, 75/35/EEC, 90/364/EEC and 93/96/EEC,* [2004] O.J. L 158/77; EC, *Council Decision 2002/772 Euratom of June 25 and September 23, 2002, amending the Act concerning the election of the representatives of the European parliament by direct universal suffrage, annexed to Decision 76/787/ECSC,* [2002] O.J. L 283/01; EC, *Council Directive 96/30 of May 13, 1996, amending Directive 94/80 laying down detailed arrangements for the exercise of the right to vote and to stand as a candidate in municipal elections by citizens of the Union residing in a Member State of which they are not nationals,* [1996] O.J.L. 122/14; and EC, *Council Directive 93/109 of December 6, 1993, laying down detailed arrangements for the exercise of the right to vote and stand as a candidate in elections to the European Parliament for citizens of the Union residing in a Member State of which they are not nationals,* [1993] O.J.L. 329/34.

Canadian proposals, all aim to ensure that migration law retains its policing role. The way European citizenship is managed ensures that European states have control over both legal migration and citizenship, and that each part of the dichotomy is now more meaningful. The sharp edge of these shifts is made clearer still in linking them directly to illegal migration.

Citizenship and illegal migration

Even as citizenship is multiplying and transforming, dualizing and deterritorial-izing, for those without citizenship, there is less than ever. The crackdown on all forms of illegal migration is translated through the citizenship law–migration law dichotomy into increased exclusion for those who are already most disadvantaged. The global crackdown means that access to new citizenships is more and more closed for those with less, and more and more open for those with more. As an increasing number of migrants are defined out of "legal" migration and into "ille-gal" migration, they lose any eligibility for citizenship. Meanwhile, dual citizenship becomes more freely available and formal legal citizenship begins, tentatively, to shed its geographies even while shoring up the embattled sovereignty of nations beleaguered by the onslaught of globalization. Citizenship law thus becomes a site to observe a sharp illustration of globalization's paradoxical nature: both inclusions and exclusions are multiplied here. It is also a site for national reconstruction, a place to counter the myth of the powerless state.

The variety of mechanisms for narrowing access to refugee law was discussed in Chapter 4. As refugee law is a surrogate protection, available when the protection due to citizens is withdrawn or fails, a restriction of refugee law amounts to a withdrawal of substituted citizenship as well. The link between refugee law and citizenship is explicit. Those who are dual citizens are required by refugee law to consider protection in each state of nationality before receiving status elsewhere. This linkage provides another illustration of the enduring power of citizenship rights in comparison to human rights. A claim that is based solely on a need for human rights protection fails unless the question of citizenship is settled.

How the increased exclusion from citizenship law accentuates other exclusions is clarified by considering again the example of gender. Crackdown measures have the effect of protecting the smuggling and trafficking markets, making refugee travel more precarious, privileging those in paid employment and fostering images of victimization. All of these factors refract gender. As the cost of smuggling increases, those with more money are advantaged, and they are more likely to be men. Early evidence about the effects of the Canada-U.S. Safe Third Country Agreement shows that this agreement affects proportionately more women than men.[57] These

---

57 Dauvergne, Angeles and Huang, *supra* note 28 at 39–40. This is because the agreement is only in effect at land borders. Proportionately more women seeking asylum enter Canada from the United States at land borders than do men.

shifts mean more men than women will have access to asylum proceedings and the eventual citizenship that process may bring. The analysis of gender is never straight-forward. Although women are disproportionately excluded from the "citizenship track" by migration crackdown measures, they are also disproportionately likely to fit the "victim" image constructed through legal measures aimed at trafficking. The potentially secure migration status that can result from this victim identity creates two kinds of risk for women: the risk that comes from engaging with traffickers and the risk that comes from constructing oneself as a victim. As I discussed in Chapter 5, legal attempts to address trafficking are paralyzed by specters of victimization. The law is moving more slowly, with less emancipatory potential here. In tandem, these legal moves erase women as anything other than victims.

Although crackdown measures are being developed, the same nations are also altering policies at the elite end of the migration spectrum, with its own gendered patterns. Recruiting those with the most education, money, work and business experience means recruiting more men than women. It is these privileged migrants who generally have the most direct track toward citizenship. The pursuit of the best and the brightest multiplies privilege exponentially, another thing at which migration law is particularly good.

At the edge of this analysis, we find the spectacle of amnesty for illegal migrants. Amnesties exist because the fiction of formal legal citizenship does not hold fast. Even as prosperous states move to close their borders more firmly, they also move to forgive this trespass. Amnesty functions as a purification ritual in a number of respects. By "amnesty" I mean any broad legal shift through which a group of people without immigration status or a legal right to remain are granted that right.[58] Amnesties may result in temporary or permanent residency status. This distinction is not particularly important, as either status puts migrants on the citizenship track by removing the stain of illegality.[59] The significant features for my brief analysis are that amnesties are granted to a group of people who clearly have no legal justification for their presence within national territory. Amnesties are always "gifts" of the state; there is no legal compulsion for them. They are structured on the basis of enumerated criteria and are often temporally limited. Amnesties achieve the important state objective of reducing the size of the extralegal population. This has the effect of instant policy success for governments concerned about an inability to control its illegal population through border-control measures. Importantly, however, amnesties have never been solely about this objective.

In thinking about the impact of globalization it is instructive to consider the basis of eligibility for an amnesty. While territorial presence is always one component of

---

58 Although individuals may also be exempted from immigration law provisions, this is a routine matter on an ad hoc basis and does not shift the law.
59 When states grant temporary residency only, they undoubtedly intend this distinction to be mean-ingful. Nonetheless, overall trends suggest that temporary status is often convertible to permanent status and thus to citizenship. Distinctions between temporary and permanent membership are increasingly flexible.

eligibility, there are often other features as well. In the mid-1960s, the United States granted amnesty based on territorial presence alone as part of the closing of the Bracero program that had brought in temporary workers from Mexico beginning in the 1940s.[60] In the 1990s, Canada granted an amnesty to people who were unsuccessful in making refugee claims, tying territorial presence with a particular type of humanitarian claim.[61] The extensive German guestworker program ended in some amnesty provisions in the 1980s.[62] In recent years both the United States and Canada have been talking about another wave of amnesties. These proposals have a more finely honed logic. In the United States the proposal was aimed at those working in jobs that were deemed unattractive to American citizens.[63] In Canada, the principal target of the plan was construction workers.[64] In other words, the amnesty proposal was in each case tied directly to a need identified in economic discourse. The Canadian day-labor construction industry is predominantly male. Even if recipients of a regularized status were also allowed to extend legal residency to their families, women and children whose status in Canada was secured in this way would, here as in the elite economic categories, have their passage to citizenship marked by dependency. The tentative American proposal is not tied to a specific industry and thus would reach more women than the Canadian plan, but the gender bias of paid employment is still present, as is evidenced by the argument that these proposals are not truly amnesties but, instead, limited programs for those who are making an economic contribution. In the Canadian plan a contribution to a particular part of the economy is required, notably not domestic work or piecework stitching, sectors where more women labor illegally. In each case, these proposals are linked to participation in the economy, especially sectors where domestic employees are in short supply. The neo-liberal economic logic of these proposals reflects the core economic logic of globalizing forces. Even as globalization is a social, cultural, or personal force, it transports an economic discourse to whichever arena it traverses.

The idea of amnesty is evidence of the impossibility of maintaining a strict separation between formal and substantive citizenship discourses. Amnesties are legal exceptions, structured to bridge the gap between "illegality" and membership, putting people on the citizenship track directly or indirectly. They convey a sense of

60 Joseph Nevins, *Operation Gatekeeper: The Rise of the 'Illegal Alien' and the Making of the U.S.-Mexico Boundary* (New York and London: Routledge, 2002); Mae Ngai, *Impossible Subjects: Illegal Aliens and the Making of Modern America* (Princeton: Princeton University Press, 2004).

61 This program was known as the Post-Determination Refugee Claimant in Canada Class, *Immigration Regulations 1978*, S.O.R. / 78-172.

62 William Rogers Brubaker, *Citizenship and Nationhood in France and Germany* (Cambridge, Mass.: Harvard University Press, 1992).

63 "A Vital Immigration Debate," Editorial, *The New York Times* (January 8, 2004) 32; Deb Riechmann, "Bush Wins Support from Mexico's President for his New Immigration Proposal," *Canadian Press* (January 12, 2004); Amy Fagan, "Democrats Offer Plan on Aliens," *The Washington Times* (January 29, 2004).

64 Maureen Murray, "Hopes, Dreams but No Status: 'You're Like a Prisoner in a Free Country,'" *The Toronto Star* (November 15, 2003); "Amnesty Encourages Illegal Immigration," Editorial, *The Gazette* (November 15, 2003).

desert, as those granted amnesty are read as already contributing to the nation, for which in contemporary times we can read as "the economy." However, amnesties also draw a significant measure of political currency from the strength of substantive citizenship. There is a public discourse of support for individuals who are law abiding and hard working and have come to this (for which substitute any) country to make better lives for themselves and their children. This migration trope is really a citizenship story. When migrants give us, as a nation, what we most want from citizens, they confound legal attempts to keep the stories separate. In other words, the beneficiaries of an amnesty are already acting as citizens. Amnesty converts substantive citizenship to formal legal citizenship. This opens another plane of struggle, as once formal citizenship is established, many beneficiaries of migration amnesties may well find that they are not fully included citizens. Nonetheless, considering the operation of this device reveals another vista on the citizenship law–migration law dichotomy. Here migration law ceases to function as rule of law because an amnesty is an exceptional act of grace. Migration law is again doing the dirty work for citizenship law, displaying law's weakness and unlegal construction, working as a purification ritual at this site, rather than disturbing the orderly function of citizenship law.

Citizenship law works in tandem with migration law as a legal expression of degrees of belonging. Once citizenship is formally established, it again fragments into degrees of substantive inclusion, but its work in constituting the border is done. Although some accounts of globalizing trends suggest a diminished role for citizenship as exclusion, attention to the border belies this suggestion. Formal, legal citizenship persists *because* of the trend toward denationalization, *because* of the potential for human rights norms to become a more meaningful statement of entitlement, and *because* the most meaningful distinction may well be between those with legal status in that state where they reside and those without it. Citizenship is an assertion by states to attempt to counter these trends. An aspiration to persist. A central part of the shift that makes migration law the last bastion of sovereignty. Citizenship law reveals that even while clinging to sovereign assertion, the newest law reforms literally tear citizenship away from the territorial nation: unhinging law and nation at their most basic joint. Chapter 9 takes up sovereignty in more detail and examines this unhinging in particular. Before moving to that analysis, however, Chapter 8 considers migration law trends in the European Union and the United States. Each of these locations contributes an important piece to any analysis of globalization and illegal migration, because in differing ways both are held up as examples of robust sovereignty at a time when sovereign power is an increasingly scarce commodity.

CHAPTER EIGHT

Myths and Giants: The influence of the European Union and the United States

Tales of globalization invariably return to one of two geographies – the European Union or the United States. In the case of Europe this turning is a romantic longing: a sense that Europe is the peaceful way of the global future. With good luck and good governance we can imagine Europe is what globalization will mean for all of us: eroding borders and diminished sovereignty, all to mutual benefit.[1] Europe is set on a course of steady expansion, spreading the blanket of strong human rights protections and robust international law ever eastward and southward. Candidate countries are eager to comply and join; enticed by the prospect of economic union, they rush to improve conditions of human flourishing. What could be better for all than to turn the globe itself into an area of freedom security and justice?[2] The United States is the twin avatar of globalization. Although the image is not exclusively rosy, the United States is the sole remaining superpower, winner of the Cold War, uncontested hegemon. In contrast to Europe, the United States is engaged in a more "direct delivery" method for the global spread of democracy and human rights. There is enormous contestation within and outside the United States about the virtues and values of its war on terror. This is a debate about methods, not about the ultimately unambiguous good of conquering terrorism and bringing the disputes it represents within an appropriately broad democratic umbrella. A parallel debate, muted since the events of September 11, 2001, but equally important, is the question of whether globalization is merely Americanization. To draw, perhaps

---

1 In Neil MacCormick's analysis, sovereignty is like virginity in that it can be lost to mutual benefit. Neil MacCormick, "Beyond the Sovereign State" (1993), 56 *Modern Law Review* 1 at 16. This analogy has a certain old-boy scallywaggish quality, but does of course invite a consideration of sexual exploitation, which is useful in considering the uneven qualities of globalization and in understanding how some sovereignties seem more important than others, and of how sovereignty maps onto questions of authority and control. MacCormick elaborates the more weighty aspects of his analysis in *Questioning Sovereignty: Law, State, and Nation in the European Commonwealth* (Oxford: Oxford University Press, 1999).

2 The *Treaty of Amsterdam amending the Treaty on European Union, the Treaties establishing the European Communities and certain related acts,* [1997] O.J.C. 340/1 [*Treaty of Amsterdam*] was signed on October 2, 1997, and brought into force on May 1, 1999. It provides the legal basis for the gradual implementation of an Area of Freedom, Security, and Justice.

unfairly, on Boaventura de Sousa Santos, the question is whether globalization shows a globalized localism, or merely a globalized Americanism.[3]

Given the importance of both the European Union and the United States to narratives of globalization, it is impossible to recount globalization and illegal migration without considering these two spaces uniquely. The reason for this is similar in each case. If neither the United States nor the European Union is participating, almost no phenomenon will be considered an aspect of globalization. This is not, of course, dictated by size alone. In matters of extralegal migration, China and India provide migrants, not regulatory structures or legal trends. This in itself reveals something of globalization's character. When legal scholars write of globalization, a significant portion of what they are talking about is law as it is known and practiced in the European Union.[4] Thus, if migration law is a key site for understanding the relationship between law and globalization, it must also be able to tell us something about Europe: to evaluate and contextualize the romantic longing for a European future. In the case of the United States, the challenge is to bring the United States within the analysis. In several of the chapters up to this point, the United States has been seen to vary from other states, for example in its engagement with human trafficking, its approach to the migration security matrix, its commitment to birthright citizenship, as well as its failure to ratify the Refugee Convention and the long-standing politicization of American refugee law. The question to confront is therefore: if the global hegemon is not fully participating in any given trend, can it still be analyzed as a meaningful trend, or is the United States simply so big and so powerful that it has the capacity to make trends through solitary action, and to move all else to the periphery? In the case of the United States, migration law is a site for understanding how globalizing forces are reshaping power.

The European Union and the United States have been present throughout the book up to this point. This chapter, however, takes a different tack by considering the two giants of globalization discretely instead of taking a migration phenomenon as a starting point. Rather than recovering the arguments and evidence of earlier chapters, here I turn to considering how the European Union and the United States contribute to the mythology of globalization. The outcome of this analysis is an understanding that in both the United States and the European Union, contemporary moves in migration law signal a recasting of the notion of sovereignty that relies on making control over population movements central. This recasting also requires a transformation of the way power is exercised, something that is being worked out differently in the United States and the European Union. Beyond this, however, these two giants also illustrate how migration law provides a counterpoint

---

3 Boaventura de Sousa Santos, *Toward a New Legal Common Sense: Law, Globalization, and Emancipation*, 2nd ed. (London: Butterworths Lexis Nexis, 2002), Chapter 5, where de Sousa Santos analyzes the distinction between globalized localisms and localized globalisms.
4 Discussed above in Chapter 3 at 34–35.

to aspects of the globalization myth. The story to be told here is not only about resistance to globalizing impeti and nation-state resilience, but also about law and the potential for its autonomy.

The chapter proceeds by considering two core samples. First, it looks at how the European Union is tackling illegal migration through harmonization of crackdown measures and asylum procedures. It then examines the seemingly disparate American phenomena of tolerance for an immense "illegal" population alongside both state and civil society initiatives aimed at fortifying the Southern border. In the concluding section, I map out connections between the European and American initiatives and lay the groundwork for the analysis of sovereignty in Chapter 9.

The fortress of freedom, security, and justice

There are several important themes in considering the evolving place of migration regulation in the architecture of the European Union. The first is that the idea of a common market was first and foremost about a common market for goods, services, and capital. Adding a common market for labor has come later. It is also important that freedom of movement for people has been understood in economists' terms, that is, movement is freed in order to allow people to work elsewhere, not to live elsewhere. Workers do, of course, also live, but that is an afterthought. The second important theme is that harmonization of migration law measures has emerged very recently and has been tied to crackdown measures. Accordingly, what are being explicitly harmonized are approaches to asylum, illegal migration, and the return of third-country nationals (otherwise known as deportation). Convergence among plans for recruiting the best and the brightest does seem to be occurring, but is coincidental or competitive, rather than part of the collective agenda. As I noted in Chapter 6, the harmonization agenda was given a considerable boost by the events of September 11, 2001, underscoring how much harmonization is about keeping people out, not letting them in.

The first firm steps toward uniting Europe were taken at the close of the Second World War. The so-called BeNeLux countries began the process of uniting as early as 1944, with governments in exile establishing the Benelux Customs Union.[5] These three nations joined with France, West Germany, and Italy to establish the European Economic Community under the Treaty of Rome in 1957.[6] This Treaty persists as the core document of the European Union, incorporating a series of significant amendments. From the outset, there has been a statement of principle

---

5 *Benelux Customs Union Agreement,* Belgium, Netherlands, and Luxembourg, September 1944. This entered into force in 1947. The BeNeLux countries are Belgium, the Netherlands, and Luxembourg.
6 The full title of the Treaty of Rome is the *Treaty Establishing the European Economic Community,* March 25, 1957, 298 U.N.T.S. 11. The European Coal and Steel Community, which created a common market for these commodities with the aim of preventing further war, was created in 1952 (*Treaty Instituting the European Coal and Steel Community,* April 18, 1951, 261 U.N.T.S. 140 (Treaty of Paris)) by the same six nations.

regarding free movement for workers.[7] It was not until the mid-1980s, however, that internal borders began to be opened. In 1985 the Schengen agreement between France, Germany, Belgium, the Netherlands, and Luxembourg began the process of breaking down internal borders and strengthening external borders.[8] This initial agreement that first aimed at reducing border checks and harmonizing regulations has expanded to develop a full abolition of internal borders and now includes twenty-eight countries.[9] The growth of "Schengenland" is primarily about traveling and commerce rather than migration.[10] The original Schengen treaty was extended by the 1990 Convention Implementing the Schengen Agreement, which came into force in 1993.[11] These conventions have now been incorporated into the core body of EU-defining law, the *acquis communautaire*.

1993 was the same year that the European Community embarked on a migration agreement in the Treaty of Maastricht.[12] This agreement also introduced the notion of European citizenship.[13] Under the title, "Free Movement of Persons, Services, and Capital," the Maastricht Treaty provided for the free movement of workers and work seekers and for a right of establishment for nationals of members states in other member states, with specific reference to rights of self-employed persons and for those providing services. This represented a considerable elaboration of the original statement in the Rome Treaty in support of the free movement of workers. The Maastricht Treaty also established the "Third Pillar" of the European Community, thereby formalizing a mechanism for intergovernmental cooperation under the heading of "justice and home affairs." Migration matters fell under

---

7 See article 48 of the original Treaty.

8 EC, *Agreement Between the Governments of the States of the Benelux Economic Union, the Federal Republic of Germany, and the French Republic on the gradual abolition of checks at their common borders*, [2000] O.J.L. 239/13.

9 All the countries of the European Union except Ireland and the United Kingdom participate in this accord. Fifteen countries are full participants; the others are partial participants. Non-EU signatories include Iceland and Norway and Switzerland, although the principles are yet to come into effect in Switzerland.

10 The Treaty of Accession 2003 contains "Schengen provisions" establishing assistance for the ten new EU states to fortify their external borders. See EC, *Act concerning the conditions of accession of the Czech Republic, the Republic of Estonia, the Republic of Cyprus, the Republic of Latvia, the Republic of Lithuania, the Republic of Hungary, the Republic of Malta, the Republic of Poland, the Republic of Slovenia and the Slovak Republic and the adjustments to the Treaties on which the European Union is founded*, [2003] O.J.L. 46/33.

11 EC, *Convention from June 19, 1990, Implementing the Schengen Agreement of 14 June 1985 between the Government of the States of the Benelux Economic Union, the Federal Republic of Germany and the French Republic on the gradual abolition of checks at their common borders*, [2000] O.J.L. 239/19.

12 7 February 1992, to take effect in November 1993. *Treaty on European Union*, February 7, 1992, O.J. 1992 No. 191/1, 31 I.L.M. 247 (Treaty of Maastricht). This treaty amends the Rome Treaty.

13 Article 8 of the 1992 consolidated treaty. As discussed in Chapter 7, citizenship of the Union is derivative in that it follows automatically from citizenship in a member state and cannot exist without such national citizenship. EU citizenship accords a right to move and reside freely (subject to treaty limitations), a right to vote in local elections once established as a resident, a right to diplomatic or consular protection from governments of other member states, and rights to petition the European Parliament and to apply to the Ombudsman. EU citizenship does not at this stage entail any enumerated duties.

this umbrella, but there were few further developments until the 1997 Treaty of Amsterdam.[14]

The Treaty of Amsterdam came into force in 1999. It launched the notion of a common area of freedom, security, and justice, and a plan of movement toward this objective was the principal achievement of the October 1999 Tampere European Council.[15] Not surprisingly given when it was constructed, the freedom, security, and justice agenda brings together matters of immigration, asylum, and crime.[16] Freedom, security, and justice are to be ensured by controlling and reducing each of these factors. For migration matters, this agreement is vital to establishing a truly European agenda. Immigration and asylum were moved, partially, from the Third Pillar to the First, making them matters of central concern and subject directly to European regulatory capacity rather than cooperation and encouragement. The Treaty of Amsterdam included a five-year transitional period, during which time both the Commission and member states could initiate regulations and the Council would act on such proposals unanimously. Following this transition, the usual procedures of Commission initiation and qualified majority voting became the norm.[17] The opening article in the detailed section on "visas, asylum, immigration, and other policies related to the free movement of persons" called for measures aimed at ensuring free movement " . . . in conjunction with directly related flanking measures with respect to external border controls, asylum and immigration [. . .], and measures to prevent and combat crime. . . . "[18]

The Treaty of Amsterdam, therefore, launched the European Union into an era of genuine cooperation in migration matters, and set the stage for making these matters central to further European expansion. Harmonization of migration regulation has made most progress in asylum, and some progress in terms of irregular migration, and legal economic migration has been significantly left in the hands of member states.[19] This gradation reflects the degree of concern over these matters. Observing the progress of harmonization over the five-year Amsterdam

---

14 *The Treaty of Amsterdam, supra* note 2.
15 This Council was held on October 15–16, 1999, in Tampere, Finland. See the Presidency Conclusions available at www.europa.eu.int/council/off/conclu/oct99/oct99˙en.htm#milestones.
16 The relevant objective set out in the revised Article B states:

> . . . to maintain and develop the Union as an area of freedom, security and justice, in which the free movement of persons is assured in conjunction with appropriate measures with respect to external border controls, asylum, immigration and the prevention and combating of crime; . . .

17 Article 73o.   18 Article 73i.
19 See for example EC, *Council Recommendation of 22 December 1995 on Harmonizing Means of Combating Illegal Immigration and Illegal Employment and Improving the Relevant Means of Control,* [1996] O.J.L. C/005. The Council and Commission action plan of December 3, 1998, set out a plan of measure to be adopted by 2004 EC, *Council and Commission Action Plan of December 3, 1998, on How Best to Implement the Provisions of the Treaty of Amsterdam on the Creation of an Area of Freedom, Security, and Justice,*[1999] O.J.C. 19/1. See also *Communication from the Commission to the Council, the European Parliament, the European Economic and Social Committee of the Regions* June 4, 2004 – *Study on the Links Between Legal and Illegal Migration* [COM (2004) 412 final].

transitional period would suggest that European states are most anxious to assert control over asylum, that asylum and illegal migration are viewed as intertwined phenomena, and that legal migration has only moderate interest to the Union itself. In these reactions, the European Union is no different from other prosperous nation-states: the move to aggregate sovereignty at the Union level carries with it a strong interest in those areas that are core to sovereignty. In order for the principles of free movement of workers throughout the Union to be fully realized, the mega-sovereign asserts control over who those workers will be.

The transitional period came to an end on the first of May 2004, the same day that ten new countries became members of the Union. One of the conditions of accession was a form of migration probation for citizens of those new member states. The usual rule of worker and work-seeker mobility throughout the Union was not immediately extended to the new members. Instead, each existing member was allowed to set its own rules for worker mobility over a seven-year phase-in period.[20] Ireland and Sweden were the only states to immediately extend mobility to new state nationals on the same terms as existing member nationals. Other states used quotas or work permits, or both, over a range of time limits.[21] Here again we see migration mobility as the last phase of harmonization, signaling both that states are most reluctant to cede control in this area, and that it is difficult to agree to terms for doing so. The case for worker mobility was argued by using the example of Iberian accession when fears of extensive migration were not subsequently realized. The argument ran, therefore, that open borders are not a threat because few are likely to move. In other words, open borders will not mean much in the end. This is born out by historical trends; only approximately 2 percent of Europeans of working age were living in an EU country other than that of their nationality in 2006, and this rate has not changed over a thirty-year period.[22] Some significant pockets of migration have developed, but it is premature to suggest that major movements will endure. For example, a series of newspaper articles have focused on the influx of Polish workers to Britain and are part of the political backdrop to Britain's renewal of its worker registration system.[23] There are also reports of an influx of migrants

20 *Supra* note 10 at Part Four, Title 1: Transitional Measures. See also EC, *Final Act to the Treaty of Accession to the European Union 2003*, [2003] O.J.L. 46/957 for a list of the amendments set by each state regarding worker mobility.
21 All limits must end in 2011. Beatrice Harper, "Commission Issues Report on Worker Mobility in the Enlarged EU" (February 23, 2006), On-line: eironline: European industrial relations observatory on-line http://www.eurofound.europa.eu/eiro/2006/02/feature/eu0602204f.html.
22 "Mobility: No Place Like Home for Most EU Citizens," *European Report* (March 28, 2006); "Austria Backs Worker Mobility Campaign but Defends Own Restrictions," *EuroNews* (February 20, 2006); "Social Policy: 2006 Designated European Year of Workers' Mobility," *European Report* (July 2, 2005).
23 Grace Hammond, "EU expansion 'Caused Wave of Immigrants,'" *Yorkshire Post* (July 21, 2006); Jeffrey Fleishman, "Looking West for Work; Young Poles Drawn to Wealthy European Nations Leave Skill Shortages in their Wake, Putting their Country's Economy in Jeopardy," *Los Angeles Times* (January 21, 2007) C1; Adam Morris, "Poles Help Fill Pews at Cathedral," *Evening News*

from 2004 accession states to Ireland, as well as evidence of a "brain drain" from the Baltic states.[24]

In December 2004, the Council of Europe committed itself to the Hague Program initiative.[25] While this Program clearly anticipated that the Treaty establishing the Constitution of Europe would soon take effect, it carefully ensured that " . . . existing Treaties provide the legal basis for Council action" in the interim. In other words, the 2005 failure of the Constitution of Europe does not directly affect progress toward Hague goals. The Program makes it clear that migration matters are now the principal political priority for the European Union. Migration matters are the first to appear in this document, and take up more than half of its space. The introduction to the Hague Program highlights the importance of migration concerns at this stage in European integration. "Illegal migration" and "trafficking and smuggling of human beings" are the first two cross-border problems named under the heading of security. Terrorism and organized crime come third and fourth. The specific objectives related to migration are listed under the heading "strengthening freedom." The question "freedom for whom?" comes quickly to mind. There are a number of objectives that relate to information sharing, ranging from developing a "common analysis of migratory phenomena" to harmonized use of biometric identifiers. Many of the specific objectives relate to asylum matters. Principal among these is the commitment to development of the Common European Asylum system, which was poised in 2004 to enter its second phase of development (item 1.3). This is to be completed by the end of 2010. Other asylum-related goals include assisting third countries to police illegal migration (item 1.6); supporting "durable solutions" and "regional protection programs," which keep asylum seekers out of EU territory (item 1.6.2); improving removal and repatriation policy (item 1.6.4);[26] and increasing border checks including considering "the feasibility of the creation of a European system of border guards" (item 1.7). The program also commits to consider improving freedom of movement for EU citizens, clearly signaling that movement within the EU is not, at present, parallel to moving around a state of which one is a citizen (item 1.1). In contrast to each of these initiatives, the quest'on of legal labor migration is left explicitly to individual states, with an accompanying call for members to reduce the informal economy as a pull factor for illegal migration (item 1.4).

(Edinburgh) (February 20, 2007) p. 21; "Leader: The Polish Immigration Lesson," *The Scotsman* (February 6, 2007) p. 29.

24 Andrew Bushe, "Immigration Pushes Irish Population to Highest Level since 1861," *Agence France Presse* (July 19, 2006); "Go West, Young Latvians," *The Irish Times* (March 25, 2006) p. 1; "Latvian Commentary: Emigration to Ireland Has Consequences in Both Countries," *BBC Monitoring International Reports* (November 30, 2005); "Emigration from Lithuania more than Double since EU Membership," *Agence France Presse* (July 13, 2006); "Lithuania: Low Salaries Cause Emigration – Poll," *Baltic News Service* (September 26, 2005).

25 Council of the European Union, General Secretariat, *The Hague Programme: Strengthening Freedom, Security, and Justice in the EU*, Texts Adopted, Rec. 16054/04 (2004). December 13, 2004, 16054/04. See also EC, *Treaty Establishing a Constitution for Europe* [2004] O.J. C310/01.

26 This objective is not explicitly linked to asylum seekers but is important in asylum policy as it related to the politically vexed matter of returning failed asylum seekers.

In December 2007, EU leaders signed the Treaty of Lisbon, which follows several years of negotiation around institutional issues and attempts to pick up where the failed Constitution left off. As this book goes to press, this latest foundational treaty is open for ratification. Its eventual, and potential, acceptance would follow with the broad trends of the early agreements, and the centrality of both European citizenship and the area of freedom security and justice. The Treaty urges continued progress towards the proposed common asylum system.[27]

Two Council Directives are the key elements in what is known as the "first phase" of a European common asylum system. The "Qualification Directive," agreed to on April 29, 2004, sets standards for refugee status and other forms of international protection and was to be transposed into national law by October 2006.[28] A second directive, agreed to on December 1, 2005, sets minimum standards in procedural matters related to granting and withdrawing refugee status and was to be transposed by December 2007.[29] Each directive, and indeed every European document that addresses the topic of asylum, affirms a commitment to international refugee law. Nonetheless, the two directives pull away from some core commitments of the international regime, and the effect of this pull is magnified by Europe's role as salutary beacon of legal globalization.

The Qualification Directive principally covers the same ground as the Refugee Convention itself. That is, it sets out who can benefit from refugee status, who will be excluded from it, when it will be withdrawn, and what rights are to be accorded to refugees. In key areas, the general tendency is to add more detail. For example, Article 4, "assessment of facts and circumstances," sets out provisions for which party is responsible for which documentation and provides guidance regarding drawing evidentiary conclusions.[30] Article 9 defines persecution and Article 10 provides

---

27 EC, *Treaty of Lisbon amending the Treaty on European Union and the Treaty establishing the European Community*, CIG 14/07. Much in keeping with earlier statements, this treaty proposes amending Article 2(2) of the EU Treaty to state:

  The Union shall offer its citizens an area of freedom, security and justice without internal frontiers, in which the free movement of persons is ensured in conjunction with appropriate measures with respect to external border controls, asylum, immigration and the prevention and combating of crime.

28 EC, *Council Directive 2004/83/EC of April 29, 2004, on minimum standards for the qualification and status of third country nationals or stateless persons as refugees or persons who otherwise need international protection and the content of the protection is granted*, [2004] O.J.L. 304/12. Only six countries (Estonia, France, Slovenia, Luxembourg, Lithuania, and Austria) had completed transposition by June 2007, and by November 2007 little additional progress had been made.

29 EC, *Council Directive 2005/85/EC of 1 December 2005 on minimum standards on procedures in Member states for granting and withdrawing refugee status*, [2005] O.J.L. 326/13. The provisions calling for legal aid in refugee appeal matters are to be transposed into national laws by December 2008.

30 Article 4(5) lists circumstances in which an applicant's account of events "shall not need confirmation" including when the applicant has made a genuine effort; when there is a satisfactory explanation for missing documents; when the story is "coherent and plausible" and does not "run counter" to other available information; when the applicant has made the application at the earliest possible time and then general credibility has been established. These evidentiary points

definitions for each of the international grounds for refugee status. These are among the most obvious examples of elements that are not present in the international law. Immediately and explicitly, or gradually through layers of interpretation, the effect of these additions will be to narrow interpretations of the refugee definition. One of the most powerful aspects of the Refugee Convention itself has been that "persecution" is not defined. This is, for example, key to the Convention's capacity to accommodate changes in human rights discourses discussed in Chapter 4. The requirement of continual reinterpretation of this term, and of its use around the globe, has led to a legal framework capable of alleviating forms of harm that were beyond the contemplation of the Convention's drafters. This is, sadly, immensely valuable, as the horrors of the Second World War did not complete the categorization of humanity's capacity for persecutory self-harm. Additional specificity will curtail the Convention's power to provide protection for those at risk of being persecuted.

To this extent, the Qualification Directive is similar to what Australia has done in legislating interpretations of "persecution," "serious crime," and "particular social group" as discussed in Chapter 4. The EU setting, however, makes these digressions more important, and this is not merely because they will be applied to tens of thousands more applications annually. It is easy to argue that Australia is simply in breach of the Refugee Convention. Although this argument can at present only be made in political rhetorical space rather than a legal forum, it is nonetheless an important advocacy tool and the prospect of some future repeal of this legislation is not entirely fanciful. The European Union's role as triumphalist of international human rights, and the status of EU law as quasi-international law, make its departures from the Refugee Convention vastly more influential. The EU's Qualification Directive amounts to a restatement of refugee law for the twenty-first century. By virtue of its application in twenty-seven nations, it will set new standards for "state practice," a vital interpretive source for international law.[31] In this respect, it works to wrest international law away from the international and to reframe it. The next step will, of course, be re-export both through the legal shadow cast directly over neighboring and aspiring states and through the jurisprudential glow of how refugee law is read in several key receiving nations.[32] The global trends toward convergence in matters of migration restriction will receive special support from this explicit harmonization.

The Qualification Directive is important in situating EU law within legal globalization. Here EU law occupies a place that is neither national law writ large, for the

---

could be more appropriately seen as procedural matters. One reason for including them in this earlier Directive may have been that there was a high degree of consensus surrounding these points and a desire to begin implementing them.

31 *Vienna Convention on the Law of Treaties*, May 23, 1969, 1155 U.N.T.S. 331 at Article 31(3)(b).

32 This shadowing effect is analyzed by Sandra Lavenex in "EU External Governance in 'Wider Europe'" (2004), 11:4 *Journal of European Public Policy* 680.

text directs nations and anticipates differences, nor international law incorporated, else why bother with a separate text. In some places, for example in discussing exclusions (Articles 12 and 17) or in setting out the principle of non-refoulement (Article 21), the Qualification Directive is close or identical to the Refugee Convention. Some of the additions beyond these redundancies demonstrate an aspiration to reign in interpretation of the internationally agreed text. In other cases, however, the Directive adds principles to international refugee law that have been elaborated elsewhere, such as in setting out a commitment to family unity (Article 23), which reflects the trend in Europe and elsewhere to protect at least a limited version of family reunion rights.[33]

Even if this Directive is ultimately no more than an intermediate step between a Europe that supports and applies international law and the Europe-of-the-future with one asylum law for all, the need to take an intermediate step is indicative of at least three points. First, it is clear that getting from refugee law as a sole and limited exception to sovereign control over borders, to handing refugee matters to a suprastate body, is a difficult matter. Second, this is further evidence that international refugee law has attained some rule of law-type qualities as discussed in Chapter 4. Third, while it is scarcely possible for Europe to forsake international law and simply proceed on its own, by its heft (including its moral authority, for international law has long had a more weighty morality than domestic law) it drags international law with it, by its teeth or in its wake as the case may be. This is particularly clear in the case of refugee law. European nations may well have decided that international refugee law is not the regime they desire, but they will have it regardless because by their actions the international is itself transformed.

It is also deeply ironic that international refugee law first defined a status available only to Europeans[34] and now is only available to those outside Europe, or at least outside the European Union.[35] The well-established critique of the Refugee Convention, asserting that it is as much about limiting state responsibility as extending it, is reinforced by the Directive, which clearly demonstrates that additional specificity makes for additional exclusions. This is embedded in the law-likeness of the refugee regime. Every line-drawing exercise results in putting some on one side

---

33 Although this is done with care to control the breadth of interpretation by limiting this to clearly defined family members (Article 2), including a limitation to the family as it existed in the country of origin.

34 This was the practical effect of the 1951 requirement that a refugee was a person who came within the definition because of "events occurring before January 1, 1951." *Convention Relating to the Status of Refugees*, July 28, 1951, 189 U.N.T.S. 150 (entered into force April 22, 1954).

35 In the Qualification Directive, refugees can only be "third country nationals." The Preamble states that the Directive is "without prejudice to the Protocol on asylum for nationals of Member States of the European Union as annexed to the Treaty Establishing the European Community." EC, *Council Directive 2004/83/EC of April 29, 2004, on minimum standards for the qualification and status of third country nationals or stateless persons who otherwise need international protection and the content of the protection granted*, [2004] O.J.L. 304/12. Denmark has declined to participate in the Qualification Directive as of July 2007.

and some on the other; every assertion of rights is only meaningful in a discursive universe where the rights can be asserted by some and not others. Injecting precision clarifies who is excluded and narrows the interpretative space for that line drawing to be incrementally adjusted.

The Qualification Directive also sets out standards for granting what is known as "subsidiary protection," an issue that has been especially vexing in the European context. At its most elementary, subsidiary protection is available to those at risk of serious harm in cases where the harm is not linked to one of the grounds in the refugee definition. In other words, the requirement of a "nexus" is removed. In addition, the term persecution is not used in the subsidiary protection definition. These moves in tandem serve to circumvent two of the most complex areas of interpretation for the refugee definition. This can be read as a straightforward simplification of complex rules built up through fifty years of interpretation. It could also be read as a rejection of the central principles of refugee protection. What is most striking in this regard, however, is that the Directive did not simply set out a new basis for surrogate state protection that would pertain only in the European Union, and thus collapse the refugee/subsidiary protection distinction. Nor did it simply enlarge the refugee definition, as has been done by other regional agreements.[36] The choice to continue this hybrid structure could even be read to reflect a desire to continue to comply with the international law, if so much else in the Directive did not pull in the opposite direction. The principal achievement, therefore, of this structure is to ensure European leadership in international refugee law, even as the European Union moves away from it.

The Procedures Directive of December 2005 is a lesser challenge to international refugee law as it largely addresses matters on which the Refugee Convention itself is silent. The Procedures Directive covers roughly two areas: safe third country principles and how refugee claims should be handled. In other words, this distinction between procedure and substance is no clearer here than anywhere else, and matters of procedure are as important to achieving legal rights as any substantive description of rights entitlement. The notion of a safe third country is at odds with those who have argued persuasively that the Refugee Convention's silence on this point means that states should not impose agreements that limit applicants' choice of state to seek asylum.[37] The safe third country rules in this Directive are extensive, while acknowledging that, at least for countries outside Europe, the

36 *Organization of African Unity: Convention on the Specific Aspects of Refugee Problems in Africa*, September 10, 1969, 1001 U.N.T.S. 45 (entered into force: June 20, 1974); OAS, Colloquium on the International Protection of Refugees in Central America, Mexico, and Panama in Cartagena de Indias, Colombia, *Cartagena Declaration on Refugees*, OR OEA/Ser.L/V/II.66, doc. 10, rev. 1, pp. 190–3 (November 22, 1984).

37 Penelope Mathew, "Australian Refugee Protection in the Wake of the *Tampa*" (2002), 96 *American Journal of International Law* 661. James Hathaway argues that the support for this proposition is weakening in recent years; see J. C. Hathaway, *The Rights of Refugees under International Law* (Cambridge and New York: Cambridge University Press, 2005) at 323–24.

notion of a safe third country is a rebuttable presumption.[38] The basic procedure for refugee determination set out in this Directive includes a personal interview, provision of reasons, the possibility of appealing, and a right to legal aid on appeal. Each of these provisions is also curtailed, sometimes quite sharply.[39] Any number of systems providing these elements will meet the requirements. The Directive establishes "guarantees for applicants for asylum" that are twinned with "obligations of the applicants for asylum" (Articles 10 and 11).[40] The Directive is evidently not a statement of individual procedural rights as it is equally attentive to the rights of the state. State rights that are closely tied to the sovereign control of borders often trump individual rights in this context.

Like the Qualification Directive, the Procedures Directive has strong potential to capture the initiative of international legal developments. This effect might be even greater in this arena, where there is not an explicit international legal text, and therefore an argument of contravention must rely more on nuance and principle. The biggest factor tending toward international leadership, however, is that Western receiving states are generally supportive at this point in time of any measure that cracks down on undesirable migration, a category to which asylum is routinely assigned. So rather than argue that the European Union, or any of its member states, is in contravention of the law, other states are much more likely to take the position that this is the best reading of the international law.

Each of these directives sets out minimum standards for states to follow, allowing in principle that more robust protections be maintained or established. Or, in the case of safe third country provisions, that more extensive lists of safe places be maintained beyond those that are commonly agreed.[41] The logic of minimum standards of course initiates a race to the bottom. It also underscores how refugee law is at odds with human rights provisions. Rather than an aspiring rhetoric, here the law is imprinted with minimalist hedging, a careful measuring of bets. Only the minimum is imbued with a law-like character. What states might do beyond this is not even hinted at. The careful detailing of procedures, exceptions, and definitions robs the texts of any inspirational quality. Furthermore, there is no indication of why these documents read as minimum standards, rather than simply as standards,

---

38 EC, *Council Directive 2005/85/EC of December 1, 2005, on minimum standards on procedures in Member States for granting and withdrawing refugee status,* [2005] O.J. L. 326/13 at paragraph 21 of the Preamble.

39 For example, Article 23 provides that states may put an applicant into an accelerated examination procedure, with reduced rights, if they have entered the country illegally. This is one of many clauses permitting an accelerated process, but it jumps out as *prima facie* contravening Article 31 of the Refugee Convention, which bars penalties for illegal entry.

40 Guarantees include receiving relevant information in a language the applicant understands, having the services of an interpreter to submit their case, being able to communicate with advisors, notice in reasonable time of the decision and its reasons. Obligations include reporting when required, handing over documents, informing the state of contact details, submitting to searches, photographs, and recording of oral statements.

41 In this case the Directive specifies maximum protection rather than minimum protection as smaller lists of "safe third countries" mean a greater number of potential claims.

unless this is to be taken as a statement that the Directives have aimed to spell out the most miserly possible application of the Refugee Convention. This might be one way to reconcile the language and content with the continued rhetorical adherence to the international rules.

It is not possible to predict in late 2007 what shape the common asylum system will assume, or what hurdles might arise in trying to establish it. What is clear now is that harmonization in European migration laws has been driven by a desire to "crack down" on extralegal movements and that harmonization in this area of border crossing has come behind other European initiatives. Harmonizing EU asylum law is not simply the final step in a progression of sovereignty transfer. There is a greater layer of complexity to be grappled with here. Member states are only moving crackdown measures to the outer border of the union, while at the same time retaining control over desirable migration and over admission to the full membership of citizenship. Indeed, as the analysis of citizenship law showed, member states have enhanced their capacity as membership gatekeepers because they now control both access to their own citizenship as well as to citizenship of the Union. The prize of membership is greater than ever. The capacity to exclude is stronger. Elspeth Guild has done important work arguing that the progression of European migration laws from the 1990s onward has been aimed at exclusion of the poor.[42] Thus here as elsewhere, globalization is turning migration status into a new marker of privilege. Not only does poverty exclude people from moving, limited mobility also reduces one's economic opportunities, fostering poverty in turn.

The specter of Fortress Europe is only partially accurate. The appetite for expansion of the area of freedom, security, and justice, as well as nation-state control over desirable migration means that the walls are malleable, but that control over malleability is solely in the hands of the state. The mechanisms for openness also disrupt a simple picture of sovereignty transfer; something more complicated is unfolding, suggesting sovereignty is not malleable in this straightforward way. This is equally true in the United States, which despite its hegemonic power has a large population of unauthorized migrants and an ongoing concern about controlling border crossing. After considering recent events along the U.S.-Mexican border, I will examine what the parallels between the European Union and the United States contribute to understanding the illegal migration and globalization.

Border law: Lessons of the U.S.–Mexico frontier

In October 2006, U.S. President Bush approved plans for the complete fortification of the U.S.–Mexican border. The notional price tag for this project ranged up to

---

42 Elspeth Guild, "The Legal Framework: Who is Entitled to Move?" and "Who is Entitled to Work and Who is in Charge?: Understanding the Legal Framework of European Labor Migration" in Didier Bigo and Elspeth Guild (eds.), *Controlling Frontiers: Free Movement Into and Within Europe* (Aldershot: Ashgate, 2005) 14 and 100.

U.S. $7 billion.[43] Major defense contractors were involved in bidding for a contract to enforce the barrier with highly sophisticated technology. These developments were one marker in the ongoing struggle by the American state to imprint control on this border. The contestation over this border, and the turn it has taken since the early 1990s, demonstrate facets of the relationship between globalization and illegal migration and how this relationship is affected by American global hegemony. The legal and policy choices made by the uncontested hegemon of globalization influence the place of illegal migration in the broad globalization script. In the early years of the twenty-first century, civil society groups in the United States have also been a vocal presence in the contestation over the southern border. Attention to these groups highlights another aspect of globalization mythology.

Illegal migration in the United States is intertwined with Mexican identity. The 1848 Treaty of Guadalupe Hidalgo, extending the American border southward into what was formerly Mexican territory, and the Mexican Revolution of 1910, which increased mobility for Mexicans, are both seminal events in the long story of migration across this border.[44] Of the estimated twelve million illegal residents of the United States, 56 percent are estimated to be Mexican nationals.[45] "Operation Wetback," which began in 1954 with one million apprehensions, targeted primarily Mexicans and added a new put-down to American English.[46] Some have argued that the innovation of the diversity visa (widely known as the green card lottery) is an initiative directed against Mexican migration.[47] The amnesty proposals of President George W. Bush's first term were directed primarily toward Mexicans.[48] The result of this intertwining is the slippage between "being Mexican" and "being illegal," which both racializes and erases Mexican identity.[49] These facts are sometimes submerged beneath the discourse of illegal migration in the United States, but inform its logic nonetheless.

While initiatives to control movement across the southern border originated in the 1920s, there was a marked shift in the nature and politics of these actions in the

43 Philip J. LaVelle, "Bush Signs Bill to Beef Up Border Security," *San Diego Union-Tribune*, October 5, 2006, p. A7.
44 This history is recounted in Joseph Nevins' *Operation Gatekeeper: The Rise of the 'Illegal Alien' and the Making of the U.S.–Mexico Boundary* (London and New York: Routledge, 2002) and in Mae M. Ngai, *Impossible Subjects: Illegal Aliens and the Making of Modern America* (Princeton, N.J.: Princeton University Press, 2004).
45 Jeffrey S. Passel, "The Size and Characteristics of the Unauthorized Migrant Population in the U.S.: Estimates Based on the March 2005 Current Population Survey" (Research Report, prepared for the Pew Hispanic Center, March 7, 2006).
46 Nevins, *supra* note 44 at 34–35.
47 See for example, Jonathan H. Wardle, "The Strategic Use of Mexico to Restrict South American Access to the Diversity Visa Lottery," (2005) 58 *Vanderbilt Law Review* 1963.
48 Discussed in Chapter 7 at 139–141.
49 Joseph Nevins, note 44 at 36, analyzes the construction of American and Mexican identities around this border and argues that "The 'border' became not only the physical line separating Mexico from the United States, but a social and legal division that empowered U.S. authorities to carry out all sorts of acts under the rubric of the law." See also Mae Ngai *supra* note 44 at 7–9.

1990s, corresponding with the worldwide crackdown on illegal migration and with the increased attention to all facets of globalization. In the early 1990s, the Border Patrol in the El Paso, Texas, sector launched a stepped-up enforcement program called Operation Hold-the-Line. In October 1994, during the first Clinton administration, Attorney General Janet Reno launched Operation Gatekeeper, focusing on the San Diego sector of the border. These campaigns were not unprecedented. The first portions of fence and guard towers had been built in 1952. President Carter had proposed extensive fencing.[50] Operation Gatekeeper, however, brought a shift in the tenor of debate and in the intensification of surveillance. It marks the beginning of the contemporary era of border enforcement – of American response to globalizing forces along the border.

The lead-up to Operation Gatekeeper reads like a primer on the popular discourse of immigration crackdown, with strong elements of economic rhetoric, security concern, and electoral politics. Governor Pete Wilson in California played a key role in pushing the national administration to act decisively against illegal migration into California as the state hit a recession during the early 1990s. During the campaign that brought Bill Clinton to power for his first term, Clinton shifted positions and announced he would agree with the first Bush administration's policy of interdicting Haitians seeking asylum. Clinton's first year in power, 1993, saw both the World Trade Center bombing by suspected unauthorized migrants and the arrival of boats of unauthorized Chinese migrants. Operation Gatekeeper was announced the month before midterm elections.[51] Its principal activities were physical fortification of the border and a pronounced increase in enforcement activities: the INS enforcement budget rose from $400 million in 1993 to $800 million in 1997; the number of Border Patrol agents in this area rose from 3,389 to 7,357 over approximately the same period.[52] In 1994, nineteen miles of the border in the San Diego sector were fenced; by 1999, fifty-two miles were fenced.[53] The activity began in the San Diego sector and gradually moved westward. Although Operation Gatekeeper is strongly linked with the Clinton regime, the heightened enforcement measures it ushered in have remained.[54]

It is impossible to evaluate the policy success of Operation Gatekeeper in terms of limiting clandestine entry across the southern border. Clearly overall numbers of extralegal migrants have continued to rise since 1994, and Mexican nationals are still the greatest proportion of those. Some effects are, however, statistically

50 Nevins, *supra* note 44 at 52 and 72.   51 Nevins, *supra* note 44 at 84–93.
52 Bill Ong Hing, "The Dark Side of Operation Gatekeeper" (2001), 7 *University of California at Davis Journal of International Law and Policy* 121 at 129.
53 Ibid.
54 The name Operation Gatekeeper is no longer being used; however, the enforcement regime launched under this title has been stepped up and subsumed under the name Operation Jump Start.

Table 8.1. *Deaths by sector for years 2002–2005*[55]

Deaths by Sector	2002	2003	2004	2005
McAllen	30	39	41	58
Laredo	15	18	22	49
Del Rio	33	23	18	12
Marfa	1	0	0	4
El Paso	9	10	18	31
Tucson	9	10	18	31
Yuma	11	15	36	51
El Centro	63	67	39	29
San Diego	24	29	15	23
Total	320	349	330	473

demonstrable. First among these is that the death toll along the border has risen markedly since 1994. This is the predictable result of making crossing in the relatively hospitable and well-populated San Diego (and El Paso) districts much more difficult. Deaths are most often reported in sparsely populated desert regions where heat, cold, and dehydration are dangers. In 1994, twenty-three deaths were reported along the California portion of the border. The following year this number jumped to 61, and by 1998 was 147, with a total of 170 for the entire national length of the border.[56] Table 8.1 shows yet further increases in subsequent years. A second discernable effect is a rise in the use and cost of smugglers ("coyotes" is the local vernacular) to assist in this crossing.[57]

Perhaps the overarching conclusion impelled by Operation Gatekeeper is that preventing illegal border crossing is close to impossible, and that coming close to full control requires draconian activities that are difficult for any liberal state to contemplate. The present Bush administration has now raised the possibility of fully fencing the border, but even the high-tech promise of what such a fence might deliver would certainly be matched by advanced technology possessed by intending migrants and the smuggling industry, not to mention air travel. Extralegal border crossing might only be defeated by "unglobalization," including halting cross-border flows and communications of all types. The idea of a fully fenced border is emblematic of the principal disparity of the early twenty-first century,

---

55 These statistics were released by the Border Patrol Offices in Washington, DC, upon request, July 2006.
56 These statistics are reported in Ong Hing, *supra* note 52 at 135–36.
57 Rey Koslowski, "Economic Globalization, Human Smuggling, and Global Governance" in David Kyle and Rey Koslowski, eds., *Global Human Smuggling: Comparative Perspectives* (Baltimore: John Hopkins University Press, 2001) at 349–50; Wayne A. Cornelius, "Controlling 'Unwanted' Immigration: Lessons from the United States, 1993–2004" (2005), 31:4 *Journal of Ethnic and Migration Studies* 775.

much as the Berlin Wall marked the terrain of the Cold War. The fencing of the U.S.–Mexican border also reflects the shift in the "us-them" parameters of exclusion. Although this fence-as-line-drawing still says much about the nation itself, it is directed not only against Mexicans, but also against all from the South. Racialization intertwines with fact resistance here, obscuring individual identity. Furthermore, it does not seek to enclose the nation, only to prevent entry from one side. Where once stood the nation, now there stands the North and prosperity itself. In both a literal and a metaphoric sense, the fence's inevitable failure reflects the paradox suggested by de Sousa Santos – this is a modern solution to a postmodern problem. In a literal sense, globalization's technologies will defeat the fence. Metaphorically, the hermetically sealed nation is the paradigm of modernity; illegal migration is perhaps its most far-reaching challenge. Under global conditions the fence appropriately mirrors the aspiration of a nation that is not sealed, but instead selectively exclusive.

The fence proposal may be a brilliant political compromise: it is soundly critiqued on all fronts.[58] For those who want more border control – and they are many – the fence is not enough. For those opposed to the immigration crackdown, the fence is its most draconian manifestation. In October 2006, Congress approved $34 billion in funding to "secure" U.S. ports and to strengthen border control.[59] The number of border agents is slated to double between 2001 and 2008.[60] The American National Guard has been bolstering border patrol activities since May 2006 while awaiting the training of 6,000 new agents.[61] Even prior to the 2006 announcement, fencing both old-tech and new was being constructed. In short, by comparison with the present, Operation Gatekeeper was a mere beginning.

Despite the massive increase in enforcement along the border, there are those who feel the government is not doing enough, not nearly enough. The U.S.–Mexican border hosts some of globalization's wealthiest civil society groups: border vigilantes. In the early years of the twenty-first century, a number of organized groups have emerged as contemporary vigilantes, seeking to both deter and punish illegal border crossers and to advocate that current government efforts are insufficient.

---

58 The proposal has been criticized by groups as diverse as the union representing border agents, Indians with traditional lands spanning the border, and both Democrats and Republicans. For some examples of these debates, see John Pomfret, "Fence Meets Wall of Skepticism; Critics Doubt a 700-Mile Barrier Would Stem Migrant Tide," *The Washington Post* (October 10, 2006), A03; Philip J. LaVelle "Bush Signs Bill to Beef Up Border Security," *The San Diego Union-Tribune* (October 5, 2006), A7; Susan Milligan, "U.S. Senate Passes Bill to Build Mexican Border Fence," *The Boston Globe* (September 30, 2006), A1; Mimi Hall, "High-tech Plan Pitched to Fight Illegal Crossings," *USA Today* (September 21, 2006), 5A; Randal C. Archibold, "Border Fence Must Skirt Objections From Arizona Tribe," *The New York Times* (September 20, 2006), A24. Scrutiny of the U.S.–Canada border has increased in recent years and the idea of further intensification is sometimes floated in the press. It would be fanciful to suggest, however, that a similar level of concern surrounds America's northern border.
59 Milligan, *supra* note 58.   60 Hall, *supra* note 58.
61 Anthony Spangler, "National Guard Assists Border Patrol; Help Frees Agents to 'Hit the Bush,'" *The Washington Post* (November 12, 2006), A06.

Two of the largest groups, each with branches in several states, are the Minuteman Project and Ranch Rescue. Each of these groups has gained national and international attention.[62] The former was founded in 2004 by ex-marine and journalist Jim Gilchrist. The group conducts what it calls "tours of duty" along the U.S.–Mexican border, but also engages in rallies and other actions at other sites.[63] Ranch Rescue (which does not post its founding date on its web site) focuses, as its name suggests, on excluding people crossing the border from adjacent private land. Its slogan is "Private property first, foremost, and always." Its activities as reported on its web site are limited to border "defense" (including building fencing) and collecting stories of those whose land has been crossed by migrants. Like the Minuteman project, there is a strong personality at the center of Ranch Rescue, Roger Barnett.[64] In June 2007, Ranch Rescue's web site was advertising the opening of a South African chapter. There are a number of other groups that have, if not a robust presence on the border, at least a cyberspace voice. These include defendourborders.com, usaborderalert.com, Arizona Border Watch, and others.

In an analysis of globalization and migration law, the most interesting thing about these groups is their relationship with the globalization script. By categorical definition, vigilantes seek to enforce the law: to outdo the state in its core endeavor. The border groups are no exception. Ranch Rescue's mission statement opens by saying that "Ranch Rescue is a volunteer organization composed of people who believe that when government fails or refuses to act, individual Citizens are obligated to act on their own."[65] The Minuteman project states that it is a "...call to voices seeking a peaceful and respectable resolve to the chaotic neglect by members of our local, state, and federal governments charged with applying U.S. immigration law."[66] Border vigilantes are convinced that the government is neglecting a core duty in failing to prevent all extralegal crossings of the border. This position, of course, directly reflects an understanding of sovereignty with border control at its center. The actions of these groups effectively move that objective from the public to the private sector, or at least signal a collapse of that traditional bifurcation. This transformation, or collapse, aligns itself with events elsewhere in globalization's

---

62 Dan Glaister, "U.S. Border Control: America's Minutemen Build their Own Fence Against Mexican Migrants: Activists Spend $1m on Symbolic Wall to Demand Sealing of the Border," *The Guardian [London]* (January 2, 2007), International Pages 21; Randal C. Archibold, "A Border Watcher Finds Himself Under Scrutiny," *The New York Times* (November 24, 2006), A1; Carolyn Lochhead, "Anti-immigration Caravan Makes it to Washington; Minuteman Project Holds Rally as Senate Ready to Debate Bill," *The San Francisco Chronicle [California]* (May 13, 2006), A3; Michelle Caruso, "Riding Shotgun on Border: Gung-ho Vols Draw Line in Sand to Halt Mex. Tide. Citizens Act as Eyes and Ears of the Border Patrol as Immigrants Take Huge Risks to Reach U.S." *Daily News [New York]* (April 9, 2006), News 22.
63 Details available from www.minutemanproject.com.   64 See www.ranchrescue.com.
65 www.ranchrescue.com/index.htm#missionstatement.
66 www.minutemanproject.com. This statement was available on the web site in September 2006 and May 2007, and is widely cited in other on-line references to the Project. By July 2007, the Minuteman Project web site had been modified.

typology. These include an analysis of globalization that suggests state power is waning, and observations of private actors as emerging power centers, as in the case of transnational corporations, for example. Much analysis of globalization has focused on the emergence of global civil society groups.[67] Typically, a thriving global nongovernmental sector is seen as a counterbalance to the democratic deficit that results from national governments increasingly losing full control over domestic policy sectors. Secondarily, civil society groups often see themselves as a site of resistance to globalization's homogenization effects and potential cultural erasures.[68] The border vigilantes fit neatly into each of these categories, and thus are an important cautionary tale for academic analysis.

Unlike many global civil society groups, border vigilantes generally are not seeking to make alliances at an international level to counter a silencing in domestic policy. They are, however, promoting a clearly articulated agenda without depending on the national government to support their actions. They also bring a particularly American element to the array of civil society groups working in active resistance to globalizing forces. There is a strong argument that the vigilante tradition is particularly American, and California and Texas, key states in the illegal migration dynamic, are longtime bases of vigilantism in the United States.[69] The strength of vigilantism is an American form of resistance to globalization. The importance of illegal migration in the United States makes this form of civil society resistance to global forces a matter for global attention. The border vigilantes have emerged in the early years of the twenty-first century, well after the commencement of a moral panic about illegal migration. While their emergence clearly reflects elements of this moral panic, it is also a harbinger of the failure of democratic politics to contain the migration debate. This is particularly important given that Western liberal democracies have functioned throughout the twentieth century using democratic compromise to contain and shape immigration politics, largely in a successful nation-building mode.[70]

---

67 Ruth Buchanan, "Global Civil Society and Cosmopolitan Legality at the WTO: Perpetual Peace or Perpetual Process?" (2003), 16 *Leiden Journal of International Law* 673; David L. Brown et al., "Globalization NGOs and Multi-Sectoral Relations," The Hauser Center for Nonprofit Organizations and the Kennedy School of Government Harvard University Working Paper No. 1, 2000; Chaime Marcuello Servos and Carmen Marcuello, "NGOs, Corporate Social Responsibility, and Social Accountability: Inditex vs. Clean Clothes," (2007) 17:3 *Development in Practice* 393; Rorden Wilkinson, "Managing Global Civil Society: The WTO's Engagement with NGOs" in Randall D. Germain and Michael Kenny, eds., *The Idea of Global Civil Society: Politics and Ethics in a Globalizing Era* (London and New York: Routledge, 2005) 156; Louise Amoore and Paul Langley, "Global Civil Society and Global Governmentality" in Randall D. Germain and Michael Kenny, eds., *The Idea of Global Civil Society: Politics and Ethics in a Globalizing Era* (London and New York: Routledge, 2005) 137.
68 See Buchanan, ibid. at 684–85.
69 Richard Maxwell Brown, *Strain of Violence: Historical Studies of American Violence and Vigilantism* (New York: Oxford University Press, 1975).
70 I have elaborated this point in *Humanitarianism, Identity, and Nation: Migration Laws of Australia and Canada* (Vancouver: UBC Press, 2005).

In contrast to the flourishing of border vigilantism, in 2006 there was an unprecedented surge in popular support for illegal migrants' rights within the United States.
This took the form of massive public rallies supporting legislation that proposed a
far-reaching amnesty, as well as other entitlements for illegal migrants.[71] The size
and strength of these rallies was a surprise even to those who supported them. This
too signals a shift in the contours of American immigration discourses. Unlike the
positions taken by the vigilante groups, the rallies largely embraced a discourse
of entitlement in the absence of law. Little distinction was made in this discourse
between legal and illegal migrants. In this sense, the tools of these advocates correspond most closely to the diffuse sense of human rights that makes strong rhetoric
but has little traction in courts. In other words, these actions were firmly in the
province of politics, where law is but an instrument. While the temporal proximity
of these events prevents a full evaluation of what they portend, they mark a clear
break with previous discourse, and strike a remarkable distance from the law. They
show at least the potential for a shift in the way illegal migrants are imagined.

These events present a complicated picture. The United States has the largest
confirmed illegal population of any prosperous migrant-receiving Western state.
In the mid-1990s, when Operation Gatekeeper was in its early days, Teitelbaum
and Weiner viewed estimates of 3.5 million illegal residents as an impressive figure
calling for extensive analysis.[72] Since that time, the estimate has at least trebled.
These estimates are, as canvassed in Chapter 2, problematic, and efforts to curtail
illegal migration necessarily make it more visible. Still, the size of this increase
means it cannot be attributed to enforcement effects alone. Over the same period
of time, the significant state power of the globe's uncontested hegemon has been
directed extensively to sealing the southern border, which remains the purported
entry point for most of the illegal population. This growth in the illegal population
of the United States corresponds with the era of globalization, as well as with the
post-Cold War shift in American refugee law.[73] Lawmakers have little appetite these
days for reducing illegal numbers through amnesty provisions, despite recurring
proposals. Illegal migration is a more politicized issue than at any previous point

71 Tim Harper, "Immigration Rallies Sweep U.S.," *The Toronto Star* (April 11, 2006) A04; Sue Anne
    Pressley, Karin Bruilliard, and Ernesto Londono, "Marchers Flood Mall with Passion, Pride; Many
    Take their First Political Step," *The Washington Post* (April 11, 2006) A01; Maura Reynolds and
    Faye Fiore, "The Immigration Debate; Across the U.S., 'We Are America'; Immigrants and their
    Supporters Call for Dignified Treatment and, above all, Legalization. Some Recite the Pledge of
    Allegiance," *Los Angeles Times* (April 11, 2006), A1.
72 Michael S. Teitelbaum and Myron Weiner, eds., *Threatened Peoples, Threatened Borders: World
    Migration and U.S. Policy* (New York and London: W.W. Norton and Company, 1995) at 18.
73 It was largely not until the end of the Cold War that the United States became a full participant
    in the international refugee law regime. American refugee law had earlier been marked strongly
    by Cold War politics, a tendency to see those leaving communist states as refugees and those
    from elsewhere as not-refugees, regardless of individual circumstance, and often in the absence of
    individual inquiries. Here too, the United States is shown to be more interested in politics than in
    law in this realm.

in time, with civil society groups marking out diverse and significant challenges to state authority. On both the government side and the civil society side, the ante has been upped in recent years. This increases rhetoric and tension, but has not decreased illegal migration in any form.

More than any other core sample, the Mexican border demonstrates the failure of modern responses to illegal migration. It also demonstrates increased state emphasis on controlling these movements. Like Europe, the United States has the capacity to define the global through solo action. In this instance, however, the action is repeatedly failing and fracturing politics in its wake. The contemporary moral panic over illegal migration is both global and local. The shifting importance of illegal migration is more than a mere globalized Americanism. Although border vigilantes, the most recent addition to the Mexican border tale, are distinctly American, their emergence intertwines with politics and law elsewhere.

The shadow of the giants

There is much in common in the story of illegal migration and globalization in Europe and the United States. Moral panic about illegal migration is firmly entrenched in both places at present. This panic predates, but fuels, the intertwining of migration law and security politics. In both places, concern about illegal migration has been met by increasing legal crackdown measures. In Europe, this has become the sole focus of the much-touted harmonization of European migration law, and it dominates the agenda for future areas of development. This pattern is mirrored in the United States, where an array of legal initiatives has been proposed, but only the most draconian have passed into law. Two closely related observations arise directly from these similarities. The first is that in the contemporary era, complete control over migration does not appear to be politically possible. The second is that this lack of control cannot be sheeted home to the human rights of migrants. These overlapping points require explanation, which I will address before turning to differences between these two giants of the global era.

At first blush, the idea that borders cannot be hermetically sealed appears preposterous. Assuming infinite resources, fences, walls, guards, and posses, it ought to be possible to close up the United States or Europe as tightly as, say, North Korea or Cuba. Even at this starting point, however, the hurdles begin to multiply. States like North Korea and Cuba are principally closed to those who wish to depart – something truly unthinkable to Western democracies – and are furthermore largely closed to flows of all kinds, including those of capital and currency upon which it is fair to say that the United States and Europe depend for their basic identity as global powers. Even among those opposed to all migration, the aspiration is not simply to close the border but rather to close the border to non-nationals with certain goals. Infinite resources may still make this possible, but at a political and economic cost so high it has not been seriously contemplated anywhere. Globalization provides the explanation for this. nation-states today derive power from their successes in managing and facilitating the global. Power can be measured by comparing the capacity that divergent states have to be actors in the global arena, rather than merely acted upon. Withdrawing from this arena – hermetically sealing borders – would equate with a loss of power and therefore be a greater threat to the nation-state than any amount of illegal migration. This leads to the conclusion that globalization has shifted key markers of state power rather than erasing them.

This shift is one key reason that migration law is such an important marker for this era of globalization. Both globalization and migration have long histories, but the EU and U.S. examples show the newness of their present condition. A key part of this is migration law, in distinction from migration. In early periods of extensive migration, the movement of people was largely unregulated, or was at least not regulated by a full mapping of the globe into closed territories with specific qualifications for entry. The stereotypical migrants of the previously most recent era of intense migration, that which opened up and populated the new settler nations, were poor, hungry, hard-working, and often persecuted at home. Most would not qualify as legal migrants today. They were also predominantly white, or have whitened with the passage of time.[74] The present is the first era of mass migration that has been met by nation-states attempting to use legal means to determine who will participate in that migration.

An impressive number of scholars have argued that states are unable to control migration because of the advance of human rights jurisprudence. This argument is put in its strongest terms by Christian Joppke, who argues that liberal states have lost ground to migrants through the courts. Joppke's version of the argument is the extreme one, and is therefore easier to critique than Jacobson's or Sassen's versions, which I have discussed in Chapter 2. At this point, however, and in relation to the power and politics of Europe and the United States, I want to press the point that the liberal state's inability to close the borders to illegal migrants has much more to do with politics and power than with the law. An impressive array of legal tools have been created and upheld to close borders to those without legal authority to enter. Neither the law itself nor support in the courts is lacking in this regard. Rather, the power that states derive from the global prevents them from comprehensive enforcement of both new and old laws for border sealing. Unauthorized migrants are not admitted on the basis of human rights pleas at the border. Asylum seekers are the only people on the move who can make claims of this nature and as I discussed in Chapter 4, measures to turn away asylum seekers have gained rather than lost momentum recently. Both the United States and the European Union are active participants in the narrowing of asylum options and the reduction of refugee

74 For example, Irish migrants to the United States were once perceived as racially inferior. In a somewhat later time Greek and Italian migrant communities were once perceived as racially distinct from Northern Europeans. All of these groups are now considered "white" for the purposes of analyzing the racial diversity of migration to North America.

rights, but are yet unable to close their borders using the instrument of law backed up, ostensibly, by the coercive power of the state.

Beyond these similarities, there are vital contrasts in the way Europe and the United States are responding to the globalization of illegal migration. These differences can best be read by considering how globalization is transforming the coupling of migration and nation, in which migration law serves as a slate for inscribing national values and identities. In Europe, illegal migration is all about asylum and in the United States it hardly is at all. This distinction links to the historical role of migration in each of these places.

The United States, more than any other, is the paradigmatic "nation of immigration." Immigration has been an overtly articulated nation-building project. The history of racism within American immigration law and policy has been legally obscured in comparison to the trajectories in Canada or Australia.[75] The present green card lottery, and its policy rationale of increasing diversity, stands as a statement of valorization of the traditional immigration mythology. This endures at an ideological level even if we accept the argument that the green card lottery aims in part to deter Mexican immigration. The capacity of the lottery to tap into this traditional ethos shores it up in the face of such critiques.[76] The traditional mythologizing of immigration shapes the present debate. In the United States, drawing a sharp line between legality and illegality of migrant claims facilitates preserving salutary immigration ideology even while sealing borders. This is also, just now, driven by straightforward geographic positioning – there are likely more individuals with plausible asylum claims who can make it to Europe by land than to the United States. For this reason the constraint on sovereignty that refugee law brings is less important in the United States.

In the modern global history of migration, Europe has been a point of departure rather than a place of arrival. It is only in the contemporary, possibly postmodern, era that European states are being transformed into nations of migration. This accounts for the obsession with asylum in moves to crack down on illegal migration in several ways. First, there is the simple story of numbers and geography. Whereas Europe has traditionally been distant from sites of extensive refugee production, this is changing as Europe itself grows and as international travel becomes commonplace. Both of these factors are globalization effects. Second, while statistics present many European nations as sites of significant immigration these days, there is not an underlying mythology of immigration. This means that it is easier to establish public and political discourses that separate immigration concerns from refugee matters. Waves of new arrivals do not need to be rhetorically distinguished, somehow, from earlier waves that now comprise the dominant population. Finally,

---

75 Sean Brawley, *The White Peril: Foreign Relations and Asian Immigration to Australasia and North America 1919–1978* (Sydney: UNSW Press, 1995); T. Alexander Aleinikoff, *Semblances of Sovereignty: The Constitution, the State, and American Citizenship* (Cambridge: Harvard University Press, 2002).
76 See *supra* note 47.

as a beacon of human rights in the global era, Europe is extending a putative welcome mat. The new directives make legal the notion that the refugee is Europe's "other," fitting neatly with a new legal text proclaiming that refugees cannot be European. These impulses converge in the public and political focus on asylum.

Ironically, as Europe struggles toward supranational form, the traditional nation-migration pairing is simply being transported to a new location, the limit of the European Union.[77] This is an innovation of sorts, pointing out that the essential exclusionary logic of "nation" need not be tied to a national form. In the United States, on the other hand, the nation-migration linkage is being significantly challenged. As I discussed in Chapter 2, this challenge calls up a strong discourse of illegal migration, which facilitates exclusion even from within the geographical national border. Both of these movements amount to a geographic shift in the deep line of inclusion and exclusion that is the hallmark of migration law, while at the same time affirming its importance. Exclusion remains vital but it need not be achieved at the national border.

Another marked distinction between the United States and the European Union is their engagement with international law. This is predictable but still informative for the goal of understanding the contours of globalization. Current European developments show Europe reaffirming its place as the center of international law. Despite an international legal landscape that is more global than in any previous era, the charge that international law is Eurocentric and has little capacity to absorb or reflect the interests of nations of the global south is substantiated by current developments pointing to the Europeanization of international refugee law. The United States, by contrast, demonstrates here as elsewhere its diffidence toward international law, especially international human rights law. This diffidence contributes to explaining why asylum has a lesser place in American political debate, as potential for constraining sovereignty derives from the international legal realm. In the United States, the tradition of refugee politics has been more closely aligned with global politics than with international law. While Europe is using international law in a way that marks that law itself as European, the United States is enforcing law in a way that makes international "law and order" particularly American. Both stances engage with law, and are suggestive for analyzing the place of law in globalization. Each core sample shows the limits of law to achieve social transformation and, at the same time, mark the global era as one in which parties from supranational politicians to civil society groups clearly desire law itself, in a purely quantitative sense.

These twinned giants of globalization each demonstrate the recasting of sovereignty as a population control issue. They also demonstrate both the importance and the failure of law to address this dilemma. Chapter 9 takes up these

---

77 This is true in spite of recent policy initiatives that have attempted to differ. For example, efforts by European states to work with sending states with the aim of curtailing illegal immigration and asylum generally.

concerns directly. My analysis of the giants concludes here by situating these core samples within the globalization narrative of Chapter 3.

Mythologies of globalization

A crucial test for migration law as a site of explanations of globalization is its capacity for meaningful insights about contemporary developments in Europe and the United States. In the European case, one can point easily to how migration harmonization matters have come to dominate the collective agenda, and, in turn, how illegal migration overshadows economic migration in this regard. The European case is also a cautionary tale about the vision of a European future for the globe. It is evident that the much-touted spread of human rights norms functions in part through neat borders, aspiring to be closed. Under the modern logic of nation, it is not evident how the emancipatory potential of human rights law could be reached – even rhetorically – without the available device of ultimate exclusion. This is the core value of migration law – that the nonmember can be excluded, on terms set by the members.

In the United States, the principal lesson drawn from illegal migration is that there is an immense and meaningful difference between tolerating a porous border and tolerating an illegal population. Although popular and political discourses in the United States evidence the pattern of other Western democracies in tying control over migration with sovereign power, on-the-ground politics suggest the border is the key site for this contestation.[78] In other words, border control is elevated over the control of an actual illegal population. This draws attention to shades of meaning within the category of illegal migration. This divergence is reflected in the strength of civil society engagement with illegal migration in 2006. In that year, the United States was the site of both unprecedented popular support of rights for migrants regardless of legal status and of intensified vigilantism along the southern border.[79] The irresolution of these contrary movements parallels the irresolution of the dilemma of illegal migration, within a politics, and law, set in the paradigm of modernity. The dilemmas of illegal migration push contemporary democracy to new limits. This contributes to ongoing policy failure and to the inability to creatively conceptualize solutions. The contradictory pressures to treat illegal populations and illegal entrants differently are very real, and the linkages between these two phenomena that make it impossible to address this contradiction coherently are linked to the structures of globalization. That global power is now as dependent on an openness of borders as on a discourse of closure, as evidenced most powerfully in the large illegal population of the globe's uncontested hegemon.

78 See Anna Pratt, *Securing Borders: Detention and Deportation in Canada* (Vancouver: UBC Press, 2005) for a discussion of the border as a discrete geo-political space.
79 A string of protests were touched off early in 2007 when President Bush declined to pardon two border patrol agents, Ignacio Ramos and Jose Campion, convicted in the shooting and wounding of a border smuggler.

The illegal population of the United States has nearly trebled since the end of the Cold War. This population must be understood in global times as a reflection of power rather than a failure of capacity. Only this recognition can pull away from the modern nation-state paradigm that paralyzes law reform.

Returning to the globalization script, the lessons of Europe and the United States clearly engage with the central strands of that story. Responses to illegal migration show how the nation-state preserves its status by adapting to new modes of power, and how the central exclusionary lines of "nation" are reinscribed at new locations both within and beyond geographical borders of the nation. The role of economic discourses and drivers is also highlighted in this story. The stark contrast between legal and illegal migration in Europe is structured along a series of beliefs about economic benefit. In the United States, a massive illegal population is tolerated, possibly even fostered, because of its immense economic contribution, a contribution that is heightened by the disparities of circumstance of the global era. The role of liberal values in the globalization script is emphasized by law and policy choices that despite all evidence to the contrary address illegal migration as a matter of individual choices. This transgression is analyzed and situated as in criminal law, as a matter of personal responsibility. The story is not, however, simply one of Americanization and globalization equating. European and American approaches to illegal migration are converging, in at least some ways, but the contemporary approach is a departure from both the American ideological embrace of migration and European states' self-perception as migrant-sending countries exclusively. This remythologizing of migration corresponds with the change in the structure and politicization of the legal texts of migration explored in Chapters 5, 6, and 7.

The final aspect of the globalization script that I identified was a focus on dilemmas of global governance. The European experience underlines the profound difficulties of attempting to address migration matters at any level other than the national. Cooperation has been slow and difficult, and focuses solely on illegality. In the United States, despite immense public and political concern, policy is being pursued in almost complete isolation from even the closest geographic neighbors. Despite the immense concentration of power, in all senses, in the United States and in Europe – as well as in the possibility of cooperation between the two – illegal migration appears ungovernable in the global era. This is a theme sometimes drawn out in globalization literature. Examples of governance challenges include the massive power of transnational corporations or the development of legal norms completely independent of the state in some aspects of the international commercial sector. Neither of these examples, however, is proceeding so quickly, and so overtly in the face of state efforts to prevent it, as the steady growth of illegal migration.

In both Europe and the United States, despite wide-ranging public opinion suggesting a variety of views are possible, the central conception of national sovereignty determines the realm of the possible – even when this is no longer coterminous with the nation itself. The transformation of sovereignty that is so central to analysis of globalization has implications for the law and its traditional tie to the nation. Reshaping sovereignty speaks directly to the rule of law and to law's emancipatory potential, as well as to preliminary inquiries into what legal concepts will travel well on globalization's terrain. It is to these questions that the concluding chapter turns.

CHAPTER NINE

Sovereignty and the rule of law in global times

In the twenty years since Joseph Carens wrote that birth in a prosperous state is the modern equivalent of feudal privilege, his statement has become truer than ever as it travels through time to the cusp of a postmodern world. This truth comes from the shifting nature of sovereignty under the pressures of globalization, and from the resulting transformation in migration laws that undercuts the individual equality of liberal legalism with a rigid hierarchy of entitlement. This chapter completes my argument about globalization and illegal migration by analyzing these shifts in three concluding movements. The first of these is to look at the picture of sovereignty that emerges in each of the core sampling chapters and to develop from this an analysis of the prospects for migration law reform. The second concluding movement is to consider what the implications of this transformed sovereignty are for the rule of law. The final movement of the chapter is to consider what migration law reveals about the place of law, more broadly, in the narrative of globalization.

Migrating sovereignty

The case that migration law is being transformed into the last bastion of sovereignty is made out in a straightforward way. There is evidence of this transformation in each of the core samples, as well as in the narratives of globalization reviewed in Chapter 3. The broad explanation for this transformation is that as the capacity for national governments to influence policy in many areas is eroded by global forces, control efforts have been concentrated on those areas that remain, ostensibly, within the direct control of national lawmakers. The importance of illegal migration, among all the migratory flows that typify the contemporary era, is linked directly to this control impulse. Illegal migration is key because it contributes to the objective of excluding even when physical borders fail to do so, and because, more than any other migration stream, it highlights states' control agenda – as well as successes and failures in achieving it. It is not novel to find sovereignty transformed. The enduring relevance of the term sovereignty is possible because of its transformative capacities. It is crucial, however, to examine the shape of contemporary transformations and to consider their consequences. This is what the core sampling studies of this book make possible.

The lesson that unites the core samples is that sovereignty is a barrier to far-reaching changes in matters of illegal migration. Sovereignty is part of the problem rather than part of the solution. It contributes to failures of policy, law, and imagination, which overlap and intersect with each other. The account of resilient state sovereignty in the global era, increasingly gaining an upper hand in the cacophony of globalization narrative, is not cause for optimism among migration advocates. Resilient state sovereignty means a reinscription of national identity and national power in matters of migration. Chapter 2's examination of the Migrant Workers' Convention revealed the reciprocal relationship between state sovereignty and migrant illegality. In that setting, sovereignty proved a barrier to creatively extending rights protections to illegal migrants. The process of international human rights drafting, and indeed the underpinnings of international law, mean that states' interests are always at the surface of these documents. In this instance, the state-driven desire to eliminate illegal migration reads like an agenda for the elimination of illegal migrants. Of course, the Convention could, at some future point, be reinterpreted against this logic. Such is the rich potential of the law. Presently, however, the Convention stands as a marker of the difficulty of using law to remedy illegality. The law is deeply implicated in creating illegality. It is at the very edge of law's potential to imagine using law to create "not-law" – a space where people could not be made "illegal."

In the analysis of sovereignty and migration law, the Refugee Convention is the most complex chapter. International refugee law both overtly constrains sovereignty and effectively remedies illegality. As such, its presence casts a shadow over each of the other core samples. This means that international refugee law has a far greater importance than asylum statistics suggest for all aspects of contemporary illegal migration. This point is worth elaborating. In the case of the Migrant Workers' Convention, refugee law is implicated because the protection that refugee status provides is superior to that provided by the Migrant Workers' Convention. Despite the human rights regime ostensibly supported by the new, migrant-tailored law, nothing in the new regime reduces the incentive for vulnerable individuals to seek refugee status. Particularly for people without legal status, refugee law continues to speak more directly to their needs – a cure for illegality and a bar to the physical inscription of sovereign power on their bodies. In the case of human trafficking and smuggling, refugee law is a similar curative. Although it is a poor and partial remedy for human trafficking, the sovereign hurdles to meaningfully addressing trafficking make refugee law the best potential remedy at present. In the case of securitized migration law, refugee law with its sovereign constraint is key to the troublesome fact resistance of the new normal security setting. In the less brave new world, refugee law is a microcosm of both the ways in which discretionary migration provisions have adapted, as well as the ways that migration law has become more law-like. Decision makers have become increasingly interested in the once near-dormant exclusionary powers of refugee law. Refugee law also intertwines with citizenship law as one path to full citizenship because of the tradition in many Western refugee-receiving countries of treating refugee status as a migration provision. Thus a resurgence of citizenship law dovetails precisely with states' desire to restrict the reach of refugee law.

Refugee law is a terrain for observing state resistance to legal limits to sovereignty. Its contemporary contours display how and why human rights are narrowed in pursuit of state goals. Refugee law is also a bridge to a less globalized past, when state responsibility toward refugees was understood in terms of opening borders rather than closing them.[1] The burden-sharing imperative of refugee law casts refugees as the rich (white) man's burden for the twenty-first century. As Tony North, 2006 president of the International Association of Refugee Law Judges, has observed, refugee law is more globalized than any other international law because judges around the globe are engaged in an ongoing daily conversation about the interpretation of its text.[2]

In matters of human trafficking, a strong defense of state sovereignty makes it impossible to craft meaningful remedies. Indeed, the worldwide crackdown on extralegal migration, itself a response to threatened sovereignty, contributes directly to circumstances that allow trafficking markets to flourish. Without strongly defended borders, the dynamics of the problem and potential remedies would shift dramatically. The trafficking setting also draws our attention to the need to shift away from the national scale in search of a remedy. Human trafficking shows us both the limits of law's power and the need to act in the absence of knowledge. Attention to the sublocal register is important for confronting trafficking, but it may not be a level at which the law can function effectively.

In the case of the migration-security matrix, sovereignty is thrown into question by the central logic of liberal states. Sovereign power is the consequence of trading individual freedom for collective safety. While this logic is driving legal developments in this area, it is also vulnerable because borders are less able to function as security screens than in earlier times. The security setting also highlights the sovereign power to act beyond the law when a matter of exceptional politics is at stake. In this setting we see a sharp turn toward rule of law ideology. This turn is linked to the potential for rule of law to become unhinged from the nation, a point I return to in the next section.

The trafficking and security settings make an important, complementary picture of the functioning of migration law. The gendering of these two settings calls this complementarity to our attention: trafficking is about victims and is feminized; security is about "bad guys" and is masculinized. There are vast numbers of people being trafficked across international borders, and comparatively few terrorists making similar journeys, yet the security-migration relationship occupies far more

1 I am grateful to Shauna Labman for this point. She canvasses the importance of this distinction in her LL.M. thesis, "The Invisibles: An Examination of Refugee Resettlement" (UBC Faculty of Law, 2007, unpublished).
2 Remarks delivered at the October 2006 Federal Court of Canada Immigration Law Retreat, Montebello, Quebec.

rhetorical space in contemporary politics. The gendering of this scenario furthers the capacity of migration law to draw clear bright lines of inclusion and exclusion: the kind of lines that are being lost or obscured as nation-states are challenged. Victimization, and its inherent feminization, allows trafficking to be separated from smuggling, and allows Western states to assign blame – outside of themselves – for border breaches and their human rights consequences. Sovereignty itself is strengthened in the migration-security rhetoric, cast as the masculinized protector at precisely the time when borders are revealed as inadequate protections, stripped of their former power. In each instance, closing the border would only alter the contours of the risk or harm, not prevent it, and yet the phenomena are understood largely in migration terms. Both settings thus are an indication of how states seek to assert sovereignty in a migration setting, even though it is transparent that the sovereign objective of sealing the border will not address the crux of either problem.

The pairing of migration law with citizenship law similarly reflects gendered patterns, and how state moves toward exclusion in tandem with globalization's economic values, are certain to affect women more sharply than men. This pairing also reveals how recent innovative transformations in citizenship law are driven by the desire to control migration, particularly illegal migration. That is, the transformation of sovereignty raises the stakes in citizenship law as well. It also shows that even though most people never change their citizenship, the logic of *all* citizenship is closely linked to its marginal category: naturalization. The inability to constrain citizenship to a legal formality offers a segue to the rule of law, to which I return in a moment. Law always contains the seeds of something more than its formal structure.

Before following that trajectory, however, I want to examine what all of this reveals about sovereignty and nation-states at the outset of the twenty-first century. It is evident that sovereignty is a resilient shape shifter and that it is central to national aspirations. It is now appropriate to say sovereignty is not so much a diagnostic characteristic of nation-states but rather an objective of nation-states. In other words, whereas it was previously possible to define sovereignty and then seek out entities that possessed it and label them as states, it is now the case that states "exist" and aspire to sovereignty, achieving it to varying degrees. This transformation in the analytic position of sovereignty accounts for Peter Fitzpatrick's observation that some states are more sovereign than others.[3] This flies in the face of the position that sovereignty used to occupy, and in the face of the formal underpinnings of much of the international legal system – the sovereign equality of states. Although power differentials between states have always been transparent, it is now sovereignty itself that is meted out in varying degrees. This also contributes to explaining the debate over sovereignty in the European Union, marked by a clamoring discussion over whether this new political form has transformed or even abolished sovereignty, or

3 See Peter Fitzpatrick, *Modernism and the Grounds of Law* (Cambridge and New York: Cambridge University Press, 2001), Chapter 4.

whether it has merely moved it. In migration terms, the European Union fractured the mirror of sovereignty along a fault line of legality and illegality, so that illegal migration is more than ever subjected to a traditional assertion of power and legal migration is ignored, thus creating an illusion of happily diminished sovereignty for the privileged.

The hierarchical arrangement of sovereign power is nowhere more evident than in the global politics of migration. The migration laws that "matter" are those of prosperous Western states. This is true for two reasons. The first is that only those states have the capacity to attempt enforcement of their laws. This is achieved partially through state power and partially through geography – there simply are not masses flowing over the borders of Western states in most instances.[4] The second is that prosperous states are the desired migration destinations of the global era. Although illegal migration is a concern around the globe, analysis and policy work concentrate largely on how Western states confront this problem, not on what India and South Africa are doing. Global inequalities are more profound than at previous points in time, and this inequality is embedded within sovereignty itself. McCormick's quip that, like virginity, sovereignty may be lost to mutual benefit, ironically averts us to the possibility that virginity may also be lost in rape or other circumstances of profound power imbalance. The impaired sovereignty of impoverished states attracts as little attention as the sex worker's allegation of rape.

Strong commitment to national sovereignty is a barrier to addressing the myriad dilemmas of illegal migration. It prevents creativity in the political realm. But its power does not stop there. The sovereign state controlling its borders is such a powerful image that it prevents us from imagining a different way of organizing regulation of global migration. As both Europe and the United States illustrate, the centrality of national sovereignty determines the realm of the possible even when this sovereignty is no longer coterminous with the nation itself. A good example of how this constraining influence operates is provided by the United Nation's ad hoc Global Commission on International Migration, which was created in 2003 and reported in 2005. This high-powered and well-resourced group had a mandate to "... provide the framework for the formulation of a coherent, comprehensive, and global response to the issue of international migration."[5] It was financed by twelve governments, two foundations, and the World Bank. It commissioned thirteen thematic studies, eight regional studies, fifty research papers, and drew on the support of forty-eight academic advisors as well as twenty-seven "experts." Ultimately, however, the recommendations of the Commission were deeply disappointing. Not only are they principally exhortatory and incremental, but they are also not

---

4 The number of asylum seekers in Germany in the 1980s were probably such an exceptional "mass." The number of illegal migrants crossing the U.S.–Mexico border is also significant. Both these instances, however, pale in comparison with migration crises of the global South.

5 Global Commission on International Migration, *Migration in an Interconnected World: New Directions for Action: Report of the Global Commission on International Migration* (Switzerland: Global Commission on International Migration, 2005) at vii.

new.[6] New ideas are hard to come by in the realm of migration regulation, and sovereignty is why. Making national sovereign power the centerpiece of migration regulation condemns policy to repetition. Yet the "old" ideas have met with profound policy failure, so proposing more of the same is most likely to lead to deeper and more far-reaching policy failure. We see this most clearly in the realm of security. The rising death toll on the United States–Mexico border cannot be the justification for a bigger fence.

Finding a way to imaginatively confront sovereignty is vital to any far-reaching change in this area, but the hurdle this represents is immense. Fitzpatrick's assertion that sovereignty is a secularized theological concept informs the scale of this task. The need to protect and defend sovereignty, even as we understand it to be shifting and transforming, is an act of faith. An aspiration to overthrow this idea is, accordingly, parallel to the transformation that accompanied the abandonment (perhaps still in train) of a Christian god as the center of Western thought. When we begin a discussion of the appropriate future direction for migration laws with the idea that these laws must first and foremost be fortified to protect and defend the states that make the laws, the options are profoundly limited, and the rights of those without citizenship can never emerge as a first order, or even a second order, consideration.

The opening of the twentieth century brought the achievement of global closure in migration regulation – the globe was by that time firmly and finally divided up into sovereign spaces with a comprehensive system of passports and visas for border crossing. Some discussion of moving migration regulation into the international sphere did occur around this time, but it was thwarted by states interested in asserting exclusive control over migration policy.[7] A century later at the outset of the twenty-first century, the kaleidoscopic network of migration regulation has again shifted so that people themselves have been made illegal. This is a crucial shift, one that is unfolding before our eyes, so close that its full implications are not yet discernable. The illegality of people erases entitlements to human rights by rendering people invisible to the law. To stretch Carens' analogy, this is the contemporary equivalent of civil death. As the global era is increasingly legalistic, invisibility to the law is a profound assignation indeed. A few decades ago, crossing borders in contravention of the law was regarded as a transgression that was not truly criminalized. It has now become a transgression more condemned than criminal acts, removing all rights. This challenges the twentieth-century mythology of migration, and the way that migration and nation have been intertwined over the past century. As a result, it also alters the meaning and import of migration regulation. This shift

---

6 The chapter on "irregular migration," for example, is subtitled "State Sovereignty and Human Security" and its first recommendation is for state and stakeholder debate about the negative consequences of irregular migration and its prevention.
7 Sean Brawley, *The White Peril: Foreign Relations and Asian Immigration to Australasia and North America 1919–1978* (Sydney: UNSW Press, 1995).

points to the relationship between sovereignty and the rule of law, to which I now turn.

Globalizing the rule of law

The transformation of sovereignty that is so central to analysis of globalization affects law's traditional tie to the nation. Reshaping sovereignty speaks directly to the rule of law and to law's emancipatory potential, as well as to inquiries into what legal concepts will travel well on globalization's terrain. It is now possible to see glimpses of how migration law could possibly become "unhinged" – in Santos' terms – from the nation-state. The cases where this is visible are few, but the potential they represent is provocative indeed. Finding such examples in migration law settings and investigating how this relationship plays out there is especially suggestive, as the intertwining of migration law and nation would previously have indicated this to be impossible. In the early years of the twenty-first century, a few cases have appeared amidst the general crackdown in Western liberal democracies that suggest potential new directions.

These cases fit with the pattern that emerged in Chapter 6. In the security setting, in at least some courts, commitment to the rule of law appears to be hardening, providing evidence that the discretionary malleability of migration law is not infinite. Faced with the exceptional politics of the current security climate, law becomes more law-like. This was clearly the case for the House of Lords in the *A* decision and for the New Zealand Supreme Court in *Zaoui*. The American jurisprudence has followed a different trajectory by moving away from the migration law setting. There is still the possibility that it will return to this setting. The 2007 Canadian decision in *Charkaoui* is instructive regarding the turn to the rule of law, and the contrast between this turn and a human-rights-based approach. The Supreme Court of Canada's reasoning rested entirely on the rights provisions of the *Charter of Rights and Freedoms*. Although the result was a partial recognition of rights breaches, the reasoning is limited and the dual possibilities of indefinite detention of foreigners and deportation to torture remain. While there is no difficulty in this decision extending rights protections to all those present, on whatever basis, in Canada, the security of citizens is still the opening line of the reasoning. Rule of law was argued, but it did not resonate with the court.

What is visible in the Chapter 6 cases is what we lawyers would hope for from the rule of law. In the House of Lords and the Supreme Court of New Zealand we see the rule of law at its substantive best. This is an introduction to the tale of the rule of law in global times. However, what is most provocative is further from the securitized setting where we would expect to find rule of law because of the proximity to the core interests of the liberal state. The protean potential of the rule of law, the possibility of a paradigm shift in its meaning for migration law, and for Western law generally, is more apparent in cases where security is in the background.

Three cases from the early years of the twenty-first century illustrate this point. These are undoubtedly not the only cases where we can catch a glimpse of this shift, but it is also true that these glimpses are few and far between.

In 2003, the Australian High Court, and both the Court of Appeal and High Court for England and Wales, required the executive to meet higher standards of procedural fairness in issues concerning refugee claimants. In each case, the respective Court set a standard that left the government with ways of pursuing its objectives in accordance with the ruling, and thus the victories are narrow ones. However, the decisions focus on the fundamental procedural rights associated with the rule of law and counter the traditionally broad discretion left to the executive branch in migration matters. Each decision addresses circumstances situated at the confluence of refugee law and illegal migration.

In *Plaintiff S157/2002 v. Commonwealth of Australia*[8] the Australian High Court read down the comprehensive privative clause, which the government had inserted into the *Migration Act* in 2001.[9] The government had sought to introduce a privative clause as early as 1997 with the objective of reducing the number of judicial review applications from Refugee Review Tribunal decisions to the Federal Court but had been unsuccessful because of opposition in the upper house of the national parliament.[10] Following the 2001 *Tampa* affair,[11] however, the main opposition party decided that as a matter of election strategy it would support the government's migration law agenda, apparently because of strong public support for the government's handling of those events.

Despite its inability to secure passage for a privative clause prior to 2001, the Australian government had introduced a series of other measures to reduce the flow of refugee cases to the courts. Most notably, in the late 1980s detention reviews were curtailed,[12] and in 1997 "breaches of natural justice" and "unreasonableness" were eliminated as acceptable grounds of judicial review in the Federal Court. In each case, challenges to the government's legislation had been rejected by the High Court.[13] Each bit of clever lawyering that widened options for asylum seekers was met by new legislation and its subsequent judicial approval. In short, although refugee litigation had a high profile in Australia for the decade preceding the

---

8 *Plaintiff S157/2002 v. Commonwealth of Australia*, [2003] HCA 2.

9 The clause reads:

   A privative clause decision: (a) is final and conclusive; (b) must not be challenged, appealed against, reviewed, quashed, or called in question in any court; and (c) is not subject to prohibition, mandamus, injunction, declaration or certiorari in any court or on any account. *Migration Legislation Amendment (Judicial Review) Act 2001* (Cth), altering s.474 of the *Migration Act 1958* (*Cth.*).

10 Phillip Ruddock, "Narrowing of Judicial Review in the Migration Context" (1997), 15 *Australian Institute of Administrative Law Forum* 13.

11 Discussed in Chapter 4.   12 Now in *Migration Act, supra* note 9 at s. 183.

13 In *Chu Kheng Lim and Ors v. Minister for Immigration Local Government and Ethic Affairs and Anor* (1992), 176 C.L.R. 1; *Abebe v. The Commonwealth; Re Minister for Immigration and Multicultural Affairs,* [1999] HCA 14, and *Minister for Immigration and Multicultural Affairs v. Eshetu,* [1999] HCA 21.

Tampa, until February 2003 the story that executives receive a high degree of judicial deference in the migration law realm had been unchallenged.

According to Chief Justice Gleeson, the ruling in *S157* turned on " . . . a basic element of the rule of law."[14] The dispute over the interpretation of the privative clause arose against the backdrop of the guarantees provided by section 75(v) of the Constitution of the Commonwealth of Australia that the High Court has an original jurisdiction to issue administrative remedies against the national government. This provision is part of Chapter III of the Constitution, which describes the parameters of judicial power and ensures the separation of powers. While the decision was unanimous, the joint judgment emphasized the importance of the text of the constitution, and referred to section 75(v) as a "textual reinforcement" of the rule of law.[15] In his separate judgment, the Chief Justice gave more direct emphasis to the rule of law. The rule of law, its nature, and its particular location within a "federal compact" are at the core of the decision.[16] The result is a ruling that reinvigorates the difficult jurisprudence of jurisdictional error as central to Australian migration law, and that therefore allowed both sides to claim victory.[17]

What is fascinating in this ruling is the assertion of the rule of law as an inviolable principle into the protracted contestation between the Australian government and the High Court over refugee matters. The decision could have been made without reference to the rule of law, on strictly written constitutional grounds (akin to the *Charkaoui* decision in Canada). Reference to the rule of law evokes something larger, grander, outside the constitution. Alternatively, it revives the notion that Australian constitutionalism has important nonwritten aspects, an idea that had been absent from recent High Court decisions. In either case, it brings the rule of law into the debate and, in contrast to the decisions of the preceding decade it says no, at least partially, to the government. This is important for two reasons. First, because in saying "no" we may yet find a mark of the turning tide. Second, as was evident in Chapters 3 and 6, the rule of law is not a passive standard but a shape shifter of long pedigree. Indeed, already in Justice Callinan's judgment, a discourse of human rights was introduced. In addition, Callinan J. specifically distinguishes "uncontestable human rights" from the concerns wrapped up in rule of law debates at the time of Australian federation, thereby reaching beyond traditional constitutional interpretation.[18] He is the only judge to write in these terms, but in doing so he names some of the public tension that swirls around the decision: what rights can refugees actually claim these days, how do they claim them

---

14 *Supra* note 8 at paragraph 5.
15 Ibid. at para. 103. The joint judgment is authored by Gaudron, McHugh, Gummow, Kirby, and Hayne JJ.
16 Ibid.
17 The court upholds what Australian public lawyers know as the *Hickman* principle, which limits the power of Parliament to oust judicial scrutiny to decisions that are within jurisdiction. The jurisdictional error distinction was abandoned in English courts in *Anisminic Ltd v Foreign Compensation Commission* [1969] 2 AC 147 (HL).
18 *Supra* note 8 at paragraph 118, 116.

and in whose courts. Callinan asserts that access to the courts is a right of "citizens" and emphasizes that "... every nation insists upon the right to determine who may enter the country, who may remain in it, who may become one of its citizens, and who may be liable to deportation."[19] Nonetheless, the context of this decision suggests that such insistence is contested.

The relationship between the rule of law and fundamental human rights that *S157* introduces but tries hard not to address is vital to the dilemmas of migration law under the pressures of globalization. Two English decisions provide a different perspective on how these two elements are related. The Court of Appeal in the case of *Q and Others*[20] upheld the decision of Justice Collins in the High Court[21] that the procedures in place to deny financial support payments to a group of asylum seekers were not fair. The Court of Appeal further found that when an asylum seeker is destitute, denying support would breach that individual's right not to be subject to inhuman or degrading treatment.[22] Before the Court of Appeal, in March 2003, the principal issue was the question of procedural fairness – a core aspect of a rule of law analysis. However, in July 2003, the High Court's decision in the case of *S, D, and T*[23] demonstrated both that the human rights aspect of the issue could well overtake the narrower procedural fairness concerns and that the battle between the executive and the courts on this question is not over.[24]

At issue was a key plank in United Kingdom's legislative crackdown on asylum seekers. In January 2003, section 55 of the *Nationality Immigration and Asylum Act 2002*[25] came into effect, removing the capacity of the Secretary of State to provide support to anyone who does not claim asylum "as soon as reasonably practicable" after arriving in the United Kingdom. The only exception is to allow the Secretary of State to take action necessary to avoid breaching the individual's rights under the European Convention on Human Rights. The accepted objective of the new provision is to ensure that those who are not genuine asylum seekers do not receive assistance and that those who have another source of support do not receive state support. The five test cases that came to court along with *Q* all involved individuals who had sought support within a day or two of arriving and included some rejections containing fairly obvious bureaucratic errors. Although some of the stories had not been believed, Justice Collins clearly pointed out that the applicants' credibility had not been adequately tested nor had they been given

19 Ibid. at paragraphs 111 and 112.
20 *The Queen on the Application of 'Q' & Others v. Secretary State for Home Department*, [2003] EWCA Civ 364 (Court of Appeal, Civil Division).
21 *Q v. Secretary of State for the Home Department* [2003], EWJ No. 718, [2003] EWHC 195 (Admin).
22 European Convention on Human Rights, s 1(3) "No one shall be subjected to torture or to inhuman or degrading treatment or punishment."
23 *The Queen on the Application of S, The Queen on the Application of D, and The Queen on the Application of T v. The Secretary of State for the Home Department* [2003], EWHC 1941 (Admin).
24 An appeal to the Court of Appeal regarding the applicant "T" was successful on the grounds that certain aspects of the test set out by the court in Q had not been met. Overall, however, the Court of Appeal affirmed its position in Q; *R(T) v Secretary of State*, [2004] 7 CCLR 53.
25 *Nationality, Immigration, and Asylum Act* 2002 (U.K.), ch 41 at s 55.

a chance to address the supposed inadequacies of their evidence. The cases of S, D, and T shared the characteristics of good test cases. The evidence regarding S included a statement from a general practitioner that he had lost thirty-one pounds (14 kilograms) since arriving in the United Kingdom and that he was severely underweight and malnourished.

The ruling in Q, like S157, contained something for both sides. Although the asylum seekers were successful in their applications for judicial review, the Court of Appeal ruling set out clear guidelines for how the government could improve its procedural approach to the denial of support and thereby bring its law within the ambit of fairness. Measures required included better signage at airports, additional training for interviewers, opportunities for applicants to address directly areas of their story the decision maker is concerned about, and individualized rather than formulaic questioning. The Court of Appeal also made clear that the degree of destitution required to trigger the European Convention on Human Rights was "lower" than that written into other related statutes and that a "real risk" of this "state of degradation" was not sufficient. Instead, the court indicated that applicants qualifying for the exceptional provision of section 55 would be "verging on" a state of degradation.[26] The requirements for fairness were set stringently by the court because "Section 55(1) is or potentially is of draconian effect...."[27] It is for this reason that the Q decision can be read as emphasizing the rule of law – it states that the government can take avowedly draconian action provided it does so "fairly."

The decision in S, D, and T illustrates, however, the potential slippage contained in this type of narrow rule of law reading of the situation.[28] This later ruling is dominated by the issue of inhuman and degrading treatment. Only one of the three applicants was successful on the fairness argument, despite Justice Kay's conclusion that signage at Heathrow did not meet the Q standards and that at least one of the rejection letters contained a straightforward bureaucratic error. All three applicants, however, were successful on the human rights argument. Justice Kay (like Justice Collins in the original Q decision) traces a jurisprudence of destitution from at least 1803[29] and concluded, echoing the words of Lord Justice Simon Brown, that "No one should be surprised if, within a short period of time, the demands of Article 3 require the relief of damage to human dignity which is caused by '...a life so destitute that...no civilized nation can tolerate it.'"[30] The tenor of this ruling is different, with this appeal to what Justice Collins had called the "law of humanity"

---

26 *Supra* note 20 at paragraph 119. The state of degradation required is drawn from *Pretty v. United Kingdom* (2002), 35 EHRR 1.

27 *Supra* note 20 at paragraph 71.

28 An earlier decision, *R (D and H) v. Secretary of State for the Home Department*, [2003] EWCA Civ 852 had suggested that the matter might be settled, and refused permission to appeal a rejection of a judicial review application on the basis of Q.

29 *R. v. Inhabitants of Eastbourne* (1803) 4 East 103 at paragraph 23.

30 *Supra* note 23 at paragraph 33.

overtaking the questions of the rule of law. The result is a much more significant constraint on governmental action.

The battle between United Kingdom's executive and judiciary over the advance of immigration law crackdown measures has not been as one-sided as that in Australia. For example, in two 1996 decisions, migrants with no legal status were given some legal protections in regard to publicly funded housing.[31] Lord Justice Staughton emotively declared, " . . . an illegal immigrant is not an outlaw, deprived of all benefit and all protection which the law affords."[32] These cases do not, however, raise the same rule of law principles as the 2003 events, nor do they check executive power.[33] The 2003 cases are distinct in that the judiciary attacks a clear executive and legislative expression of intent.

Asylum seekers – as completely nonrights-bearing strangers – have also had some victories prior to the 2003 cases. The decision of the European Court of Human Rights in *D v. The United Kingdom*[34] is the most far-reaching. *D* is based not in a rule of law ideology, but straightforwardly in Article 3 of the European Convention on Human Rights. In *D*, the court held that it would be inhuman to expel an unlawful alien in the terminal stages of AIDS-related illness to a place with no adequate medical treatment, no shelter, and no family support. Importantly, the receiving state itself would not be in breach of Article 3 (were it a signatory), the inhumanity arising instead from the act of return in the particular combination of circumstances. Subsequent United Kingdom courts have been uneasy with the *D* ruling. In *N v. The Secretary of State for the Home Department*,[35] Lord Justice Laws emphasized the "territoriality" principle of the European Convention on Human Rights and characterized the *D* decision as an exception to an exception, based more in compassion than in right.[36] Ms. N, a Ugandan national suffering from AIDS, found no relief in Article 3. In *N*, the rule of law is not invoked. Here again we see that the rule of law itself may well be equally or even more important to positive outcomes for those without domestic legal right than any human rights provision. Second, *N* demonstrates the point that any advancement based on rule of law that *Q* and *S, D, and T* represent is not yet a fully established trend. It is instead a vision on the horizon.

These cases themselves are not enormous victories, providing as they do the capacity to implement draconian measures in accordance with the rule of law.

---

31 *Castelli v. City of Westminster*, [1996] EWJ 4254 (CA); *Akinbolu v. Hackney BC*, [1996] NLOR No 3383 (CA).
32 *Castelli*, ibid. at paragraph 68.
33 Vital in each case was the fact that the applicants had initially had some valid form of permission to remain in the United Kingdom, and that the immigration bureaucracy had not taken any action to remove them. More importantly for the argument I am making here, the rule at stake – that an illegal migrant is not a "person" for the purposes of some provisions of the Housing Act 1985 – is one of judicial rather than executive construction. *R v. Hillingdon London BC ex parte Streeting*, [1980] 1 WLR 1425; *R v. Environment Sec ex parte Tower Hamlets*, [1993] QB 632.
34 (146/1996/767/964)   35 [2003] EWCA Civ 1369.
36 Ibid. at paras. 37 and 38, as well as elsewhere in the judgment.

Nonetheless, *S, D, and T* also says that the state cannot leave people to starve, even when it is convinced they have cheated and lied, that they have evaded the law and that they seek to continue to do so. The clear bright "us-them" line of the border is disturbed here, ever so slightly. The *S, T, and D* decision would not have been possible without the *Q* ruling. That is, a narrowly framed rule of law assertion opened the space for a much broader human rights analysis. While this relies on the European Convention of Human Rights, it also draws on the expansive capacity of the rule of law itself.

A further illustration of this role for the rule of law is seen in a 2006 decision of the High Court for England and Wales.[37] In *Karas*, Justice Munby ruled that detention of a couple who had claimed asylum and been declined was an infringement of the rule of law. Karas and his wife had been in England for many years by the time the government attempted to deport them in October 2004; indeed they had met there in 1999. Karas himself had had an ongoing engagement with the immigration bureaucracy, reporting regularly as required over a period of years. When the decision was made to remove them to Croatia, immigration officials came to their home after dark, at 8:30 P.M., and took them into custody with the aim of putting them on a flight early the next morning. The removal was stalled when the wife made an independent claim for asylum in the middle of the night. Justice Munby concluded that the government's decision making surrounding the detention aimed to ensure that the pair was unable to communicate with their solicitors and would not have access to the courts. He felt that the Secretary of State had declined a straightforward request to provide alternative reasons, and commented on " . . . the surprisingly insouciant manner in which the Secretary of State has chosen to conduct his defense of these claims."[38]

Although arguments were put relying on several enumerated rights, it is the rule of law principles that carry the ruling. Justice Munby cites a series of cases emphasizing that "access to legal advice is one of the fundamental rights enjoyed by every citizen under the common law"[39] and declines to distinguish "citizens" from others in so doing. He concludes that the case reveals " . . . at best an unacceptable disregard by the Home Office of the rule of law, at worst an unacceptable disdain by the Home Office for the rule of law, which is as depressing as it ought to be concerning."[40] This turn of reasoning is not necessary to ground the outcome the Justice is pursing. There is ample precedent in international human rights law to ground the principles of access to legal advice and to courts. Instead this reasoning seems to meet Justice Munby's clear condemnation for the course of action followed by bureaucracy. Thus rule of law expresses condemnation more powerfully than human rights language.

---

37 *Karas & Anor, R (on application of) v. Secretary of State for the Home Department* [2006] EWHC 747 (Admin).
38 Ibid. at para. 53.   39 Ibid. at para. 74.
40 Ibid. at para. 87.

A similar point can be made about the U.S. Court of Appeals for the Seventh Circuit decision in *Zhen Li Iao v. Alberto R. Gonzales*. The court does not use the language of rule of law, but appeals to the same principles. Judicial review is granted because of errors below: "We do not decide that Li is entitled to asylum; that is a decision for the immigration authorities to make. But she is entitled to a rational analysis of the evidence by them".[41] What is remarkable about this case is that Justice Posner, writing for the unanimous court, uses it as an opportunity to comment on "six disturbing features of the handling of this case that bulk large in the immigration cases we are seeing,"[42] and concludes the judgment by stating:

> We do not offer these points in a spirit of criticism. The cases that we see are not a random sample of all asylum cases, and the problems that the cases raise may not be representative. Even if they are representative, given caseload pressures and, what is the other side of that coin, resource constraints, it is possible that nothing better can realistically be expected than what we are seeing in this and like cases. But we are not authorized to affirm unreasoned decisions even when we understand why they are unreasoned.

At one level, these cases illustrate the same point demonstrated by the security-migration matrix in Chapter 6: contemporary pressures on migration law are altering its nature and rendering it more law-like. What is more explicit here, however, is the rule of law functioning with a frame of reference that is not the nation itself. In each of these cases, the rule of law is appealed to in spite of the boundary of the nation. Where a straightforward adherence to Australian national text would have sufficed, rule of law predominates; where human rights text could have done the job, rule of law does it differently. The source of judicial recognition of a space for marginal migrants within the law is embedded within the nature of law itself. This gestures toward the emancipatory potential of law, achieved through the unhinging of law and nation and the potentially robust nature of the rule of law. It is also notable that in each of these cases, access to the courts is linked to an asylum claim, demonstrating the importance of a constraint on sovereignty for prying apart the law and nation boundary.

The unhinging of law and nation is key to shifting the bounds of migration law. In each of these cases, judicial explication of rule of law begins within national frameworks (constitutional text, historical common law) but moves beyond them. While the refugee claimants before these courts could and did make arguments based on the text of the Refugee Convention (and in England on the additional basis of the European Human Rights Convention), these arguments are not won because of international human rights norms or standards. They are won because of something inherent in the law. This is a key distinction because it suggests

---

41 *Zhen Li Iao v. Alberto R. Gonzales* 400 F. 3d 530, U.S. App Lexis 3921 (7th Cir. 2005) at 533.
42 Ibid.

a transformation in legal legitimacy. The claims asserted here do not depend on states' commitments at an international level, nor on law as a defining – in the sense of limiting – feature of the community. They appeal instead to law behaving "as it ought." This speaks to understanding rule of law in its robust sense, as embodying standards of treatment for those who come before it that are distinct from rights claims but that protect individual interests.

A crucial issue for this emerging transition in the rule of law is where to locate its legitimacy. International law norms are justified by states' voluntary commitments to them; domestic state law has diverse legitimation structures, democratic governance the most common for the states under discussion here. Peter Fitzpatrick's account of a shifting authority for international law norms is useful at this juncture. Recalling his argument (see Chapter 3) that international law now appears to be drawing authority from an existent ethical community, a community of law, we may look to such a community as a source of rule of law norms unhinged from the nation itself. The norms articulated in these cases share much with Fitzpatrick's values of equality, freedom, and impartiality. A robust reading of the rule of law, not tied to national limits or national volition, is new terrain for those who would migrate "illegally." Illegal migration, a creature of the law, is always and necessarily a creature of *domestic* law. International legal statements, by contrast, focus on rights to move rather than on restrictions.[43] Rule of law that is not tied to a national frame offers the potential of a source of substantive protection, which has some degree of distance from the structure that creates, recreates, and endlessly reifies the problem of illegal migration. Where might we find the existent ethical community that can make this reach of the rule of law possible? Is it existent or merely on the verge of being conjured into being? The jurists in *S157* and in *Q, and S, D, and T Karas* and possibly even *Zhen Li Iao* are sometimes a part of it. Those for whom their arguments resonate are also part of it. This ethical community is itself a partial, sometimes, creation of globalizing forces. Of the capacity for communication around the globe about how and what the law "ought." The community is of course normative – an ethics cannot be otherwise.

There are two important pitfalls to explore in the idea of unhinging rule of law from nation. The first is to tackle the thorny issue exposed by Boaventura de Sousa Santos. One of globalization's effects is simply more and more legalization of everything everywhere. Chapter 8 showed this plainly: globalization coincides with a desire for law. This is not a liberating trend; its overall tendency is restrictive. If rule of law breaking free of state bounds is no more than an outgrowth of this legalization, it will have no emancipatory potential. The key here is to consider whether rule of law is expanding in its thick or thin iteration. The narrow shelf of rule of law that is contained in the proliferation of law itself is scarcely cause

---

43 See for example Colin Harvey and Robert P. Barnidge Jr., "The Right to Leave One's Own Country under International Law," (Paper prepared for the Global Commission on International Migration, September 2005).

for optimism. Optimism comes only from the persistent inability to separate this narrow version from a more robust reading, and from the appreciation that rule of law is always both versions at the same time. There may be a terrain of contestation over which version will prevail in a given setting, but growth of rule of law, as opposed to simply legal text, has the seeds of emancipatory potential embedded within it. What may become of these seeds is unclear; the cases here show a glimpse of emancipatory change – of the potential to use law against itself, to create spaces where the law can hear the arguments of "illegal" voices.

The other pitfall to explore here is to consider why this is not an argument for and about human rights. The response to this concern is presented throughout the book, but it is worthwhile recapitulating at this point to demonstrate how it fits into the argument about a transformation in the rule of law. Human rights arguments have worked poorly for those without a legal right to be present. It has proven remarkably difficult to separate a legal right to be present within a state from a right to simply "be." Furthermore, rights arguments have tended to trigger rights-based responses from states, drawing on states' sovereign right to exclude non-nationals and to close borders. At one level, a reading of the rule of law that is not hinged solely to the nation offers the potential of altering this disappointing pattern in human rights arguments. This is what happened in the English High Court in the *S, D, and T* decision. At another level, the argument must run that "humans" are well blanketed with human rights entitlements at present. More law written on paper is hardly likely to offer up new solutions. What is required instead is a transformation in the meaning of these commitments, or, alternatively, creative new sources of protection for "humans." The rule of law – at its best – offers both. It may open a space in which human rights for those outside the law could take root.

If the law could be unhinged from nation, even partially, even as a glimpse, what would this import for the transformation of sovereignty? The transformation of migration law into the last bastion of sovereignty reveals sovereignty to be linked to both power and identity. Sovereignty is a mode of exercising power. Even as states shift their sovereign ambitions to border control, this aspiration is revealed to be impossible, or at least impossible to align with the myriad of other ways in which "being a state" is achieved at this historical juncture. Sovereignty is about exclusivity in control. Whereas migration law was initially, a century ago, characterized by extensive domains of unbridled sovereign power, these domains are now being narrowed by the transformation of migration law itself. In short, the most recent change in how states seek to use migration law is generating pressures that make this aspiration harder to achieve. The tension that results raises the question of whether sovereignty itself can be unhinged from nation. As a means of exercising power, this is surely the case. The problem may be that sovereign power could well be increased by doing this, rather than decreased. Law and sovereignty have been intertwined and mutually referencing terms. Although sovereign power is possible without rule of law, rule of law is the legitimating marker of modern,

Western sovereignty. Migration law provides a glimpse here of a movement toward a postmodern alignment. The consequence may well be an increase in concentrations of sovereignty in such a way that while it no longer maps directly to the border of the nation, it remains glued to the logic of inclusion and exclusion that nation epitomized in modern times. This insight reaches well beyond considerations of how illegal migration and globalization are interrelated, pointing us to the broader question of how law itself fits into globalization.

The current state of migration laws indicates that sovereignty has some possibility of being unhinged from nation. This shift in turn can pull law away from its relationship with nation, but such rending could not be painlessly achieved. Thoroughgoing reform of migration laws, in a way that would decenter state sovereignty, appears both politically impossible *and* the only way to achieve changes that respect and protect individuals trapped in the overlapping cycles of illegal migration. If sovereignty, the well-traveled shape shifter, can be moved in this way, rule of law must surely be able to make a similar transition. The problem, however, is that rule of law rests on a legitimation structure, and sovereignty does not. Although democratic liberalism does provide such a structure for sovereign power, it is unnecessary to sustain the concept in tact. This challenge is not so easily met in the case of rule of law. Is rule of law a rich enough idea to exist – constraining excesses of power and meaningfully protecting individuals – as a free-floating concept, neither national nor international? Its emancipatory potential would seem to hinge on the capacity to constitute a meaningful existent and ethical community as a touchstone for globalizing rule of law. This notion is potentially emancipatory, but not certain to be so as the existence of such a community remains optimistic rather than assured. Poised between a modern and postmodern world, it requires us to think of a community as something formed by values of equality, freedom, and impartiality rather than people. This might not be possible. Attempting to address the question of how the rule of law may function in a globalized future pushes us toward the broader question of how law fits into the narrative of globalization – a fitting place to conclude.

Law in global times

I began this book with the assertion that migration law, and in particular the illegalizing of migration, had unique characteristics intertwined with our understandings of globalization that made it a key site for investigating the central claims of globalization theory and for illustrating the place of law in globalization. Each of the core sample chapters engages part of this argument and Chapter 8, looking at the European Union and the United States, tackles the full argument systematically. Here, I take up the more general point that illegal migration shows us key features of globalized law.

Migration law demonstrates that the question of whether and how nations remain relevant is fought out in the texts and politics of migration regulation.

This point, more than any other, is key to each of the core samples. These samples also show that while globalization tends toward being a liberal and economic discourse, it fails to be exclusively so. This is partially because states, collectively, fail in their ambition to control all migration. The increasing illegalization of people migrating is some evidence of this lack of control, even while illegal migration is often explained, or defined, in economic terms. For example, illegal migration is often cast as a matter of supply and demand, to take the most facile case. This presentation of illegal migration shows both the hegemony of economic analysis of the global and the inability of that same analysis to fully explain this increasingly important phenomenon. The failure of human rights law to alleviate dilemmas of illegal migration highlights the limits of globalization's embrace of liberal values. Like the economic analysis, the primacy of a liberal transmission belt loses its explanatory capacity as illegal migration increases.

The dynamics of illegal migration compellingly reveal how fragile and tentative any movement toward global governance is at this point in time. On its face, illegal migration is a quintessentially global issue. Moreover, domestic regulation exemplifies repeated policy failure and lack of innovation. Despite all of this, there have been no serious attempts to regulate migration globally. Instead there is an emphasis on migration as a matter of individual decision making. Such analysis is an apology for domestic policy failure. It turns the analytic gaze toward the local rather than the global sphere. In an area where global governance would seem a logical and untested option, gestures toward it are almost completely absent. This suggests an important conclusion about the nature of globalization. If global governance is developing in a range of areas, but not the policy domain where the core of sovereignty rests, we can conclude that prosperous nation-states are quite successfully resisting globalization, but poor nations are not. Global forces have fractured the fiction of the sovereign equality of states in this setting more comprehensively than in any other, including the realm of global finance and borrowing. This adds a new and more potent dimension to the growth of global inequality that accompanies the global era. It is another of globalization's paradoxes.

One of the insights of the interrelationship between globalization and illegal migration is a reinforcement of the value of William Twining's idea that a first pass test of legal globalization is the extent to which legal concepts "travel well"; in other words, resonate meaningfully in diverse global settings. "Illegal migration" is such a concept. While Chapter 2 demonstrated the difficulty of pinning down a precise definition of illegal migration, there is a coherence to the widespread moral panic in spite of this imprecision. Unlike Twining's example of corruption that passes into incomprehension as we attempt to take it across borders and cultures, illegal migration does not lose its shape. Indeed, over the past two decades of worldwide crackdown measures, the contours of illegal migration are firming rather than fraying. While illegal migration can be analyzed on other planes – social, political, economic – it is at its core a legal concept. Without law, it disappears. Its ability to travel well identifies it as a prototypical case of legal globalization. As such, following

Twining's analysis, it meets the test of generalizability that is central to theorizing law in global, or as Twining prefers, cosmopolitan settings.[44] This indicates that where migration law was recently a marginal category of administrative law, it now engages the key jurisprudential debates of the global era. As such, it commands more scrutiny.

Another important lesson that can be drawn from migration law is that law has its own substance in global terms. It is not a mere tool for achieving particular state, or other actor, objectives, and even when deployed as such, it may be spectacularly ineffective *as law*. This insight is not new for jurisprudes, but has been slow to seep into other analyses of globalization, most of which take place beyond the rarified terrain of legal theory. It is important in situating law in the global sphere to grapple with the distinction between law as a written text and law imbued with law-like characteristics, chief among which is a commitment to the rule of law. This distinction is key to understanding the partial and constrained autonomy of law. As we can just begin to see in questions of illegal migration, rule of law can have its own substance and can therefore pull the law in unanticipated directions. The account of globalization that points to the proliferation of human rights instruments or the growth of a new *lex mercatoria* provides only a starting point for understanding what law means for the global era.

At this starting point, we observe two things. First, the legalization that each of these trends represents shows the global era as typified by law as code, privileging law that mirrors the form of state law, even when the source of such code is located elsewhere than the state. To the extent that law is distinguished from other social ordering by its formality, form matters. This prevalence shows the state form of power extended even as states are challenged. Global law shores up the state in this way even when that is not its explicit objective. A second point drawn from these twinned trends is that the shrinking of the globe is being partially achieved through an elevation of law as a social ordering mechanism. Trust in the law is a global act of faith. Where community differences, or what it was once fashionable to express as "cultural relativism," were formerly posited as a barrier to "global" law this opposition is waning, at least in the areas of human rights and economic law. Law is elevated to the position of that singular system of social ordering that can bridge the gap of cultural differences. Law, in this analysis, becomes the thing that facilitates the global. This elevation is to be distinguished from utilizing law as a mere modus operandi of the global: law not only facilitates transactions but also works to make transactions imaginable.

In earlier eras, large global accumulations of power were united by nonlegal social ordering mechanisms. The Holy Roman Empire or the European colonial era come to mind here. Religious or cultural homogeneity, organic or enforced, were part of the equation. Law certainly assisted colonial empires, but was deeply

---

44 William Twining, "The Province of Jurisprudence Re-examined" in Catherine Dauvergne, ed. *Jurisprudence for an Interconnected Globe* (Aldershot: Ashgate, 2003) 13 at 28–29.

intertwined with cultural value in these settings. The common law carried to the corners of the British Empire, the colonial reach of the French Napoleonic civil code, or the reach of Spanish and Dutch legal systems are suggestive examples.[45] In the cases of human rights law and economic law, law is being asserted as a global unifying force that crosses rather than carries the markers of other ordering systems. This vision of law is troubling. A critique of law's inability to be free of its cultural setting is being developed in discussions of the Western roots of human rights law, or the American underpinnings of economic regulation.[46] This critique is important, and goes to our understanding of globalization as culturally imperial, uneven, and biased. It is equally important to consider that law in action – that is when it functions as law rather than merely as rhetoric – is hermeneutic. Law can be a global ordering system, but its application is ever local. Its meaning is interpreted and reinterpreted, applied and reapplied. Law cannot be deployed in a globalizing era simply to achieve state objectives; it also changes those objectives, and through repeated interpretation reaches into the future in unpredictable ways.

The proliferation of legal text itself does little to increase hermeneutic dilemmas. For this reason, human rights on the books are not truly the complicating factor for state actions in global contexts. Law can appear as a mere instrument when it is observed rather than applied. This provides further evidence of how it is that law is becoming an act of faith. When law is held up in this way, it becomes an object of secular idolatry. We worship at the altar of convention drafting. If people are suffering, so goes the reasoning, we must not yet have made the right laws. Through the wondrous impartiality and replicability of law, we can solve the problems of the globe. In this rendition, law becomes almighty.

This is what Peter Fitzpatrick warned of in his cautionary tale on sovereignty: We are skipping over the step of aspiring to the transcendental and positing instead law itself as the object of worship. It is not worthy. We have forgotten the problems that law cannot solve, and nowhere is this forgetting plainer than in the matrices of illegal migration. Asking that the law do everything risks overlooking its limits, and in such overlooking, failing to charge it with appropriate tasks.

The stock story of globalization both overbloats law beyond its sustainable limits and overlooks its core. Regardless of its area or aims, law is at its substantive best

45 John R. Schmidhauser traces the imperialist reach of the legal systems of conquest and colonization in "Legal Imperialism: Its Enduring Impact on Colonial and Post-Colonial Judicial Systems" (1992), 13:3 *International Political Science Review* 321.
46 Examples include Costas Douzinas, *The End of Human Rights: Critical Legal Thought at the Turn of the Century* (Oxford: Hart Publishing 2000); Peter Fitzpatrick, "Terminal Legality? Human Rights and Critical Being" in Peter Fitzpatrick and Patricia Tuitt, eds., *Critical Beings: Law, Nation, and the Global Subject* (Aldershot: Ashgate Press, 2004) 119; Sundhya Pahuja, "Rights as Regulation: The Integration of Human Rights" in Bronwen Morgan, ed., *The Intersection of Rights and Regulation: New Directions in Sociolegal Scholarship* (Aldershot: Ashgate, 2007); Sundhya Pahuja, "Post-Colonial Approaches to International Economic Law" (2000), *Hague Yearbook of International Law* 123; Dimity Kingsford Smith, "Networks, Norms, and the Nation States: Thoughts on Pluralism and Globalized Securities Regulation" (2003) in Catherine Dauvergne, ed., *Jurisprudence for an Interconnected Globe* (Aldershot: Ashgate, 2003) 93.

when functioning as rule of law. What rule of law may mean in matters of illegal migration was discussed earlier. Here it remains to consider the place of rule of law in fitting law together with globalization. The central question emerging in that earlier discussion was the dilemma of legitimation for rule of law. This dilemma replicates aspects of the debate about globalization and democratic deficit. In that debate, the concern is that while social ordering increasingly occurs at the supranational level, mechanisms for democratic accountability in the global sphere have not grown apace with regulatory capacity. Regarding the rule of law, the question is if rule of law is adapting to extend beyond the borders of the nation, if it is to become a free-floating, global concept, what are its appropriate touchstones? Into this space, Fitzpatrick appears to offer the existent ethical community of the global. This is an enormously attractive proposition. But I am sometimes afraid of where we will find it and how we will know it. Still, it is worth imagining further. Alternatively, the rule of law may find its touchstone in the ways that our understanding of law is emerging in global settings. This is less extravagant, and therefore less eloquent, but need not be fully separated from the ethical community of the global.

What are we in the process of learning that could serve this understanding of the rule of law as well as help us to know a global ethical community of the law? This is an enormous question, but even asking it demonstrates an advance in analysis. Our knowledge thus far may include understanding that many people have a faith in law that is mirrored only by a faith in scientific knowledge. We can work to understand the tenets of this faith. These will include that the law has its own substance, its own logic, which allows it, sometimes, to play against the interests of power. Our knowledge also includes an understanding that law cannot function as law at a solely global level; it is local by its nature.[47] Law can in this sense be global only in its rhetorical mode, where it is closest to being a false idol. This observation is central to private international law with its core questions of jurisdiction, choice of law, and enforceability. Thus globalizing law is an ongoing conversation between global and local that alters both those settings. Refugee lawyers know this better than anyone does, as refugee law's local interpretations interact with meaning in the global sphere on a daily basis. Our knowledge must also comprehend the hegemony of the state form of law, even as pluralism of substance and setting increases. Attuning to state form is vital because it shows us the hard work necessary to achieve the promise of law's emancipatory potential. This knowledge must therefore be used to drive a wedge between law and nation to create a space for interests other than state interests. On those days when I despair of finding the existent ethical community that can both legitimate and emancipate law under global conditions, I console myself with this less ambitious knowledge. By collecting these touchstones we can

---

47 William Twining's evocative analysis of the "clean water" dilemma is a memorable illustration of this point. In "The Province of Jurisprudence Re-examined," *supra* note 44, he discusses the debate that ensued following a commitment to enforce human rights norms for prisoners in a hypothetical impoverished country beginning with the ostensibly easy step of providing clean water for prisoners. The lesson of his parable is the complexity of making law meaningfully local.

accomplish a great deal. And along this path we may yet encounter that better community.

Mindful of this understanding of law and the rule of law, we can return to the question of illegal migration. The opening of the twenty-first century is marked by a widespread, indeed growing, acceptance that people themselves can be "illegal." This contemporary commonplace ought to be a linguistic perversity. As sovereignty is the uncontested barrier to meaningful, far-reaching reform in this area, efforts to think beyond it, and without it, are vital. Only when this thinking is beginning to take shape can law-reform initiatives be built from it. Such fledgling reform efforts could alternately feed on and bolster the emerging paradigm shift of the rule of law. This task is, at present, at the very limits of the collective imagination of Western states and Western advocates, and even of my own imagination. Nevertheless, it is clear that decentering sovereignty is the only way forward. The constraint of refugee law has opened space for transformation of the rule of law. Changes elsewhere would reduce the immense pressure on refugee law to contain and remedy all illegal migration. In citizenship law, sovereignty could be decentered by conceptualizing citizenship as belonging to individuals, not a pure creation of the state to bestow or withhold. The new horizon of deterritorialization could be radically expanded in this way. In matters of human trafficking, reform would start from holding states responsible for the trafficking markets they foster, rather than for prosecutions. The remedy of permanent status for victims must be taken seriously as one way of achieving this. In the security frame, we must abandon the legal fiction that our borders are what is protecting us. This fiction, and the fact resistance that sustains it politically, foster harmful legal postures without increasing safety. The potential of thinking differently about illegal migration is breathtaking, even if its theoretical supports remain shaky. Nothing that we are currently doing about illegal migration holds much potential for serious change. A leap beyond what we can currently imagine is not only a risk worth taking, it is the only way forward from here.

Bibliography

STATUTES AND INTERNATIONAL LEGAL MATERIALS

Agreement Between the Government of Canada and the Government of the United States of America for Cooperation in the Examination of Refugee Status Claims from Nationals of Third Countries (Safe Third Country Agreement), United States and Canada, December 5, 2002 (entered into force December 29, 2004).

Anti-Terrorism Act, S.C. 2001, c. 41.

Anti-terrorism, Crime, and Security Act 2001 (U.K.), 2001, c. 24, s. 21.

Australian Citizenship Act 1948 (Cth.).

Australian Citizenship Act 2007 (Cth. No. 20 of 2007).

Australian Citizenship Amendment (Citizenship Testing) Act 2007 (Cth. No. 142 of 2007).

Benelux Customs Union Agreement, Belgium, Netherlands, and Luxembourg, September 1944 [entered into force in 1947].

Bill C-18, *The Citizenship of Canada Act*, 2nd Sess., 37th Parl., 2002 (Second Reading November 8, 2002).

"Bossi-Fini" Law, (Italy), no. 189 of July 30, 2002.

Canada Border Services Agency Act, S.C. 2005, c. 38.

Communication from the Commission to the Council, the European Parliament, the European Economic and Social Committee of the Regions June 4, 2004 – *Study on the Links Between Legal and Illegal Migration* [COM (2004) 412 final].

Constitution of Ireland, 1937.

Convention Against Transnational Organized Crime, GA Res. 217(I), UN GAOR, 55th Sess., Supp. No. 49, UN Doc. A/RES/55/25 (2000) 44.

Convention for the Protection of Human Rights and Fundamental Freedoms, November 4, 1950, 213 U.N.T.S. 221, Eur. T.S. 5.

Convention for the Suppression of the Traffic in Persons and the Exploitation of the Prostitution of Others, December 2, 1949, 96 U.N.T.S, 271.

Convention on the Elimination of All Forms of Discrimination Against Women, March 1, 1980, 1249 U.N.T.S. 13 (entered into force September 3, 1981).

Convention Relating to the Status of Refugees, July 28, 1951, 189 U.N.T.S. 150 (entered into force April 22, 1954).

EC, *Act concerning the conditions of accession of the Czech Republic, the Republic of Estonia, the Republic of Cyprus, the Republic of Latvia, the Republic of Lithuania, the Republic of Hungary, the Republic of Malta, the Republic of Poland, the Republic of Slovenia and the Slovak Republic and the adjustments to the Treaties on which the European Union is founded*, [2003] O.J.L. 46/33.

EC, *Agreement Between the Governments of the States of the Benelux Economic Union, the Federal Republic of Germany and the French Republic on the gradual abolition of checks at their common borders*, [2000] O.J.L. 239/13.

EC, *Convention from June 19, 1990, Implementing the Schengen Agreement of June 14, 1985, between the Government of the States of the Benelux Economic Union, the Federal Republic of Germany and the French Republic on the gradual abolition of checks at their common borders*, [2000] O.J.L. 239/19.

EC, *Council and Commission Action Plan of December 3, 1998, on How Best to Implement the Provisions of the Treaty of Amsterdam on the Creation of an Area of Freedom, Security and Justice* [1999] O.J.C. 19/1.

EC, *Council Decision 2002/772 Euratom of June 25 and September 23, 2002, amending the Act concerning the election of the representatives of the European parliament by direct universal suffrage, annexed to Decision 76/787/ECSC*, [2002] O.J.L. 283/01.

EC, *Council Directive 93/109 of December 6, 1993, laying down detailed arrangements for the exercise of the right to vote and stand as a candidate in elections to the European Parliament for citizens of the Union residing in a Member State of which they are not nationals*, [1993] O.J.L. 329/34.

EC, *Council Directive 96/30 of May 13, 1996, amending Directive 94/80 laying down detailed arrangements for the exercise of the right to vote and to stand as a candidate in municipal elections by citizens of the Union residing in a Member State of which they are not nationals*, [1996] O.J. L. 122/14.

EC, *Council Directive of 2004/38 of the European Parliament and of the Council of April 29, 2004, on the right of citizens of the Union and their family members to move and reside freely within the territory of the Member States amending Regulation (EEC) No. 1612/68 and repealing Directives 64/221/EEC, 68/360/EEC, 72/194/EEC, 73/148/EEC, 75/34/EEC, 75/35/EEC, 90/364/EEC and 93/96/EEC*, [2004] O.J.L. 158/77.

EC, *Council Directive 2004/83/EC of April 29, 2004, on Minimum Standards for the Qualification and Status of third country nationals or stateless persons as refugees or persons who otherwise need international protection and the content of the protection is granted*, [2004] O.J.L. 304/12.

EC, *Council Directive 2005/85/EC of December 1, 2005, on Minimum Standards on Procedures in Member States for Granting and Withdrawing Refugee Status*, [2005] O.J.L. 326/13.

EC, *Council recommendation of December 22, 1995, on harmonizing means of combating illegal immigration and illegal employment and improving the relevant means of control*, [1996] O.J.L. C/005.

EC, *The Hague Programme: Strengthening Freedom, Security, and Justice in the European Union*, [2005] O.J.L. 53/01.

EC, *Final Act to the Treaty of Accession to the European Union 2003*, [2003] O.J.L. 46/957.

EC, *Treaty Establishing a Constitution for Europe*, [2004] O.J.C. 310/01.

Gangmaster Licensing Act 2004 (U.K.), 2004, c. 11.

Human Rights Act (U.K.), 1998, c. 42.

Immigration Act 1987 NZ 074 (commenced April 21, 1987).

Immigration and Naturalization Act, 8 U.S.C.

Immigration and Refugee Protection Act, S.C. 2001, c. 27.

Immigration and Refugee Protection Regulations S.O.R./ 2002–227.

Immigration Regulations 1978, S.O.R. / 78–172.

International Agreement for the Suppression of the White Slave Traffic, May 18, 1904, 35 Stat. 1979, 1 L.N.T.S. 83.

International Convention on the Protection of the Rights of all Migrant Workers and Members of their Families, GA Res. 45/158, UN GAOR, 45th Sess., Supp. No. 49A, UN Doc. A/45/49 (1990) 261 (entered into force July 1, 2003).

International Covenant on Civil and Political Rights, December 19, 1966, 999 U.N.T.S. 171; Can. T.S. 1976 No. 47, 6 I.L.M. 368 (entered into force March 23, 1976).

India, *Citizenship Act of 1955*.

Migration Act 1958 (Cth).

Migration Amendment (Excision from Migration Zone) Act 2001 (Cth).

Migration Amendment Regulations 2005 (No. 6) (Cth.).

Migration Legislation Amendment Act (No.1) 2001 (Cth.).

Migration Legislation Amendment Act (No. 6) 2001 (Cth.).

Nationality, Immigration, and Asylum Act 2002 (U.K.), 2002, c. 41.

The North American Free Trade Agreement Between the Government of Canada, the Government of Mexico, and the Government of the United States, December 17, 1992, Can. T.S. 1994 No. 2, 32 I.L.M. 289 (entered into force January 1, 1994).

OAS, Colloquium on the International Protection of Refugees in Central America, Mexico, and Panama in Cartagena de Indias, Colombia, *Cartagena Declaration on Refugees*, OR OEA/Ser.L/V/II.66, doc. 10, rev. 1, pp. 190–3 (November 22, 1984).

Organization of African Unity: Convention on the Specific Aspects of Refugee Problems in Africa, September 10, 1969, 1001 U.N.T.S. 45 (entered into force: June 20, 1974).

Protocol Against the Smuggling of Migrants by Land, Sea, and Air, Supplementing the United Nations Convention against Transnational Organized Crime, GA Res. 55/25(III), UN GAOR, 55th Sess., Supp. No. 49, UN Doc. A/45/49 (2001) 65 (entered into force January 28, 2004).

Protocol to Prevent, Suppress, and Punish Trafficking in Persons, Especially Women and Children, Supplementing the United Nations Convention against Transnational Organized Crime, GA Res. 25(II), UN GAOR, 55th Sess., Supp. No. 49, UN Doc. A/45/49 (2001) 60 (entered into force December 25, 2003).

Protocol Relating to the Status of Refugees, December 16, 1966, 606 U.N.T.S. 267 (entered into force October 4, 1967).

Provisions governing the right to vote of Italian citizens abroad, Law 459 of December 27, 2001, Official Journal No. 4 of January 5, 2002.

Trafficking Victims Protection Reauthorization Act of 2003, Pub. L. No. 108–193, 117 Stat. 2875 (2003).

Treaty Establishing the European Economic Community, March 25, 1957, 298 U.N.T.S. 11 (Treaty of Rome).

Treaty Instituting the European Coal and Steel Community, April 18, 1951, 261 U.N.T.S. 140 (Treaty of Paris).

Treaty of Amsterdam amending the Treaty on European Union, the Treaties establishing the European Communities, and certain related acts, [1997] O.J.C. 340/1.

Treaty on European Union (Maastricht), February 7, 1992, O.J. 1992 No. 191/1, 31 I.L.M. 247.

Treaty of Lisbon amending the Treaty on European Union and the Treaty establishing the European Community, CIG 14/07.

Uniting and Strengthening America by Providing Appropriate Tools Required to Intercept and Obstruct Terrorism Act of 2001, Pub. L. No. 107–56, 115 Stat. 272.

Universal Declaration of Human Rights, GA Res. 217 (III), UN GAOR, 3d Sess., Supp. No. 13, UN Doc. A/810 (1948).

Victims of Trafficking and Violence Protection Act, Pub. L. No. 106–386, 114 Stat. 1464 (2000) (codified at 22 U.S.C. § 7101).

Vienna Convention on the Law of Treaties, May 23, 1969, 1155 U.N.T.S. 331 (entered into force January 27, 1980).

JURISPRUDENCE

A v. Secretary of State for the Home Department (2004), [2005] 2 A.C. 68 (H.L.).

Abebe v. The Commonwealth; Re Minister for Immigration and Multicultural Affairs, [1999] HCA 14.

Akinbolu v. Hackney BC, [1996] NLOR No 3383 (CA).

Almrei v. Canada (Minister of Citizenship and Immigration), [2005] 3 F.C.R. 142 (C.A.).

Anisminic Ltd v. Foreign Compensation Commission, [1969] 2 AC 147 (HL).

Bouianova v. Canada (Minister of Employment and Immigration), [1993] F.C.J. No. 576.

Canada (Attorney General) v. Ward, [1993] 2 S.C.R. 689, 103 D.L.R. (4th) 1.

Canada (Minister of Employment and Immigration) v. Chiarelli, [1992] 1 S.C.R. 711.

Canadian Council for Refugees et. Al. v. Her Majesty the Queen 2007 FC 1262.

Castelli v. City of Westminster, [1996] EWJ 4254 (CA).

Chahal v. United Kingdom (1996), V Eur. Ct. H.R. Rep. Judgments & Dec. 1831, 23 E.H.R.R. 413.

Charkaoui (Re), [2005] 2 F.C.R. 299 (C.A.).

Charkaoui v. Canada (Citizenship and Immigration), 2007 SCC 9, [2007] 1 S.C.R. 350.

Chen and Zhu v. Secretary of State for the Home Department, C-200/02, [2004] E.C.R. I-9925.

Chu Kheng Lim and Ors v. Minister for Immigration Local Government and Ethnic Affairs and Anor (1992), 176 C.L.R. 1 (High Court of Australia).

Clark v. Martinez 125 S.Ct. 716 (2005).

D v. The United Kingdom, (146/1996/767/964).

Hamdan v. Rumsfeld 125 S. Ct. 2749 (2006).

Hamdi v. Rumsfeld, 542 U.S. 507 (2004).

Harkat (Re) (2005), 340 N.R. 286, 2005 FCA 285.

Hoffman Plastic Compounds v. National Labor Relations Board 535 U.S. 137 (2002).

Jaballah v. Canada (Minister of Citizenship and Immigration), 2004 FC 299.

Karas & Anor, R (on application of) v. Secretary of State for the Home Department [2006] EWHC 747 (Admin).

Katkova v. Canada, [1997] F.C.J. No. 29.

Khadr v. Canada (Attorney General), 2006 FC 727, [2006] 142 C.R.R. (2d) 116, 268 D.L.R. (4th) 303.

Kioa v. West (1985), 150 C.L.R. 550 (H.C.A.).

Minister for Immigration and Multicultural Affairs v. Eshetu, [1999] HCA 21.

Legal Consequences of the Construction of a Wall in the Occupied Palestinian Territory, Advisory Opinion, I.C.J. Reports 2004, p. 136.

N v. the Secretary of State for the Home Department, [2003] EWCA Civ 1369.

Nottebohm Case (Lichtenstein v. Guatemala) (Second Phase), [1955] I.C.J. Rep. 4.

Padilla v. Hanft, 423 F.3d 386 (4th Cir. 2005).

Plaintiff S157/2002 v. Commonwealth of Australia, [2003] H.C.A. 2, 211 C.L.R. 476.

Pretty v. United Kingdom (2002), 35 EHRR 1.

'Q' & Others v. Secretary State for Home Department, [2003] EWHC 195, [2003] EWJ No. 718, (Admin).

The Queen on the Application of 'Q' & Others v. Secretary State for Home Department [2003], EWCA Civ 364.

The Queen on the Application of S, The Queen on the Application of D, and the Queen on the Application of T v. The Secretary of State for the Home Department [2003] EWHC 1941, 100(36) L.S.G. 39 (Admin).

R(T) v Secretary of State [2004] 7 CCLR 53 (C.A.).

R v. Environment Sec ex parte Tower Hamlets, [1993] QB 632.

R v. Hillingdon London BC ex parte Streeting, [1980] 1 WLR 1425.

R. v. Inhabitants of Eastbourne (1803) 4 East 103. 102 E.R. 769.

R v. Governor of Durham Prison, ex parte Hardial Singh, [1984] 1 W.L.R. 704 (Q.B.).

R (D and H) v. Secretary of State for the Home Department, [2003] EWCA Civ 852.

Rasul v. Bush, 542 US 466 (2004).

Reference re Secession of Quebec, [1998] 2 S.C.R. 217.

Ruddock v. Vardalis, [2001] FCA 1329, 110 FCR 491.

Sharma v. Hindu Temple & Others (1990) EAT/253/90.

Suresh v. Canada (Minister of Citizenship and Immigration), 2002 SCC 1, [2002] 1 S.C.R. 3, 208 D.L.R. (4th) 1.

Tan Te Lam v. Superintendent of Tai A Chau Detention Center (1996), [1997] A.C. 97.

Victorian Council for Civil Liberties Incorporated v. Minister for Immigration and Multicultural Affairs, [2001] FCA 1297, 110 FCR 452.

Zaoui v. The Attorney-General and Ors (2004), [2005] 1 N.Z.L.R. 577 (S.C.).

Zhen Li Iao v. Alberto R. Gonzales, 400 F. 3d 530, U.S. App Lexis 3921 (7th Cir. 2005).

SECONDARY MATERIALS

Abramson, Kara. "Beyond Consent, Toward Safeguarding Human Rights: Implementing the United Nations Trafficking Protocol" (2003), 44 *Harvard International Law Journal* 473.

Agamben, Giorgio. *Homo Sacer: Sovereign Power and Bare Life*, trans. by Daniel Heller-Roazen (Stanford: Stanford University Press, 1995).

Aleinikoff, T. Alexander. *Semblances of Sovereignty: The Constitution, the State, and American Citizenship* (Cambridge: Harvard University Press, 2002).

Amoore, Louise, and Paul Langley. "Global Civil Society and Global Governmentality" in Randall D. Germain and Michael Kenny, eds., *The Idea of Global Civil Society: Politics and Ethics in a Globalizing Era* (London and New York: Routledge, 2005) 137.

Anderson, Benedict. *Imagined Communities: Reflections on the Origin and Spread of Nationalism*, rev. ed. (London and New York: Verso, 1991).

Askola, Heli. "Violence Against Women, Trafficking, and Migration in the European Union" (2007), 13:2 *European Law Journal* 204.

Australia, Department of Immigration and Multicultural Affairs, *Population Flows: Immigration Aspects 2004–2005 Edition* (Commonwealth of Australia, 2006).

Australia, Department of Immigration and Multicultural Affairs, *Population Flows: Immigration Aspects 2005–2006 Edition* (Commonwealth of Australia, 2007), online: Australian Government, Department of Immigration and Citizenship: Publications, Research and Statistics, http://www.immi.gov.au/media/publications/statistics/popflows2005-6/index.htm.

Barber, Benjamin. *Jihad vs. McWorld* (New York: Times Books, 1995).

Benhabib, Seyla. *The Claims of Culture: Equality and Diversity in the Global Era* (Princeton: Princeton University Press, 2002).

Berman, Harold J. "The Western Legal Tradition in a Millennial Perspective: Past and Future" (2000) 60 *Louisiana Law Review* 739.

Bigo, Didier. *Polices en réseaux: l'expérience européenne* (Paris: Presses de la Fondation Nationale des Sciences Politiques, 1996).

Blay, Sam, and Andreas Zimmermann. "Recent Changes in German Refugee Law: A Critical Assessment" (1994), 88:2 *American Journal of International Law* 361.

Bond, Patrick. "Top Down or Bottom Up? A Reply" in David Held et al., eds., *Debating Globlization* (Cambridge: Polity Press, 2005).

Bosniak, Linda. "Citizenship Denationalized" (2000), 7 *Indiana Journal of Global Law Studies* 447.

Brawley, Sean. *The White Peril: Foreign Relations and Asian Immigration to Australasia and North America 1919–1978* (Sydney: UNSW Press, 1995).

Brouwer, Evelien. "Immigration, Asylum, and Terrorism: A Changing Dynamic Legal and Practical Developments in the EU in Response to the Terrorist Attacks of 11.09" (2003) 4 *European Journal of Migration and Law* 399.

Brown, David L. et al. "Globalization NGOs and Multi-Sectoral Relations," The Hauser Center for Nonprofit Organizations and the Kennedy School of Government Harvard University Working Paper No.1, 2000.

Brown, Richard Maxwell. *Strain of Violence: Historical Studies of American Violence and Vigilantism* (New York: Oxford University Press, 1975).

Brownlie, Ian. *Principles of Public International Law* (Oxford and New York: Oxford University Press, 2003).

Brubaker, William Rogers. "Introduction" in William R. Brubaker, ed., *Immigration and the Politics of Citizenship in Europe and North America* (Lanham: University Press of America, 1989).

_____. *Citizenship and Nationhood in France and Germany* (Cambridge, Mass.: Harvard University Press, 1992).

_____. *Nationalism Reframed: Nationhood and the National Question in the New Europe* (Cambridge: Cambridge University Press, 1996).

Brysk, Alison, and Gershon Shafir eds. *People Out of Place: Globalization, Human Rights, and the Citizenship Gap* (New York: Routledge, 2004).

Buchanan, Ruth. "Global Civil Society and Cosmopolitan Legality at the WTO: Perpetual Peace or Perpetual Process?" (2003) 16 *Leiden Journal of International Law* 673.

Buchanan, Ruth, and Rebecca Johnston. "The 'Unforgiven' Sources of International Law: Nation-building, Violence and Gender in the West(ern)" in Doris Buss and Ambreena Maji, eds., *International Law: Modern Feminist Approaches* (Oxford: Hart Publishing, 2005).

Buzan, Barry, Ole Waever, and Jaap de Wilde. *Security: A New Framework for Analysis* (London: Boulder, 1998).

Carens, Joseph. "Aliens and Citizens: The Case for Open Borders" (1987), 49 *The Review of Politics* 251.

_____. "Open Borders and Liberal Limits" (2000), 34 *International Migration Review* 636.

_____. "Refugees and the Limits of Obligation" (1992), 6 *Public Affairs Quarterly* 31.

_____. "Who Belongs? Theoretical and Legal Questions About Birthright Citizenship in the United States" (1987) 37 U.T. Fac. L. Rev. 413.

Chirinos, Alexandra. "Finding The Balance Between Liberty and Security: The Lords' Decision on Britain's Anti-Terrorism Act" (2005), 18 *Harvard Human Rights Journal* 265.

Citizenship and Immigration Canada. *Facts and Figures: Immigration Overview: Permanent and Temporary Residents 2004* (Ottawa: Minister of Public Works and Government Services Canada, 2005).

Clarke, Desmond M. "Nationalism, The Irish Constitution, and Multicultural Citizenship" (2000), 51.1 *Northern Ireland Legal Quarterly* 100.

Commission of Inquiry into the Actions of Canadian Officials in Relation to Maher Arar. *Report of the Events Relating to Maher Arar: Analysis and Recommendations* (Ottawa: Public Works and Government Services Canada, 2006).

Cornelius, Wayne A. "Controlling 'Unwanted' Immigration: Lessons from the United States, 1993–2004" (2005), 31:4 *Journal of Ethnic and Migration Studies* 775.

Crock, Mary. "In the Wake of the *Tampa*: Conflicting Visions of International Refugee Law in the Management of Refugee Flows" (2003), 12 *Pacific Rim Law and Policy Journal* 49.

Crock, Mary, and Ben Saul. *Future Seekers: Refugee and the Law in Australia* (Sydney: Federation Press, 2002).

Cronin, Kathryn. "A Culture of Control: An Overview of Immigration Policy-Making" in James Jupp and Marie Kabala, eds., *The Politics of Australian Immigration* (Canberra: Australian Government Publishing Service, 1993).

Currie, John. *Public International Law* (Toronto: Irwin Law, 2001).

Dauvergne, Catherine. "Beyond Justice: The Consequences of Liberalism for Immigration Law" (1997), 10 *Canadian Journal of Law and Jurisprudence* 323.

_____. "Amorality and Humanitarianism in Immigration Law" (1999), 37 *Osgoode Hall Law Journal* 597.

_____. "Citizenship, Migration Laws, and Women: Gendering Permanent Residency Statistics" (2000), 24 *Melbourne U.L. Rev.* 280.

_____. "The Dilemma of Rights Discourses for Refugees" (2000), 23 *University of New South Wales Law Journal* 56.

_____. "New Directions for Jurisprudence" in Catherine Dauvergne, ed., *Jurisprudence for an Interconnected Globe* (Aldershot: Ashgate Press, 2003).

_____. "Making People Illegal" in Peter Fitzpatrick and Patricia Tuitt, eds., *Critical Beings: Law, Nation, and the Global Subject* (Aldershot: Ashgate Press, 2004).

_____. "Refugee Law and the Measure of Globalization" (2005), 22:2 *Law in Context* 62.

_____. "Sovereignty, Migration, and the Rule of Law in Global Times" (2004), 67 *Modern Law Review* 588.

_____. *Humanitarianism, Identity, and Nation: Migration Laws of Australia and Canada* (Toronto and Vancouver: UBC Press, 2005).

_____, Leonora Angeles, and Agnes Huang, *Gendering Canada's Refugee Process* (Ottawa: Status of Women Canada, 2006).

Dauvergne, Peter. "Globalization and the Environment' in John Ravenhill, ed., *Global Political Economy* (Oxford: Oxford University Press, 2005) 370.

Davis, Michael C. "Human Rights and the War in Iraq" (2005), 4 *Journal of Human Rights* 37.

Della Porta, Donatella. "The Social Bases of the Global Justice Movement: Some Theoretical Reflections and Empirical Evidence from the First European Social Forum," United Nations Research Institute for Social Development, Civil Society and Social Movements Programme Paper Number 21, December 2005.

Demleitner, Nora V. "The Law at a Crossroads: The Construction of Migrant Women Trafficked into Prostitution" in David Kyle and Rey Koslowski, eds., *Global Human Smuggling: Comparative Perspectives* (Baltimore: John Hopkins University Press, 2001).

Department of Immigration Multicultural and Indigenous Affairs (2003), *Annual Report 2002–03.*

Douzinas, Costas. *The End of Human Rights: Critical Legal Thought at the Turn of the Century* (Oxford: Hart Publishing 2000).

Dummett, Ann, and Andrew Nicol. *Subjects, Citizens, Aliens, and Others: Nationality and Immigration Law* (London: Weidenfeld and Nicolson, 1990).

Düvell, Franck, ed. *Illegal Migration in Europe: Beyond Control?* (New York: Palgrave MacMillan, 2006).

Dworkin, Ronald. *Law's Empire* (Cambridge, Mass.: Harvard University Press, 1986).

Findlay, Mark. *The Globalization of Crime: Understanding Transnational Relationships in Context* (New York and Cambridge: Cambridge University Press, 1999).

Fitzpatrick, Joan. "Trafficking As a Human Rights Violation: The Complex Intersection of Legal Frameworks for Conceptualizing and Combating Trafficking" (2003), 24 *Michigan Journal of International Law* 1143.

Fitzpatrick, Peter. "Introduction" in Peter Fitzpatrick, ed., *Nationalism, Racism, and the Rule of Law* (Aldershot: Dartmouth Press, 1995).

_____. *Modernism and the Grounds of Law* (Cambridge and New York: Cambridge University Press, 2001).

_____. "Terminal Legality? Human Rights and Critical Being" in Peter Fitzpatrick and Patricia Tuitt, eds., *Critical Beings: Law, Nation, and the Global Subject* (Aldershot: Ashgate Press, 2004).

_____. "'Gods Would Be Needed . . .': American Empire and the Rule of (International) Law" (2003), 16 *Leiden Journal of International Law* 429.

————. "'We know what it is when you do not ask us': The Unchallengeable Nation" (2004), 8 *Law/Text/Culture* 263.

————. "Bare Sovereignty: *Homo Sacer* and the Insistence of Law" in Andrew Norris, ed., *Politics, Metaphysics, and Death: Essays on Giorgio Agamben's Homo Sacer* (Durham: Duke University Press, 2005) 49.

Forcese, Craig. "Through a Glass Darkly: The Role and Review of 'National Security' Concepts in Canadian Law" (2006), 43 *Alberta Law Review* 963.

Foster, Michelle. *International Refugee Law and Socio-Economic Rights: Refuge From Deprivation* (Cambridge and New York: Cambridge University Press, 2007).

Fuller, Lon L. *The Morality of Law*, rev. ed. (New Haven and London: Yale University Press, 1969).

Futo, Peter, Michael Jandl, and Liia Karsakova. "A Survey of Illegal Migration and Human Smuggling in Central and Eastern Europe" (2005), 21 *Migration and Ethnic Studies* 35.

Gallagher, Anne. "Human Rights and the New UN Protocols on Trafficking and Migrant Smuggling: A Preliminary Analysis" (2001), 23 *Human Rights Quarterly* 975.

Galloway, Donald. "Liberalism, Globalism, and Immigration" (1993), 18 *Queen's L.J.* 266.

————. *Essentials of Canadian Law: Immigration Law* (Concord, Ont.: Irwin Law, 1997).

Gellner, Ernest. *Nations and Nationalism* (Ithaca, New York: Cornell University Press, 1983).

Gessner, Volkmar, and Ali Cem Budak, eds. *Emerging Legal Certainty: Empirical Studies on the Globalization of Law* (Aldershot and Brookfield, VT: Ashgate Publishing, 1998).

Gibney, Matthew, and Randall Hansen. "Deportation and the Liberal State: The Forcible Return of Asylum Seekers and Unlawful Migrants in Canada, Germany, and the United Kingdom," UNHCR Working Paper No. 77, 2003.

Ghosh, Bimal. *Huddled Masses and Uncertain Shores: Insights into Irregular Migration* (Boston: Martinus Nijhoff Publishers, 1998).

Giddens, Anthony. *The Consequences of Modernity* (Stanford: Stanford University Press, 1990).

————. *Runaway World: How Globalization is Reshaping Our Lives* (New York: Routledge, 2000).

Gill, Stephen. "Globalization, Market Civilization, and Disciplinary Neo-liberalism" (1995), 24 *Millennium* 3.

Global Commission on International Migration. *Migration in an Interconnected World: New Directions for Action: Report of the Global Commission on International Migration* (Switzerland: Global Commission on International Migration, 2005).

Goldman, David B. "Historical Aspects of Globalization and Law" in Catherine Dauvergne, ed., *Jurisprudence for an Interconnected Globe* (Aldershot: Ashgate Press, 2003).

Goodwin-Gill, Guy. *The Refugee in International Law* (Oxford: Clarendon Press, 1996).
_____. "Refugees: The Functions and Limits of the Existing Protection System" in Alan Nash, ed., *Human Rights and the Protection of Refugees Under International Law* (Halifax: Halifax Institute for Research and Policy, 1988) 149.
Government of Canada, *Securing an Open Society: Canada's National Security Policy* (Ottawa: Privy Council Office, April 2004).
Guild, Elspeth. "The Legal Framework: Who is Entitled to Move?" in Didier Bigo and Elspeth Guild, eds., *Controlling Frontiers: Free Movement Into and Within Europe* (Aldershot: Ashgate, 2005).
_____. "Who is Entitled to Work and Who is in Charge?: Understanding the Legal Framework of European Labour Migration" in Didier Bigo and Elspeth Guild, eds., *Controlling Frontiers: Free Movement Into and Within Europe* (Aldershot: Ashgate, 2005).
Hage, Ghassan. *White Nation: Fantasies of White Supremacy in a Multicultural Society* (Sydney: Pluto Press, 1998).
Harrington, John. "Citizenship and the Biopolitics of post-Nationalist Ireland" (2005), 32.3 *Journal of Law and Society* 424.
Harris, Nigel. *Thinking the Unthinkable: The Immigration Myth Exposed* (New York and London: IB Tauris, 2002).
Harvey, Colin and Robert P. Barnidge Jr. "The Right to Leave One's Own Country under International Law," (Paper prepared for the Global Commission on International Migration, September 2005).
Hathaway, James. *The Law of Refugee Status* (Toronto and Vancouver: Butterworths, 1991).
_____. *The Rights of Refugees Under International Law* (Cambridge and New York: Cambridge University Press, 2005).
Hathaway, James and Alexander Neve. "Making International Refugee Law Relevant Again: A Proposal for Collectivized and Solution-Oriented Protection" (1997), 10 *Harvard Human Rights Journal* 115.
Hathaway, Oona. "Do Human Rights Treaties Make a Difference?" (2002), 11 *Yale Law Journal* 1935.
Held, David. "Law of States, Law of Peoples: Three Models of Sovereignty" (2002), 8 *Legal Theory* 1.
_____. *Global Covenant: The Social Democratic Alternative to the Washington Consensus* (Cambridge and Malden, Mass.: Polity Press, 2004).
Held, David and Anthony McGrew. "Globalization and the Liberal-Democratic State" in Yoshikazu Sakamoto, ed., *Global Transformation: Challenges to the State System* (Tokyo and New York: United Nations University Press, 1994).
_____. *Globalization/Anti-Globalization* (Cambridge and Oxford: Polity Press, 2002).
Held, David, Anthony Barnett, and Caspar Henderson, eds. *Debating Globalization* (Cambridge: Polity Press, 2005).

Held, David et al. *Global Transformations: Politics, Economics, and Culture* (Cambridge: Polity Press, 1999).

Hickman, Tom R. "Between Human Rights and the Rule of Law: Indefinite Detention and the Derogation Model of Constitutionalism" (2005), 63.4 *Modern Law Review* 655.

Hirst, Paul and Grahame Thompson. *Globalization in Question: The International Economy and the Possibilities of Governance*, 2nd ed. (Malden, Mass.: Polity Press, 1999).

Hobsbawn, Eric J. *Nations and Nationalism since 1780: Programme, Myth, Reality*, 2nd ed. (Cambridge: Cambridge University Press, 1992).

Hobsbawn, Eric and Terence Ranger. *The Invention of Tradition* (Cambridge and New York: Cambridge University Press, 1983).

Huntington, Samuel. "Clash of Civilizations" (1993), 72:3 *Foreign Affairs* 22.

Hurrell, Andrew and Ngaire Woods. "Globalization and Inequality" (1995), 24 *Millennium* 447.

International Organization for Migration (IOM). *World Migration 2005: Costs and Benefits of International Migration* (Geneva: International Organization for Migration, 2005).

Jacobson, David. *Rights Across Borders: Immigration and the Decline of Citizenship* (Baltimore: John Hopkins University Press, 1996).

———. "Courts Across Borders: The Implications of Judicial Agency for Human Rights and Democracy" (2003), 25 *Human Rights Quarterly* 74.

Jandl, Michael. "The Estimation of Illegal Migration in Europe" (2004), 41 *Studi Emigrazione/Migration Studies* 141.

Jayasuriya, Kanishka. "Globalization, Law, and the Transformation of Sovereignty: The Emergence of Global Regulatory Governance" (1999), 6 *Indiana Journal of Global Legal Studies* 435.

Joerges, Christian and Navraj Singh, eds. *Darker Legacies of Law in Europe: The Shadow of National Socialism and Fascism over Europe and Its Legal Traditions* (Oxford: Hart Publishing, 2003).

Joppke, Christian. "Immigration Challenges the Nation State" in Christian Joppke, ed., *Challenge to the Nation State: Immigration in Western Europe and the United States* (New York: Oxford University Press, 1998).

———. "Why Liberal States Accept Unwanted Immigration" (1998), 50 *World Politics* 266.

Kapur, Ratna. "The 'Other' Side of Globalization: The Legal Regulation of Cross-Border Movements" (2003), 22:3–4 *Canadian Woman Studies* 6–16.

Keely, Charles B. "Demography and International Migration" in *Migration Theory: Talking Across Disciplines* (New York and London: Routledge, 2000) 43.

Kempadoo, Kamala. "Victims and Agents: The New Crusade against Trafficking" in Julia Sudbury, ed., *Global Lockdown: Race, Gender, and the Prison-Industrial Complex* (New York: Routledge, 2005).

Kingsford Smith, Dimity. "Networks, Norms, and the Nation State: Thoughts on Pluralism and Globalized Securities Regulation" in Catherine Dauvergne, ed., *Jurisprudence for an Interconnected Globe* (Aldershot: Ashgate Press, 2003) 93.

Kneebone, Susan. "Women Within the Refugee Construct: 'Exclusionary Inclusion' in Policy and Practice – the Australian Experience" (2005), 17 *International Journal of Refugee Law* 7.

Kobayashi, Audrey. "Challenging the National Dream: Gender Persecution and Canadian Immigration Law" in P. Fitzpatrick, ed., *Nationalism, Racism, and the Rule of Law* (Aldershot and Brookfield, VT: Dartmouth Press, 1995).

Koslowski, Rey. "Economic Globalization, Human Smuggling, and Global Governance" in David Kyle and Rey Koslowski, eds., *Global Human Smuggling: Comparative Perspectives* (Baltimore: John Hopkins University Press, 2001).

Kymlicka, Will. *Multicultural Citizenship: A Liberal Theory of Minority Rights* (Oxford: Oxford University Press, 1995).

Kymlicka, Will and Wayne Norman. "The Return of the Citizen: A Survey of Recent Work on Citizenship Theory" (1994), 104 *Ethics* 352.

Labman, Shauna. "The Invisibles: An Examination of Refugee Resettlement" (LL.M. Thesis, UBC Faculty of Law, 2007) [unpublished].

Larson, David Allen. "Understanding the Cost of the War Against Iraq and how that Realization Can Affect International Law" (2005), 13 *Cardozo Journal of International and Comparative Law* 387.

Lavenex, Sandra, "EU External Governance in 'Wider Europe'" (2004),11:4 *Journal of European Public Policy* 680.

Lawson, Theresa. "Sending Countries and the Rights of Women Migrant Workers: The Case of Guatemala" (2005), 18 *Harvard Human Rights Journal* 225.

Lechener, Frank and John Boli, eds. *The Globalization Reader* (Malden: Blackwell Publishing, 2004).

Legomsky, Stephen. *Immigration and the Judiciary: Law and Politics in Britain and America* (Oxford: Clarendon Press, 1987).

––––––. "Employer Sanctions: Past and Future" in Peter Duignan and Lewis H. Gann, eds., *The Debate in the United States Over Immigration* (Stanford, Calif.: Hoover Institution Press, 1998).

Levene, Rachael. *Irregular Migrant Workers in the UK: A Story of Marginalization* (LL.M. Thesis, University of British Columbia Law School, 2005) [unpublished].

Lewis, N. Douglas. *Law and Governance: The Old Meets the New* (London: Cavendish, 2001).

Lister, Ruth. *Citizenship: Feminist Perspectives* (Basingstoke: Palgrave Macmillan, 2002).

Macklin, Audrey. "Refugee Women and the Imperative of Categories" (May 1995), 17.2 *Human Rights Quarterly* 213.

––––––. "A Comparative Analysis of the Canadian, U.S., and Australian Directives on Gender Persecution and Refugee Status" in Doreen Indra, ed., *Engendering*

Forced Migration: Theory and Practice (New York and Oxford: Berghan Books, 1999).

_____. "Borderline Security" in Ronald J. Daniels, Patrick Macklem, and Kent Roach, eds., *The Security of Freedom: Essays on Canada's Anti-Terrorism Bill* (Toronto: University of Toronto Press, 2001).

_____. "Dancing Across Borders: Exotic Dancers, Trafficking, and Immigration Policy," (2003) 37 *International Migration Review* 464.

_____. "Exile on Main Street: Popular Discourse and Legal Manoeuvres around Citizenship" in Law Commission of Canada, ed., *Law and Citizenship* (Vancouver: UBC Press, 2006) 22.

Marr, David and Marian Wilkinson, *Dark Victory* (Sydney: Allen and Unwin, 2003).

Marshall, T. H. *Citizenship and Social Class* (Cambridge: Cambridge University Press, 1950).

Mathew, Penelope. "Australian Refugee Protection in the Wake of the *Tampa*" (2002), 96 *American Journal of International Law* 661.

MacCormick, Neil. *Questioning Sovereignty: Law, State, and Nation in the European Commonwealth* (Oxford: Oxford University Press, 1999).

_____. "Beyond the Sovereign State" (1993), 56 *Modern Law Review* 1.

Mendes, Errol and Ozay Mehmet. *Global Governance, Economy, and Law: Waiting for Justice* (London and New York: Routledge, 2003).

Millbank, Jenni. "The Role of Rights in Asylum Claims on the Basis of Sexual Orientation" (2004), 4 *Human Rights Law Review* 193.

Nevins, Joseph. *Operation Gatekeeper: The Rise of the 'Illegal Alien' and the Making of the U.S.–Mexico Boundary* (New York and London: Routledge, 2002).

Ngai, Mae. *Impossible Subjects: Illegal Aliens and the Making of Modern America* (Princeton: Princeton University Press, 2004).

Ohmae, Kenichi. *The End of the Nation State: The Rise of Regional Economies* (London: Harper Collins, 1995).

Ong, Aihwa. *Flexible Citizenship: The Cultural Logics of Transnationality* (Durham and London: Duke University Press, 1999).

_____*Buddha Is Hiding: Refugees, Citizenship, the New America* (Berkeley and Los Angeles: University of California Press, 2003).

Ong Hing, Bill. "The Dark Side of Operation Gatekeeper" (2001), 7 *University of California at Davis Journal of International Law and Policy* 121.

Orford, Anne. *Reading Humanitarian Intervention: Human Rights and the Use of Force in International Law* (Cambridge: Cambridge University Press, 2003).

Pahuja, Sundhya. "'Normalizing' Pathologies of Difference: The Discursive Functions of International Monetary Fund Conditionality" in Lyndsay M. Campbell et al., eds., *International Intersections: Law's Changing Territories: Papers Presented at Green College, University of British Columbia, April 3–May 2, 1998* (Vancouver: University of British Columbia, Faculty of Law, Graduate Program, 1998).

_____. "Post-Colonial Approaches to International Economic Law" (2000), *Hague Yearbook of International Law* 123.

_____. "Rights as Regulation: The Integration of Development and Human Rights" in Bronwen Morgan, ed., *The Intersection of Rights and Regulation: New Directions in Sociolegal Scholarship* (Aldershot: Ashgate, 2007).

Passel, Jeffrey S. "The Size and Characteristics of the Unauthorized Migrant Population in the U.S.: Estimates Based on the March 2005 Current Population Survey" (Research Report prepared for the Pew Hispanic Center, March 7, 2006).

Pateman, Carole. *The Disorder of Women: Democracy, Feminism, and Political Theory* (Stanford, Calif.: Stanford University Press, 1989).

Phuong, Catherine. "Enlarging 'Fortress Europe:' EU Accession, Asylum, and Immigration in Candidate Countries" (2003), 52 *International and Comparative Law Quarterly* 641.

Pratt, Anna. *Securing Borders: Detention and Deportation in Canada* (Vancouver: UBC Press, 2005).

Randall, Melanie. "Refugee Law and State Accountability for Violence Against Women: A Comparative Analysis of Legal Approaches to Recognizing Asylum Claims Based on Gender Persecution" (2002), 25 *Harvard Women's Law Journal* 281.

Rawls, John. "Justice as Fairness: Political not Metaphysical" (1985), 14 *Philosophy and Public Affairs* 223.

Razack, Sherene. *Looking White People in the Eye: Gender, Race, and Culture in Courtrooms and Classrooms* (Toronto: University of Toronto Press, 1998).

Reich, Robert B. *The Work of Nations: Preparing Ourselves for 21st Century Capitalism* (London: Simon & Schuster, 1983).

Ritzer, George. *The McDonaldization of Society* (Thousand Oaks, Calif.: Pine Forge Press, 2004).

Rothwell, Donald. "The Law of the Sea and the MV *Tampa* Incident: Reconciling Maritime Principles with Coastal State Sovereignty" (2002), 13 *Public Law Review* 118.

Rubenstein, Kim. "Citizenship in a Borderless World" in A. Anghie and G. Sturgess, eds., *Legal Visions of the 21st Century: Essays in Honour of Judge Christopher Weeramantry* (The Hague: Kluwer Law International Publishers, 1998).

_____. "Citizenship, Sovereignty, and Migration: Australia's Exclusive Approach to Membership of the Community" (2002), 13 *Public Law Review* 102.

_____. *Australian Citizenship Law in Context* (Sydney: Law Book Company, 2002).

Rubenstein, Kim and Daniel Adler. "International Citizenship: The Future of Nationality in a Globalized World" (2000), 7 *Indiana Journal of Global Legal Studies* 519.

Ruddock, Phillip. "Narrowing of Judicial Review in the Migration Context" (1997), 15 *Australian Institute of Administrative Law Forum* 13.

Ruggie, John Gerrard. "Territoriality and Beyond: Problematizing Modernity in International Relations" (1993), 47 *International Organization* 139.

Salt, John. *Current Trends in International Migration in Europe* (Strasbourg: Council of Europe, 2001).

Sassen, Saskia. *Losing Control? Sovereignty in an Age of Globalization* (New York: Columbia University Press, 1996).

———. *Globalization and Its Discontents* (New York: New York Press, 1998).

Schmidhauser, John R. "Legal Imperialism: Its Enduring Impact on Colonial and Post-Colonial Judicial Systems" (1992), 13:3 *International Political Science Review* 321.

Servos, Chaime Marcuello and Carmen Marcuello. "NGOs, Corporate Social Responsibility, and Social Accountability: Inditex vs. Clean Clothes" (2007), 17:3 *Development in Practice* 393.

Shachar, Ayelet. *Multicultural Jurisdictions: Cultural Differences and Women's Rights* (Cambridge and New York: Cambridge University Press, 2001).

———. "The Race for Talent: Highly Skilled Migrants and Competitive Immigration Regimes" (2006), 81 *NYU Law Review* 148.

Simpson, Gerry. "The War in Iraq and International Law" (2005), 6 *Melbourne Journal of International Law* 167.

Slaughter, Anne-Marie. *A New World Order* (Princeton: Princeton University Press, 2004).

Smith, Anthony. *The Ethnic Origins of Nations* (Oxford: Blackwell Publishers, 1986).

———. *National Identity* (London and New York: Penguin, 1991).

Smith, Dimity Kingsford. "Networks, Norms, and the Nation States: Thoughts on Pluralism and Globalized Securities Regulation" (2003) in Catherine Dauvergne, ed., *Jurisprudence for an Interconnected Globe* (Aldershot: Ashgate, 2003).

Soltesz, Susan, "Implications of the Conseil Constitutionnel's Immigration and Asylum Decision of August 1993" (1995), 18:1 *Boston College International and Comparative Law Review* 265.

Sousa Santos, Boaventura de. *Law Against Law: Legal Reasoning in Pasargada Law* (Cuernavaca: Centro Intercultural de Documentacion, 1974).

———. "The Law of the Oppressed: The Construction and Reproduction of Legality in Pasargada" (1977), 12 *Law and Society Review* 5.

———. *Toward a New Legal Common Sense: Law, Globalization, and Emancipation*, 2nd ed. (London: Butterworths LexisNexis, 2002).

———. *Toward a New Legal Common Sense: Law, Globalization, and Emancipation*, (London: Routledge, 1995).

Soysal, Yasemin. *Limits of Citizenship: Migrants and Postnational Membership in Europe* (Chicago: University of Chicago Press, 1994).

Spijkerboer, Thomas. *Gender and Refugee Status* (Aldershot, England and Burlington, VT: Ashgate, 2000).

Taylor, Savitri. "The Importance of Human Rights Talk in Asylum Seeker Advocacy: A Response to Catherine Dauvergne" (2001) 24 *University of New South Wales Law Journal* 191.

Teitelbaum, Michael S. and Myron Weiner, eds. *Threatened Peoples, Threatened Borders: World Migration and U.S. Policy* (New York and London: W.W. Norton and Company, 1995).

Thompson, Grahame. "The Limits of Globalization: Questions for Held and Wolf" in David Held et al., eds., *Debating Globlization* (Cambridge: Polity Press, 2005).

Tomkins, Adam. "Readings of *A v. Secretary of State for Home Department*" [2005], *Public Law* 259.

Torpey, John. *The Invention of the Passport: Surveillance, Citizenship, and the State* (Cambridge: Cambridge University Press, 2000).

Tuitt, Patricia. *False Images: Law's Construction of the Refugee* (London and East Haven, CT: Pluto Press, 1996).

Turner, Bryan, ed. *Citizenship and Social Theory* (London: Sage Press, 1993).

Twining, William. *Globalisation and Legal Theory* (London: Butterworths, 2000).

_____. "The Province of Jurisprudence Re-Examined" in Catherine Dauvergne, ed., *Jurisprudence for an Interconnected Globe* (Aldershot: Ashgate Press, 2003).

U.K. H.C., Environment, Food, and Rural Affairs Committee, *Gangmasters, Fourteenth Report of Session 2002–2003* (London: The Stationary Office Limited, 2003).

U.K. H.L., European Union Committee, *Handling EU Asylum Claims: New Approaches Examined* (Eleventh Report) (London: The Stationery Office Limited, 2004), on-line: UK Parliament: Publications & Records, http://www.publications.parliament.ukpa/ld200304/ldselect/ldeucom/74/74.pdf.

U.K. H.C., Home Affairs Committee, *Asylum Applications* (Second Report) vol.1 (London: The Stationary Office Limited, 2004), on-line: UK Parliament: Publications & Records, http://www.publications.parliament.uk/pa/cm200304/cmselect/cmhaff/218/218.pdf.

U.K. Select Committee on Environment, Food, and Rural Affairs, *Memorandum Submitted by the Transport and General Workers Union* (2004).

UNHCR. *2005 Global Refugee Trends: Statistical Overview of Populations of Refugees, Asylum- Seekers, Internally Displaced Persons, Stateless Persons, and Other Persons of Concern to UNHCR* (Geneva: UNHCR, 2006).

UNHCR. Field Information and Coordination Support Section, Division of Operational Services, *Asylum Levels and Trends in Industrialized Countries, 2006: Overview of Asylum Applications Lodged in European and Non-European Industrialized Countries in 2006* (Geneva: UNHCR, 2007), on-line: UNHCR –The UN Refugee Agency: Statistics, http://www.unhcr.org/statistics/STATISTICS/460150272.pdf.

UNHCR. *Guidelines on International Protection No.7: The Application of Article 1A(2) of the 1951 Convention and/or 1967 Protocol Relating to the Status of Refugees to Victims of Trafficking and Persons at Risk of Being Trafficked*, April 7, 2006. HCR/GIP/06/07. On-line: UNHCR Refworld, http://www.unhcr.org/cgi-bin/texis/vtx/refworld/rwmain?docid=443679fa4.

UNHCR. *The International Convention of Migrant Workers and its Committee: Fact Sheet Number 24 (Rev. 1)*, Office of the United Nations High Commissioner for Human Rights (2005).

United Nations. *International Migration 2006* (United Nations Publication, 2006), on-line: Department of Economic and Social Affairs: Population division, http://www.un.org/esa/population/publications/2006Migration_Chart/Migration2006.pdf.

United Nations Development Program. *Human Development Report 2003 Millennium Development Goals: A Compact Among Nations to End Human Poverty* (New York and Oxford: Oxford University Press, 2003).

U.S. Immigration and Naturalization Service, *Estimates of Unauthorized Immigration Population Residing in the United States: 1990–2000* (Office of Policy and Planning, 2003).

U.S., State Department, *Trafficking in Persons Report 2000* (U.S. State Department, 2000).

U.S., State Department, *Trafficking in Persons Report 2001* (U.S. State Department, 2001).

U.S., State Department, *Trafficking in Persons Report 2002* (U.S. State Department, 2002).

U.S., State Department, *Trafficking in Persons Report 2003* (U.S. State Department, 2003).

U.S., State Department, *Trafficking in Persons Report 2004* (U.S. State Department, 2004).

U.S., State Department, *Trafficking in Persons Report 2005* (U.S. State Department, 2005).

U.S., State Department, *Trafficking in Persons Report 2006* (U.S. State Department, 2006).

U.S., State Department, *Trafficking in Persons Report 2007* (U.S. State Department, 2007).

U.S. United States Government Accountability Office, *Better Data, Strategy, and Reporting Needed to Enhance U.S. Antitrafficking Efforts Abroad* (GAO-06-825) (Washington D.C.: United States Government Accountability Office, 2006).

U.S. White House, "The National Security Strategy of the United States of America" (September 2002), on-line: The White House, http://www.use.gov/nsc/nssal.html.

Vedsted-Hansen, Jens. "Non-admission Policies and the Right to Protection: Refugees' Choice versus States' Exclusion?" in Frances Nicholson and Patrick Twomey, eds., *Refugee Rights and Realities: Evolving International Concepts and Regimes* (Cambridge and New York: Cambridge University Press, 1999).

Von Brenda-Beckmann, Franz, Keebet von Brenda-Beckman, and Anne Griffiths, eds. *Mobile People, Mobile Law: Expanding Legal Relations in a Contracting World* (Aldershot and Burlington: Ashgate Publishing, 2005).

Voronina, Natalia, "Outlook on Migration Policy Reform in Russia: Contemporary Challenges and Political Paradoxes" in Roger Rodríguez Rios, ed., *Migration Perspectives Eastern Europe and Central Asia* (Vienna: International Organization for Migration, 2006).

Walzer, Michael. *Spheres of Justice: A Defense of Pluralism and Equality* (New York: Basic Books, 1983).

Wardle, Jonathan H. "The Strategic Use of Mexico to Restrict South American Access to the Diversity Visa Lottery" (2005), 58 *Vanderbilt Law Review* 1963.

Weiss, Linda. *The Myth of the Powerless State: Governing the Economy in a Global Era* (Cambridge: Polity Press, 1998).

Wiener, Jarrod. *Globalization and the Harmonization of Law* (London and New York: Pinter, 1999).

Wilkinson, Rorden. "Managing Global Civil Society: The WTO's Engagement with NGOs" in Randall D. Germain and Michael Kenny, eds., *The Idea of Global Civil Society: Politics and Ethics in a Globalizing Era* (London and New York: Routledge, 2005).

Wilke, Christiane. "War v. Justice: Terrorism Cases, Enemy Combatants, and Political Justice in U.S. Courts" (2005), 33 *Politics and Society* 637.

Wolf, Ronald Charles. *Trade, Aid, and Arbitrate: The Globalization of Western Law* (Aldershot and Burlington, VT: Ashgate Publishing, 2004).

Young, Tom. "'A Project to be Realized': Global Liberalism and Contemporary Africa" (1995), 24 *Millennium* 527.

Index

Books in the Series (*continued from p. iii*)

Moffat: *Trusts Law: Text and Materials*
Norrie: *Crime, Reason and History*
O'Dair: *Legal Ethics*
Oliver: *Common Values and the Public-Private Divide*
Oliver & Drewry: *The Law and Parliament*
Picciotto: *International Business Taxation*
Reed: *Internet Law: Text and Materials*
Richardson: *Law Process and Custody*
Roberts & Palmer: *Dispute Process ADR and the Primary Forms of Decision Making*
Seneviratne: *Ombudsmen: Public Services and Administrative Justice*
Stapleton: *Product Liability*
Tamanaha: *Law as a Means to an End: Threat to the Rule of Law*
Turpin: *British Government and the Constitution: Text, Cases and Materials*
Twining: *Globalisation and Legal Theory*
Twining: *Rethinking Evidence: Exploratory Essays*
Twining & Miers: *How to Do Things with Rules*
Ward: *A Critical Introduction to European Law*
Ward: *Shakespeare and Legal Imagination*
Zander: *Cases and Materials on the English Legal System*
Zander: *The Law Making Process*